William Blair

Joseph the Seer

His prophetic mission vindicated, and the divine origin of the Book of Mormon

defended and maintained

William Blair

Joseph the Seer
His prophetic mission vindicated, and the divine origin of the Book of Mormon defended and maintained

ISBN/EAN: 9783337295448

Printed in Europe, USA, Canada, Australia, Japan

Cover: Foto ©Lupo / pixelio.de

More available books at **www.hansebooks.com**

JOSEPH THE SEER;

HIS

PROPHETIC MISSION VINDICATED,

AND THE

DIVINE ORIGIN

OF

THE BOOK OF MORMON DEFENDED AND MAINTAINED;

BEING A REPLY

BY ELDER WILLIAM W. BLAIR,

Of the Reorganized Church of Jesus Christ of Latter Day Saints,

TO ELDER WILLIAM SHELDON,

Of the Second Adventist Society.

PLANO, ILLINOIS:
PRINTED AND PUBLISHED BY THE BOARD OF PUBLICATION OF THE REORGANIZED
CHURCH OF JESUS CHRIST OF LATTER DAY SAINTS.
1877.

PREFACE.

The severe trials to which the Truth of God has been subjected in all the past, have always resulted well in bringing its high importance, its essential impregnability, and its perpetual beauties into clearer, grander light, disclosing more plainly its deep, and broad, and immovable foundations. They have also resulted well in revealing the dark and delusive ways of error, ways so common to the conceited, the self-sufficient, and the bigot, who, with blind heart, and clamorous tongue, or pen, would compel all others into their mazy lines of thought, and into their devious and inconsistent modes of religious, moral, social, and scientific conduct. Truth gains and error loses in every fairly conducted conflict.

Such, we trust, will be the ultimate fruits of the recent malevolent attack of Rev. William Sheldon upon the faith and doctrines of the Latter Day Saints, to which we reply in the following pages. Truth will arise and prevail.

Mr. Sheldon, in his arguments, draws heavily on various anti-Mormon writers, from Howe to Ann Eliza. From these he takes his cue; and from their productions he obtains his chief enlightenment, and his loftiest inspirations; yet, notably, he fails to give them their proper credits. This literary piracy will be found to be quite in keeping with the general tenor of his work, as we proceed.

It will also be seen that he is a prince among cavilers, and that he is as feeble in his sophisms as he is fertile in invention. He builds, with affected seriousness, his men-of-straw; and then, with self-complacent, pompous puffs, topples them over, and then applauds himself for decisive victories.

He attempts, with persistent zeal, to make the Book of Mormon and the Inspired Translation claim for themselves what they do not claim, viz., that *all* their historical and epistolary parts were written with unerring precision, and infallible accuracy, and under the fullest and highest measure of inspiration; but in this attempt he fails, miserably.

He seeks to force upon the standard writings of the Church such sense and meaning as are utterly foreign and contrary to them; and this he does, evidently, with the base purpose of making them appear false and contradictory.

We regret that Mr. Sheldon has quoted our works so inaccurately, and that he has cited passages so incorrectly; for it tends to perplex the reader, both as respects his statements, and, possibly, in respect to our answers; beside which it places him in the attitude of either a heedless, or a lawless controversialist.

It is quite impossible in these pages to notice more than the major and more important part of the objections urged by Mr. Sheldon; and this we cannot do in a manner nearly so extended as we could wish, and as we know their importance demands; but we have undertaken to reply to all those of any real force or value.

If in anything in this work we have descended to too low a plane in our argument, our main apology is, that we thought it best, in the interests of truth, to follow our opponent wherever he went, in order to flash the true light upon his dark and crooked ways, and thus disclose his errors.

We have frequently emphasized passages quoted, and we have done so in order to call special attention to the matter under consideration; but we disclaim any intention of thereby changing the sense of such passages.

We submit our work to the careful and considerate attention of the reader, asking that it be judged upon the merits of its *facts*, and not upon the excellency of its diction, or the beauty and finish of its periods.

We regret its brevity, and its imperfections; especially when we consider the weighty matters of which it treats.

We have written it in the interests of truth—diamond truth—and for the promotion of the righteousness of God among men, and to further the cause of "full salvation." And with this consciousness we send it out, humbly asking for it the best blessings of heaven, a respectful reception among men, and a fair hearing by all into whose hands it may come.

THE AUTHOR.

PROPHETIC MISSION OF JOSEPH SMITH VINDICATED,

AND THE

DIVINE ORIGIN OF THE BOOK OF MORMON MAINTAINED,

AND DEFENDED.

CHAPTER I.

We have recently read in the *World's Crisis* for July, 1875, a lengthy article, entitled "Mormonism Examined; or, Was Joseph Smith a Divinely Inspired Prophet?" from the pen of Elder Wm. Sheldon, a minister of the Advent Church, and sometime editor of the *Christian Advent Times,* and more recently his book entitled "Mormonism Reviewed," and feeling that they should be answered, we now undertake this review.

Mr. Sheldon doubtless availed himself of all the arguments hitherto used by opponents of the Latter Day Work, selecting such as he thought he could use with effect, and has then added to them an occasional one that has at least the merit of being new. His affected fairness is painfully apparent, while his false inferences, his bald mis-statements, and his frequent false and garbled quotations, place him in an unpleasantly low rank among controversialists. This we very much regret, as from a brief acquaintance with the gentleman we had expected of him better things. His course adds but another to the long list of evidences, stretching down through the ages, that men, when they have an end in view, usually, spare no effort, and use without scruple any means to attain it—"the end [with them] justifies the means."

We are not averse to criticism, but, on the contrary, admire it when it is conducted with fairness and skill; but when it degenerates into quibbling, low trickery, and contemptible pettifoggery, then the less of it the better.

We have no quarrel with any for not believing as we do; all may believe as they think best, and we are morally bound to respect them in that right; for the right of private judgment, and the fact of personal responsibility, are inherent in man, and ordained of God. What we ask, and all that we ask, is, for others to bear in mind that the Latter Day Saints, as well as themselves, should be respected in their rights, and be treated in respect to their *faith* and *works*, honestly, fairly and courteously.

As for Mr. Sheldon,—the propriety of his efforts, the strength of his arguments, the piety of his motives, and the extent of his success in proving that "Mormonism" is false in its foundations and in its leading facts,—the reader must form his own judgment as we progress.

Mr. Sheldon postulates the following: "The claims of Mormonism to divine origin, stand or fall with a correct answer to the simple question, Was Joseph Smith a true prophet;" and he then attempts to prove that there are historical errors in the Book of Mormon, assuming that if there are, then Joseph Smith, who translated the book, must be a false prophet. This claim is certainly a novel one.

To make a translator responsible for the truth or falsity of the facts he translates, is probably an original idea with Mr. S., and one that he feels is quite indispensable to his success. Sensible, fair-dealing people, hardly think of holding Pope responsible for the truth or falsity of Homer's Illiad, or Odyssey, because he translated them; nor would they hold the translators of the Bible responsible for the character of its contents, but only for the faithfulness with which they performed their work of translation.

Now, the Book of Mormon in more places than one admits that there *may be* errors and imperfections in it. It does not claim absolute perfection as to its contents in all, and in every respect. Its *historical* parts do not claim to be written by revelation, or by such measure of inspiration as to exclude errors and defects in language, and style; nor does it claim to be absolutely correct in *all* its historical dates. Nephi, the very first writer in the book is conscious that through his inherent "weakness" his record might be, possibly, faulty. He says.

"If I do err, even did they err of old; not that I would excuse myself because of other men, but because of the weakness which is in me, according to the flesh."—1 Nephi 5: 47.

That some of the sacred historians "of old" did "err" in some of their writings is too well known to need any argument to prove it, as may be seen by comparing the historical books of the Old Testament. Nor is the New Testament free from this defect. One instance may suffice for this place. In Acts, 1 : 18, 19, we are told that Judas obtained for betraying Christ, money with which he bought a field; but in Matthew 27 : 5, 6, 7, we are told that the chief priests with that money bought the field. So of Paul, 1 Cor. 10 : 8, compare Num. 25 : 9. Here are conflicts, which with others that occur, prove that the writers of the New Testament history made some mistakes—they did "err" in, at least, a few things.

Mr. S. quotes the Book of Nephi:

"And it came to pass in the thirty-fourth year, in the first month, in the fourth day of the month, * * * then behold there was darkness upon the face of the land." * * * And it came to pass that it did last for the space of three days."—Nephi 4: 2.

This, Mr. S. claims, was the time of Christ's crucifixion, as predicted by the Lamanite prophet Samuel; and, that its occurring on the "fourth day" of the "first month," instead of the fourteenth day of the first month, Jewish time, proves the account false, the Book of Mormon untrue, and Joseph Smith, its translator, a false prophet. Now, if Mr. S. had read and honestly considered the preceding paragraph, he might have spared us the necessity of exposing what savors strongly of craftiness, and even downright trickery. It reads:

"It was a just man who did keep the record; * * * and now it came to pass, if there was no mistake made in the reckoning of our time."

Here is a frank admission of a *possible* error in the record, as to time. Why did not Mr. S. cite this qualifying statement? Evidently because he knew that his argument would thereby be stripped of its force.

The Nephites reckoned time under three different eras; the first dating from Lehi's exodus from Jerusalem,—1 Nephi, 1 : 2. Jacob 1 : 1, etc.; the next dating with the beginning of the reign of the Judges,—Alma, 1 : 1; 2 : 1; also, book of Nephi, 1 : 1; and the next with the birth of Christ,—Book of Nephi 1 : 6–8. Whether their *months* were after the Jewish style, or not, is uncertain. Their months may have begun with the going out of Lehi and his family from Jerusalem. As to whether "the first month," of Nephi 4 : 2, was really intended for Jewish time, or for time peculiar to the Nephites, it is not our province now to determine. Whatever the time was, Jewish or Nephite, the writer of the book does not claim that it was absolutely correct. Joseph Smith translated it as he found it; and the correctness or incorrectness of those dates cannot affect the truthfulness of Joseph Smith's calling.

TIME OF CHRIST'S BIRTH.

Mr. S. next affirms that "the Book of Mormon locates the birth of Christ too late in the world's history to harmonize with the Bible," because it is stated in 2 Nephi 11 : 4, that the Messiah should come in six hundred years from the time that Lehi left Jerusalem, which was in the first year of King Zedekiah's reign. Mr. S. enters into a lengthy argument to prove that the birth of Christ occurred "just five hundred and fifty-three years from the first of Zedekiah."

As to the precise number of years between those events, chronologists differ. All that seems necessary now is to find what was intended by the statement in question; for it is a wise maxim that "the thing *intended*, is the thing said." The text reads:—

"For according to the words of the prophets, the Messiah cometh in six hundred years from the time that my father left Jerusalem."

Here is a text similar in structure, in which the Lord said to Abraham:—

"Thy seed shall be a stranger in a land that is not theirs, and shall serve them; and they shall afflict them four hundred years."—Gen. 15 : 13.

Now, In Ex. 12 : 40, it is said, "The sojourning of Israel, who dwelt in Egypt, was four hundred and thirty years." Here is a difference of *thirty years*, when we descend to verbal niceties, between the time as promised, and the recorded time of history. Will Mr. S. impeach the Almighty, or invalidate Bible history, because of this discrepancy! The grounds here presented are much better for his doing so, than are his supposed grounds for invalidating the testimony of Nephi. For in one case there is an admitted verbal difference, of thirty years, while in the other there is not. What was evidently intended in the promise to Abraham, was, that about four hundred years, in round numbers, would measure Israel's captivity in Egypt. So in regard to the "six hundred years" predicted by Nephi, a fair interpretation would be that "in about six hundred years."

But we need not dwell upon this, for it is a well known fact that there is quite a difference of opinion about the date of our Savior's birth, and Mr. S.'s statement is only his personal opinion about that matter. Tegg, editor of "The Chronology, or Historian's Companion," makes it about six hundred and four years from the first of Zedekiah. Rollin makes it about six hundred; Usher, Petavius, Jackson, Hales, and Bunsen, near the same; and, as we have seen, Mr. S. fixes it at just *precisely* "five hundred and fifty-three," a difference of *forty-seven years*. It may be well to remark that Mr. S. reaches *his* very precise figures, by means of *his* forced interpretation of Daniel 9 : 25. Mr. S. and his fellows, have devoted not a little labor to "the time question," for the last twenty-five or more years; and, if they succeed as well in the future as they have in the past, they will convince others, even if they fail to convince themselves, that they know but little in reckoning time. Their erroneous methods of interpretation, which have involved them in serious blunders and painful mistakes, proclaim them "blind guides;" especially upon questions of time. "By their fruits ye shall know them."

That Mr. S. has gone wide of the mark, as is usual, in stating that it was but five hundred and fifty-three years from the first of Zedekiah to the birth of Jesus, we will now proceed to show, and that, too, in part, from this same prophecy of Daniel:

"*Seventy weeks* are determined upon thy *people* and upon thy *holy city*, to finish the transgression, and to make an end of sins, and to make reconciliation for iniquity, and to bring in everlasting righteousness, and to seal up the vision and prophecy, and to anoint the Most Holy. Know therefore and understand, that from the going forth of the commandment to *restore and to build Jerusalem*, unto the Messiah the Prince, shall be *seven weeks, and three score and two weeks;* the *street* shall be *built* again, and the *wall*, even in *troublous times*. And after *three score and two weeks* shall Messiah be cut off, but not for himself: and the people of the prince that shall come shall destroy the city and the sanctuary; and the end thereof shall be with a flood, and unto the end of the war desolations are determined. And he shall confirm the covenant with many for *one week*; and in the midst of *the week* he shall cause the sacrifice and the oblation to cease, and for the overspreading of abominations he shall make it desolate, even until the consummation, and that determined shall be poured upon the desolate."—Dan. 9 : 24–27.

That the days composing these periods signify so many years of common time we fully believe.

Now, it should be carefully noted that the "seventy weeks," (or four hundred and ninety years), are divided into periods of "seven weeks, and threescore and two weeks," (or four hundred and eighty-three years), leaving "the week," or, "one week," (seven years), as the last and concluding period. Now, "from the going forth of the commandment to *restore* and to *build Jerusalem* unto the Messiah, the Prince, shall be seven weeks, and threescore and two weeks,"—or four hundred and eighty-three years. This certainly does not relate to the commandment of Cyrus to *build the temple* as Mr. S. claims, for that was issued, according to Rollin, (Hist. Cyrus, ch. 1, art. 3, sec. 2.), A.D. 536, or about from five hundred and sixty-two to five hundred and sixty-seven years before "Messiah the Prince" was manifested, which evidently occurred at his baptism by John, (see John, 1 : 29–41), and with this agrees the dates in the Bible, Ezra 1 : 1. The "commandment" predicted was clearly that one which should *effect* the restoration of Jerusalem and the Jews, and eventuate in the building up of their city—"the street," "and the wall"—and all this "even in troublous times," for such are the terms of the prophecy. Twenty years after the decree of Cyrus, in the sixth year of Darius, "the temple was finished and dedicated," but "the *walls* remained as the Assyrians had left them" at the close of the terrible seige seventy years before—(*a*). Fifty-eight years after the temple was dedicated, or "B.C. 457, Ezra arrived from Babylon with a caravan of Priests, Levites, Nethinims, and lay people."—*Ibid*. This was by the commandment of Artaxerxes [Longimanus],—Ezra 7 : 1–28. And the effect of this "commandment" was to restore Jerusalem to its former state, before the captivity, in respect to its civil government, and religious services:

"And thou, Ezra, after the wisdom of thy God, that is in thine hand, set magistrates and judges, which may judge all the people that are beyond the river, all such as know the laws of thy God ; and teach ye them that know them not. And whosoever will not do the law of thy God, and the law of the king, let judgment be executed speedily upon him, whether it be unto death, or to banishment, or to confiscation of goods, or to imprisonment."—Ezra 7: 25, 26.

It is true that the building of "the street," and "the wall" did not take place till about *thirteen* years after this, in the twentieth of Artaxerxes, or about B.C. 444–5, but the "commandment to *restore* and to build Jerusalem" was given to Ezra. This work of building "the wall" was done when Nehemiah was Governor of Judea. Neh. 2. And this building was done "even in troublous times," for

* "They which builded on the wall, and they which bare burdens, with those that laded, every one with one of his hands wrought in the work, and with the other hand held a weapon. For the builders, every one had his sword girded by his side, and so builded."—Neh. 4 : 17, 18.

(*a*) Bible Dict., Smith, Art. Jerusalem.

Now, "from the commandment" of Artaxerxes to Ezra, to "restore" Jerusalem to its former religious and civil estate, (which we see went forth about B.C. 457), to the announcement of "Messiah the Prince," (John 1 : 29–41) A.D. 30, would be four hundred and eighty-seven years. From this take off four years for the fact that our A. D. begins, it is said, four years after Christ was born, and this would leave just four hundred and eighty-three years, or, "seven weeks, three score and two weeks."

That "the week"—the last period—"in the midst" of which "he shall cause the sacrifice and the oblation [under the law] to cease" measures the three and a half years of Christ's active ministry, the terminating of the law of sacrifices by the sacrifice of himself on the cross, (Heb. 10 : 4–12, &c.), with the three and a half years of his ministers fruitful labors in establishing the New Covenant among the Jews, is very probable, if not conclusive.

And further; that the "seven weeks"—or forty-nine years—refer to the peculiar period immediately following the "going forth of the commandment to restore and to build Jerusalem," is, I think, quite evident; and that the period of "threescore and two weeks"— or four hundred and thirty-four years—are to be added to the forty-nine years, making four hundred and eighty-three years, thus bringing us to the times when the Messiahship of Jesus was announced, I also think is beyond question; but of this we have not time to write at length.

Rollin, whose chronological dates differ from those of Usher, Hales, Haydn, and others, thinks the beginning of the "seventy weeks" should date from the twentieth of Artaxerxes, instead of the seventh, for the reason that at that time Nehemiah was appointed governor of Judea, and specially commissioned, by decree of the King, to build the *walls* of Jerusalem—(*b*). If Rollin's Chronology were correct his position would be good. He locates the seventh of Artaxerxes B.C. 467, instead of B.C. 457, as Usher, and others; and the twentieth of Artaxerxes B.C. 454, instead of B.C. 445, as Usher and others. But we believe the "seventy weeks" dates from the commandment to Ezra.

Having discovered very near, if not the exact year to date the beginning of the famous "seventy weeks," we now have to look after that period between either the seventh or the twentieth of Artaxerxes, and the first of Zedekiah, in order to learn how long it was from the

(*b*) See Hist. of the Persians and Grecians, Chap. 1. Sec. 6.

latter to the birth of Christ; for that is the point upon which Mr. S. claims that he has wrecked the authenticity of the Book of Mormon, and the prophetic mission of Joseph, the Seer. From the first of Zedekiah, (2 Chron. 36 : 10), to the seventh of Artaxerxes—and the "commandment" to Ezra to "restore" Jerusalem,—(Ezra 7 : 7), is one hundred and forty-two years. To this add four hundred and fifty-seven and we have five hundred and ninty-nine years to A.D. 1. Or, taking Rollin's dates, we have the last of Zedekiah in B.C. 589, to which the eleven years of his reign should be added, and we have six hundred years to A.D. 1, instead of "just five hundred and fifty-three years from the first of Zedekiah to Messiah," as is so boastfully claimed by Mr. S.

We could wish that the chronology of the past was more perfect, but imperfect as it is we can approximate the truth, and that answers the practical purposes of the case. In the confessed defective state of chronology, especially that prior to A.D. 30, we are quite safe in trusting the dates of the Book of Mormon. They may be trusted as safely, at least, as any. One thing we have demonstrated, and that is, that Mr. S. has grievously erred in his statements on time, in his interpretation of Daniel, and in these bitter and groundless charges against the authenticity of the Book of Mormon and the prophetic character of Joseph the Seer. In his malevolent haste, he has plunged, as we have seen, into an error of *forty-seven years* in reckoning time; and he also errs in his statement that "the first year of Zedekiah began the seventy years captivity," (of the Jews). It began in the reign of Jehoiakim, in the fourth year, or about B.C. 606—(*c*).

PLACE OF CHRIST'S BIRTH.

In the next place, Mr. S. undertakes to show that the Book of Mormon is false from its statement that Christ should be born "at Jerusalem."—(Alma 5 : 2). Now, if Mr. S. had quoted the context, the reader of his article could have seen at a glance what was meant by Alma. I will quote it, "And behold, he shall be born of Mary, at Jerusalem, *which is the land* of our forefathers." We have no apologies to offer for the grammatical construction of this passage; what we wish to know is, *what it means*. That it refers more especially to the vicinity of, and not necessarily to the very limits within the city, is, I think, quite apparent. The word *at*, is a prep-

(*c*) *Vide* Jer. 25 : 11-18; 2 Chron. 36 : 5-7; Rollin, Hist. Assyrians, Chap. 2.

osition; and primarily signifies *nearness, presence;* as, *at the sea; at the grave; at the river;* etc., etc. Some suppose, and not without reason, that Bethlehem, of Judea, the birth-place of our Savior, was a suburb of Jerusalem, and could, in that sense, be reckoned a part of Jerusalem. Mr. S. states that "the Bible often affirms that he was born at Bethlehem." We deny it. It often affirms that he was born *in* Bethlehem.

When considering the import of the text in question, it should be borne in mind that Alma was many thousand miles away from the place of which he speaks, and therefore his description of it, relatively, was eminently proper, and sufficiently plain for all but those who would "make a man an offender for a word."

MELCHIZEDEK PRIESTHOOD.

Mr. S. says, that "the Book of Mormon clashes with the Bible in its claims concerning the Melchizedek priesthood under the law."

It does claim that there were many besides Melchizedek who were priests of the Melchizedek order, not "under the law," though some of them lived during the times of "the law."

Mr. S. argues, substantially, that Israel had no other than Aaronic priests, and they only under the law. Moses was a priest, (Ps. 99 : 6), and officiated as such, (Ex. 24 : 4-8), before Aaron and his sons were set apart to minister in the priest's office, (Ex. 28 : 1). Now, as there are but two orders of priesthood mentioned in the Bible, we think that he must be assigned to one of those two orders. And inasmuch as he held priestly authority and power over both Aaron and his sons, before and after they were set apart, are we not forced to conclude that he held the higher priesthood,—the Melchizedek?

Certainly, Mr. S., rash as he is, will not dare say that Moses was not a priest; nor can he with truth say that he was an Aaronic priest. To what order *he* would assign him it is difficult to conjecture; yet of one thing we may rest assured, he will not allow that he was a Melchizedek priest, for that would utterly spoil his argument; for he claims that *only* Melchizedek and Christ were priests of that order. If Moses belonged to neither the Melchizedek nor the Aaronic orders, then he *must* have belonged to some other order. Will Mr. S. please arise and explain; for he would have it that only Christ and Melchizedek belonged to the one order; and, only Aaron and his sons to the other; nevertheless Moses was a priest of God, and the leading type of Christ. Will Mr. S. say that he was a sort of provisional priest,—a make-shift, and belonging to no order?

We believe that Moses was truly a priest, and that he was not an Aaronic priest, either, but that he was a Melchizedek priest, and hence was a fit type of the Lord Christ. Abel was evidently a priest, (Gen. 4:3-5); so also was Noah, (Gen. 8:20, 21); so Abraham, (Gen. 22:13); and so Jacob, (Gen. 31:54; 46:1); so also was Job, (Job 1:5; 42:8), who, it is probable, was not a Hebrew. Nor is this all, for Jethro was evidently a priest, accredited and honored of God; for,—

"Jethro, Moses' father-in-law, took a burnt offering and sacrifices for God; and Aaron came, and all the elders of Israel, to eat bread with Moses' father-in-law before God."—Ex. 18:12.

That this eating "bread" was a religious ceremony, (like the sacrament under the gospel), and not ordinary feasting, is seen in the fact that it was done "before God," under the administration of a "priest," and at a season when this priest offered "a burnt offering and sacrifices *for God*."

Furthermore, that Jethro was a priest accepted and ordained of God, is seen in the fact that Aaron, and all the elders of Israel, honored his ministrations by their presence, and did "eat bread" with him, which they would not have done if he had not been a priest of God ministering in righteousness. That he was a priest of God is further evident from the fact that he "rejoiced for all the goodness which the Lord had done to Israel," (Ex. 18:9), in delivering them from Egypt; and from the fact that he said, "Blessed be the Lord who hath delivered you out of the hand of the Egyptians;" and from the still greater fact, that he gave to Moses important, acceptable, and highly enlightened counsel in regard to the organization and government of Israel. To Moses he said:

"Hearken now unto my voice, I will give thee counsel, and God shall be with thee; * * * So Moses hearkened to the voice of his father-in-law, and did all that he said."—Ex. 18:19, 24.

Certainly an idolatrous priest would not have proffered counsel, especially such wise counsel. And, it is furthermore certain that Moses would not, for one moment, have received counsel from any other than a priest of God. To say that Jethro was an idolatrous priest would be to say that God taught superior wisdom to his own minister, Moses, through an idolator.

Inasmuch then as Jethro was a priest of God, he, too, must have belonged to one of the two orders—Melchizedek, or Aaronic. If we say that he was an Aaronic priest, we deny the Bible account; but if we say, that he was a Melchizedek priest, then we say, that which is, we think, conclusive to every intelligent, unprejudiced mind.

Besides those priests already mentioned there were others, not of the order of Aaron, who did minister before the Lord with acceptance, between Moses and Christ: Samuel, (1 Sam. 7:9); David, (2 Sam. 6:18); Elijah, (1 Kings 18:30–38). These, with others, officiated as priests with favor before the Lord; for the Lord answered their ministrations with blessing. And, inasmuch as all these aforementioned persons, some of whom were not even of Israel, did minister in the rites, ceremonies, and ordinances of the priesthood, both before and after the times of Moses, either by the commandment, or with the approval of God, is it unreasonable, or contrary to the Scriptures to believe, or claim, that God did call persons on this continent, in ancient times, to minister in the priesthood, as is taught in the Book of Mormon? But enough on this topic for the present; we shall have occasion to consider the subject of the priesthood at greater length ere we conclude this review.

TITHES.

Another huge stumbling-stone, one upon which Mr. S. proposes to wreck Mormonism, he finds in the saying of Alma, that "our father Abraham paid tithes of one tenth part of all he possessed." Alma 10:1. Mr. S. tells us that "tithes" "means a tenth." This we deny. "Tithes" means *tenths'*, or *may* mean a *tax*, a *revenue* arising from tithings; and this latter is clearly the sense in which Alma wished to be understood. The word "tithes" may mean the sum total of what is gathered by tithing, as an amount of revenue gathered under the order of tithing. Mr. S. says the text from Alma, "Our father Abraham paid tithes of one-tenth part of all he possessed," states, in effect, that Abraham paid "a tenth of one tenth part of all ;he possessed ,* * * which would be only a hundredth." Now we venture the assertion, that no sensible, honest person, unless he be blinded by prejudice, would ever put such a construction upon the passage. The manifest meaning of the passage is this: Abraham paid tithes *composed of one tenth part of all that he possessed.*

Here is a text from Deut. 26 : 12, which we present for the future consideration and critical labor of Mr. S. Perhaps we may next hear of his undertaking to prove Moses a false prophet, and the Bible a humbug, because the text is so very like the offensive one from Alma: "When thou hast made an end of tithing all the tithes of thine increase the third year." This was the commandment to the *people* of Israel, and refers directly to the manner in which they should pay their tithing as may be further seen from Deut. 14 : 28. Would it not be consistent now for Mr. S. to set himself vigorously at it to write another work, warning the people against Moses and the Bible, because that in the Bible Moses instructs Israel in "tithing all the tithes" of their increase? Mr. S., with his critical tact, could easily prove the Bible false, and Moses an impostor! Why, Moses! you command "tithing all the tithes!" You are as faulty as Alma! Why—that would give you only a "tenth of one tenth part, which would be only a hundredth!" Leaving this matter between Moses and Mr. S., we pass on.

AARONIC PRIESTHOOD.

Mr. S. objects that, "The Book of Mormon locates the Aaronic priesthood among the descendants of Manasseh, instead of Levi, in opposition to the Bible." It should be borne in mind that this particular priesthood is called the *Aaronic* or *Levitical*, in order to distinguish it from the higher or Melchizedek; and because that in the *organized kingdom* or *commonwealth* of Israel, it was delegated to Aaron and his seed. But we are not aware of any passage in the Bible that would prevent the scattered branches of Israel, or those who become "Abraham's seed, and heirs according to the promise," from holding and exercising the same or similar priesthood authority as did Aaron and his seed, with, or without the ceremonial law. But how does Mr. S. know that those of Manasseh's seed whom he mentions were professedly priests of the Aaronic order? They do not claim to be of that order; and the Latter Day Saints do not claim that they were. Mr. S. simply *assumes* as much, and then undertakes to prove it by quoting,

"And it came to pass that I, Nephi, did consecrate Jacob and Joseph, that they should be priests."—2 Nephi 4: 5.

There is here not even the slightest hint that they were Aaronic priests. As we have before seen, there were many priests among the people, both before and after the giving of the law, who were not called Aaronic priests.

God never had a special people whom he did not bless with priesthood privileges and powers, whether during the times of the Patriarchs, or from Moses to Christ, or under the gospel dispensation. And inasmuch as the Nephites were a righteous people and specially favored of God, it is but reasonable to suppose that they would enjoy the privileges and benefits of the priesthood. It is not impossible or improbable, that the Nephites held priesthood similar, or identical with that of Aaron. The text is silent on this point, yet Mr. S. *assumes* that it claims Aaronic priesthood. But of this priesthood matter, more hereafter.

SECOND COMING OF CHRIST.

The next objection urged is, that "the Book of Mormon conflicts with the Bible in locating the second coming of Christ in the past," because it states that Christ appeared to the Nephites "within a year after his crucifixion."—Book of Nephi 5 : 5. Christ said,

"Other sheep I have, which are not of this fold; [in Judea] them also I must bring, and *they shall hear my voice*."—John 10 : 16.

Now, inasmuch as he was "not sent but unto the lost sheep of the house of Israel," (Matt. 15 : 24), it must follow that the "other sheep" were "of the house of Israel," and they not in Judea. Christ's ministry *before* his crucifixion was confined to Judea; so that the fulfillment of this promise must have been accomplished *after* his crucifixion, and in *another locality* than Judea, and to others of "the lost sheep of the house of Israel" than those dwelling in Judea. The Book of Mormon, and that only, affords the true meaning of Christ's words, and in that we find an easy and rational solution of the otherwise unanswerable questions as to *when, where*, and *how*, this promise of Jesus had its fulfillment. For it states (Book of Nephi 7 : 2) that Jesus, after his resurrection did minister in teaching a branch of the "lost sheep," the Nephites on this continent. Christ certainly appeared to Paul some years after he had ascended to the Father, for Paul testifies: 1 Cor. 15 : 8:

"And last of all he was *seen of me also*, as of one born out of due time."

Now it is evident that Paul saw him as truly and as literally as did any of the apostles. This is the sense of his testimony. Again:

"Have I not *seen* Jesus Christ our Lord?"—1 Cor. 9 : 1.

"The God of our fathers hath chosen thee, that thou shouldest know his will, and *see that Just One*, and shouldest hear the voice of his mouth."—Acts 22: 14.

These texts teach the personal appearing of Jesus to Paul. But further:

"And the night following *the Lord stood by him*, and said, Be of good cheer, Paul; for as thou hast testified of me in Jerusalem, so must thou bear witness also at Rome."—Acts 23: 11.

That Paul actually *saw* the Lord Jesus on earth, personally, we further learn from the direct testimony of Barnabas.

"But Barnabas took him, [Paul], and brought him to the apostles, and declared unto them how he had *seen the Lord* in the way, and that he had spoken unto him."—Acts 9: 27.

This puts the matter beyond question, that Paul not only saw the "light from heaven" and "heard *a* voice," but that he likewise actually and literally saw the Lord Jesus, and heard "the voice of *his mouth*," "in the way" going to Damascus, *i. e.*, in the highway.

It seems from Eusebius that the early Christians believed that Christ appeared to many, after his ascension. He says:

"Besides these, ['Cephus,' 'the twelve,' 'five hundred brethren at once,' 'James'], there still was a *considerable number* who were apostles in imitation of the twelve, such as Paul himself was, he [Paul] adds, saying, 'afterwards he appeared to all the apostles.'"—Eccl. Hist. 42.

By this we learn that these last mentioned "apostles" were others besides the first "twelve" and Paul, and they, too, saw Christ. Again, Paul says he appeared unto "the twelve;" *i. e.*, evidently, after his ascension, for, after the death of Judas there was but "the eleven," until after the ascension. And again, Paul says he appeared to "above five hundred brethren at once." The facts of history favor the idea that there was no assemblage after the crucifixion, of so many Saints, (especially *brethren*), until after the ascension. Evidence is abundant that our Savior appeared, personally, to many in Judea, after his ascension. Mr. S. says this appearance to Paul "was a vision;" by which he probably means *a trance*, ecstasy, or spiritual view. That the word often signifies this, we know; but in Paul's case it certainly signifies something different, as is apparent from the different descriptions given of it. The first and most natural meaning of the word *vision* is literal, natural, *actual sight*. In this sense it is used, no doubt, in respect to Paul's seeing Christ; also in Luke 24 : 23, where it is said that certain women "had also seen a *vision* of angels, which said that he was alive." That this is the true sense may be seen by consulting Luke 24 : 4–10. So also of Luke 1 : 11, 22, where Zachariah saw the angel Gabriel, "on the right side of the altar of incense," in "a vision." Why should it be thought strange that Christ appeared on earth after his ascension, and before his second coming? We read in the Scriptures of his appearing to some many years before his first coming, such as to Nebuchadnezzar, for instance:

"Lo, I see four men loose, walking in the midst of the fire, and they have no hurt; and the form of the fourth is like the Son of God."—Dan. 3: 25.

Again, to Abraham, Gen. 18 : 13, 17, 20, 26, 30; to Jacob, Gen. 32 : 30, and to Moses, Ex. 3 : 2, 4, Ex. 6 : 3. Of these last mentioned appearances, and others, Eusebius makes these judicious remarks,—

"That the divine word, therefore, pre-existed and appeared, if not to all, at least to some, has been thus briefly shown."—Eccl. Hist. 18.

He further says, (what must be evident to every candid, intelligent mind), that,

"To suppose these divine appearances were the forms of subordinate angels and servants of God, is inadmissible; since, as often as any of these [angels] appeared to men, the Scriptures do not conceal the fact in the name, expressly saying that they were called not God, nor Lord, but [only] angels."—Eccl. Hist. 17.

Now, inasmuch as Christ appeared to his people before his first advent, and to Paul, and others in Judea, after his resurrection and ascension, it is not unscriptural, nor incredible, that he, after his ascension, should appear to his people on this continent, as stated in the Book of Mormon, especially when we consider his promise, that "other sheep" than those in Judea should *hear his voice*. Christ's *first* coming was to *dwell with*, and *minister for his people;* and his *second* coming is for the same purpose. His appearance at divers times after his ascension, including his resurrection, can no more be called his second or third coming, than his various appearances before his incarnation could be called his first coming. Christ did "appear" to Paul, and doubtless to others after his ascension; and he will "appear" again to all his Saints, at his glorious coming and kingdom to dwell with them in regal power and glory forever and ever. These events will differ, not in regard to their literality, or being personal; but in the surrounding circumstances, and in the results.

"THE SCRIPTURE WHICH SAITH."

Mr. S. next finds a "clash," where there is none; and in this he evidently strives to excel. He says.

> "In the book of Ether, sixth chapter, purporting to have been written many centuries before the first advent, and to have been translated and transcribed by Moroni, we read concerning 'the scripture which saith, there are they who were first, who shall be last; and there are they who were last, who shall be first.' Mark this point, [says Mr. S.], as none of the Old Testament Scriptures were then written, what scriptures can here be referred to but those in the New Testament, where we find similar language."

In reply we have to say, first, that the Old and New Testaments do not contain *all* the scriptures as Mr. S. would seem to claim; and in the second place, the words he quotes are the words of Moroni, who lived four hundred years after Christ, and not the words of Ether, as he falsely claims; and lastly they are not the words of the New Testament at all.

"NO VARIABLENESS."

He next objects:

> "In the fourth chapter of the book of Mormon we read, 'For do we not *read* that God is the same yesterday, to-day, and forever; and in him is no variableness, neither shadow of changing?' Yes, [says Mr. S.], we 'read' it, but where? In the New Testament, which claimed to be unknown to Mormon."

If Mr. S. had been as eager to learn the genuine spirit and doctrine of the Book of Mormon as he has been to conjure up faults, and to manufacture errors, he would have found divers places where the sentiments of the passage he quotes are written.

In Mosiah 1:8, is a passage having this import; and in Nephi 11:1: "I am the Lord, I change not;" and in 2 Nephi 12:7: "I am the same yesterday, to-day and forever;" and then in Alma 5:3: "Neither doth he vary from that which he hath said; neither hath he a shadow of turning from the right to the left." Moroni professed to quote only the *sense* of what they *read*, and not letter for letter; and surely, he had abundant grounds, as we have seen, from the records of his fathers.

In the next place he objects to the following passage found in Moroni 8:2: "The whole need no physician, but they that are sick;" "language borrowed, [he says], from the Savior."

Now the text, with its context, reads as follows:

> "And the word of the Lord came to me [Mormon] *by the power of the Holy Ghost*, saying, Listen to the words of Christ, your Redeemer, your Lord and

your God. Behold, I came into the world, not to call the righteous, but sinners to repentance; *the whole need no physician, but they that are sick;* wherefore little children are whole, for they are not capable of committing sin."

Here we see that the passage does not purport to be "borrowed" from any place, but that it was a direct revelation from Christ to Mormon.

If we are to condemn the Book of Mormon because sentiments and phrases are found in it similar to those found in the Old and New Testaments, then we may condemn the book of Micah, because in its fourth chapter there is found a prophecy similar in sense and *letter* to that found in Isaiah, second chapter. We may go further and condemn the Bible because in it are phrases and sentiments similar to those found in the Brahmin's Veda, which claims to be the oldest of books, and which was compiled as early, at least, as B. C. 1200. In it is a prayer similar to that taught by our Savior, "O God have mercy, give me my daily bread."—Rig-Veda 6 : 47. Shall we say that because Jesus taught similarly, that he, therefore, "borrowed" from the Veda? We should, if we adopted the reasoning of Mr. S. Again, (Rig-Veda 9 : 113, 7): "Where life is free, in the *third heaven of heavens*, where the worlds are radiant, there make me immortal." The logic of Mr. S. would make David and Paul *borrow* some of these ideas, and some of this language, from the Rig-Veda!

ZEND-AVESTA.

Again; in the Zend-Avesta there are many ideas and phrases similar to what is found in both the Old and New Testaments. Of this Dr. Haug remarks:

"The Zoroastrian religion exhibits a very close affinity to, or rather identity with, several important doctrines of the Mosiac religion and Christianity."—Chips from a German Workshop, p. 125.

There is one place in it where the Supreme Spirit proclaims himself "I am who I am;"—a similar name to that of Jehovah given by him, Ex. 3 : 14. Now, shall we argue from these coincidences that the Scriptures of the Old and New Testaments, or any part of them, have been copied—"borrowed"—from those ancient books? The fallacious method of reasoning adopted by Mr. S. would force us to do so. The Book of Mormon claims that the same God who inspired the prophets and seers in Judea, inspired prophets and seers in America, whose writings we find in the Book of Mormon.

This being true, it is no wonder that we find the same general ideas, the same doctrines and phrases in the Book of Mormon, that we find in the Bible. Of this the Lord says:

"Wherefore, I speak the same words unto one nation like unto another. And when the two nations shall run together, the testimony of the two nations shall run together also. And I do this that I may prove unto many, that I am the same yesterday, to-day, and forever; and that I speak forth my words according to mine own pleasure."—2 Nephi 12 : 7.

Will Mr. S. have us believe that two or more revelations from God to as many different persons, at as many different times, touching the same things, *must differ* in sentiment, and in phraseology!

It would seem so, for he is condemning the Book of Mormon on the ground that in it are found sentiments and phrases similar to those found in the Bible.

CHRISTIAN.

Here comes another insurmountable stumbling block in the way of Mr. S. He says:

"The Book of Mormon blunders into the claim that about one hundred years before the first advent, the name 'Christian' was in common use on this continent; thus clashing with the Bible which affirms, 'the disciples were first called Christians at Antioch.'—Acts 11: 26."

That the disciples upon the eastern continent were "first called Christians at Antioch," we do not deny; and that this was all that Luke intended, must be apparent to every fair-minded reader. Luke did not claim to write by revelation or prophecy; and as a historian he only wrote of facts as he knew and believed them. He referred only to those connected with the Church of Christ on the Eastern Continent, and did not profess to know or write of matters beyond that. But the statement that people on this continent were called Christians, even "one hundred years before the first Advent," Mr. S. cannot disprove. The very *name*, as well as the doctrine and mission of Christ, was known hundreds of years before the first Advent. So also that other prominent New Testament name of our Savior,—"Son of God." If the leading New Testament names of our Savior were known and *used* so long before the first Advent, why should it be thought incredible that one of the leading New Testament names of his disciples should likewise be known and used equally as long before? The Nephites foreknew the name, and mission, and peculiar doctrines of Christ, hundreds of years before the Advent, and they lived in conformity with his gospel, and why might they not be called by a name in their language that was the exact equivalent of the English word "Christian?" For my part I can see no reason against it, but, on the other hand, many good reasons for it. Eusebius informs us that:

"The very *name* of Jesus, as also that of *Christ*, was honored by the pious prophets of old. * * * Moses attaches the name of our *Savior Jesus Christ;* * * * the prophets that lived subsequently to these times, also plainly announced Christ before by *name*."—Eccl. Hist., pp. 21, 22.

Again he says:

"For as the name *Christians* is intended to indicate this very idea, that a man, by the *knowledge* and *doctrine* of Christ, is distinguished by modesty and justice, by patience and a virtuous fortitude, and by a profession of piety towards the one and only true and supreme God; all this was no less studiously cultivated by *them* than by us."—p. 26.

Moses, we are told by Paul, esteemed "the reproach of [for] Christ greater riches than the treasures of Egypt." Moses, then knew something of Christ and of his doctrine, as did, no doubt, some of his people.

THE PLATES.

Mr. S. next undertakes to make a conflict between the Book of Mormon and the testimony of Joseph, in regard to the disposal of the plates after Joseph translated them. The Book of Mormon says concerning Joseph:

"Wherefore, when thou hast read the words which I have commanded thee, and obtained the witness which I have promised thee, then shalt thou seal up the book again and hide it up unto me."

Now, Mr. S. says that it is claimed by Mr. John Taylor that the plates "when he [Joseph] got through translating, they were delivered again to the angel." "So [says Mr. S.], he did not hide up the plates, as stated in the Book of Mormon." The Book of Mormon does not state, nor even intimate, the *manner* in which Joseph was to "hide up" the plates. There are very many ways in which we may "hide up" plates, or other things, without putting them into the ground as is urged by Mr. S.

To hide up anything is to conceal it, to secure it, or screen it from public observation. This was certainly done when the plates were put into the hands of the angel.

THE THREE DISCIPLES.

Mr. S. objects that Jesus is made to say to three of his disciples:

"Ye shall never endure the pains of death; but when I come in my glory,

ye shall be changed in the twinkling of an eye, from mortality to immortality."
—Nephi 13: 3.

And that:

"In the next paragraph it is added, 'whether they were mortal or immortal, from the day of their transfiguration I know not.' * * * Nephi says he did not know whether they were mortal or immortal—equivalent to saying that he did not know whether Christ lied or told the truth."

It is not infrequent that people, even disciples of Christ, are told that which they do not fully understand when told. Jesus told his disciples in Judea to go and "preach the gospel to every creature;" yet it required no less than a miracle, and another command, to make Peter *know*, fully, the nature and scope of his mission, (Acts 10 : 19–35). Jesus foretold the facts of his death and resurrection, yet his disciples did not *intelligently* believe him on this point, till after his resurrection and appearance unto them.

Mr. S., who professes to be a disciple of Christ, does not believe in a pre-millennial kingdom, yet Christ plainly teaches it in Matthew 25 : 1; 13 : 47–49, and elsewhere. Mr. S. also believes that the Adventists are the "wise virgins" of Matthew 25 : 4, and that they, since A.D. 1833, have been sounding the midnight cry; whereas Christ says the midnight cry comes *to* [not from] the wise, as well as to the foolish virgins, and that it finds them asleep, or slumbering. Mr. S. believes also that while they have been sounding the midnight cry, for the past forty or more years, Christ, "the bridegroom tarried;" whereas Christ says, that after the midnight cry is made there is no tarrying, and, that so sudden would be the coming of the bridegroom, that the foolish virgins would not have time to get the needed oil to fill their lamps. Now, because Mr. S. and his co-religionists believe contrary to what Christ says, or because they at least fail to believe what he does say, would it not be indelicate, not to say unchristian-like, for us to charge that their want of intelligent belief is "equivalent to saying they did not know whether Christ lied or told the truth?" We think so.

PEOPLE OF ZARAHEMLA.

Here another terrible fault is conjured up. He says:

"The first chapter of the Book of Omni represents Mosiah as going from the land of Nephi to Zarahemla, about three hundred years after Nephi reached America; 'and they discovered a people who were called the people of Zarahemla. Now there was great rejoicing among the people of Zarahemla; and also Zarahemla did rejoice exceedingly because the Lord had sent the people of Mosiah with the plates of brass which contained the record of the

Jews.' In the next paragraph we are told, [says Mr. S.], their language had become corrupted; and they had brought no records with them; and they denied the being of their Creator; and Mosiah, nor the people of Mosiah could understand them. Yet, [says Mr. S.], the same paragraph tells us that they came out of Jerusalem at the time Zedekiah was taken to Babylon—about three hundred years previously. At this time they rejoiced that the Lord had sent Mosiah, and yet did not believe that there was a Lord *in existence*. Glad of the records, yet could not understand each other's language—their language having been so corrupted in a little over three hundred years."

A more shameful effort at garbling texts is seldom, if ever, seen than this. It would put the most unblushing infidel critic to shame. Amaleki records the fact, that Mosiah, being warned of God, fled out of the land of Nephi, and went to the land of Zarahemla, both he and others who accompanied him.

"And they discovered a people who were called the people of Zarahemla. Now, there was great rejoicing among the people of Zarahemla; and also Zarahemla did rejoice exceedingly, because the Lord had sent the people of Mosiah with the plates of brass which contained a record of the Jews."

This "great rejoicing" took place evidently, not when the people were first discovered by Mosiah and his company, but when the people of Zarahemla became acquainted thoroughly with the new immigrants,—their doctrines and their tidings,—as we shall further see:

"Behold, it came to pass that Mosiah discovered that the people of Zarahemla came out from Jerusalem at the time that Zedekiah, king of Judah, was carried away into Babylon. * * * And *at the time that Mosiah discovered them*, they had become exceeding numerous. Nevertheless, they had many wars and serious contentions, and had fallen by the sword from time to time, and their language had become corrupted; and they had brought no records with them; and they denied the being of their Creator; and Mosiah, nor the people of Mosiah, could understand them. But it came to pass that Mosiah caused that they should be taught in his language."

There is nothing contradictory in this brief narrative; neither anything impossible or incredible. Amaleki first states the fact of the discovery of Zarahemla and his people, and then states, as one of the results, that there was "great rejoicing." But he does not intimate that this rejoicing took place immediately upon the discovery, but after the people of Zarahemla could understand Mosiah and his people, and had been instructed by them. Furthermore, it was *at the time* of their discovery, and also before it, that the people of Zarahemla denied the being of their Creator; and at that time it was that "the people of Mosiah" could not understand them.

Mr. S. argues that it is incredible that these two peoples, having a common origin, coming from the same country about three hundred years before, could have so corrupted their language as not to understand each other. If Mr. S. was instructed in philology, or was very observant of current facts, he would know that there was nothing improbable in it; especially when we consider that they of Zarahemla "brought no records with them." Language changes constantly among all nations, and among some far more rapidly than with others; and that, too, where they have an extensive literature —or "records." It would be next to impossible for the English speaking nations of to-day to understand the English of but a few hundred years ago. So great have been the changes of language in England, alone, that people from one shire cannot well understand those of another. The languages of men, like their forms of religion, are subject to rapid and extensive change. Max Muller, M. A., Fellow of All Souls' College, Oxford, England, a competent authority says:

"The meaning of words changes imperceptibly and irresistibly. Even where there is a literature, and *a printed literature*, like that of modern Europe, four or five centuries work such a change that few even of the most learned divines in England would find it easy to read and to understand accurately a theological treatise written in England four hundred years ago. The same happened, and happened to a far greater extent, in ancient languages. Nor was the sacred character, attributed to certain writings, any safeguard."—*Chips From a German Workshop*, p. 130.

These facts amount to conclusive proof in favor of what is said in regard to the language of the people of Zarahemla having become so corrupted, as stated by Amaleki.

PLATES OF ETHER.

Mr. S., in the following, undertakes to show that there are very damaging contradictions in the Book of Mormon in its statements concerning the plates written and hid up by Ether. Now it should be borne in mind that one class of these statements is prophetic,—fortelling what should occur with the plates,—another, giving *commands* touching their disposal; and, lastly, the purely historical account of their origin, transmission, and final disposition. Whilst the first claims to be fully inspired, the latter makes no such claim. Prophecy and history are two quite different things. The one claims absolute divine perfection, in its sense, its import, and in all its facts; while history—Bible history—Scripture history—seldom makes such claim. Scripture history claims to be *essentially* true in its statements, but it does not usually claim to have been written with such full measure of the Holy Spirit as to secure it against verbal errors, and even errors in some of its minor and unimportant *facts*.

DEFECTS IN SCRIPTURE HISTORY.

When we reflect one moment upon the discrepancies—omissions and contradictions—between the *Books of the Chronicles* and the *Books of the Kings*, between the four several gospels, and between the four gospels and the *Acts;* also between the *Acts* and the *Old Testament* history, we see the folly of claiming for the writers of those books what they never claim for themselves, *i. e.*, full and absolute inspiration.

As to prophecy, holy men and women speak as they are "moved upon by the Holy Ghost;" but history is a narration of matters as the writers know them, understand them, and believe them. Hence Luke (1 : 13), thought it good to write what he knew, and believed, and had a "perfect understanding of," as it had been delivered to him by those who "from the beginning were eye-witnesses and ministers of the word. Luke did not claim to write by direct revelation from God to himself, but simply what he had learned from persons who were, as he believed, competent witnesses. Luke omits many facts found in the three other gospels, but these omissions do not invalidate anything he may have written, and no one but a quibbling critic would argue as much. The evangelists differ widely in regard to the crucifixion and resurrection of Christ, yet this difference arises mainly, if not entirely, from omissions—some failing to write just the same things that were written by others. In the *Acts* three different accounts are given of the conversion of Saul, (9 : 3-20; 22 : 6-16; 26 : 12-18). In these there is considerable discrepancy, and some direct contradiction. This could not occur if all Scripture history was fully and perfectly inspired of God. Again Paul, that faithful, devoted servant of Christ, takes occasion to inform us that some of his writings were not indited under the inspiration of the Holy Spirit.—(1 Cor. 7 : 6, 12, 25, 40; 2 Cor. 8 : 8; 11 : 17, &c.)

Now, inasmuch as Bible historians did not always profess to write under the full inspiration of God's unerring Spirit, are we justified in demanding of those who wrote Scripture history on this continent, that their historical writings shall be so fully and perfectly inspired of God, as to be absolutely full and complete, and without error in letter, or defect in matter? We think not. Such a claim by those versed well in Scripture matters exhibits unfairness, prejudice, or ignorance. But we do not admit the contradictions claimed by Mr. S. We utterly deny them, except, possibly, in one point, and that one of no essential historical value.

He says:

1. "Moroni says the plates found by the people of Limhi were kept by king Benjamin, that the world should not see them; but the Book of Mosiah says that the people of Limhi did not find the plates till after king Benjamin was dead.

2. "Moroni testifies that they were not to be translated till after Christ was 'lifted up upon the cross;' but the book of Mosiah informs us that they were translated by king Mosiah, 'and caused to be written,' even hundreds of years before the crucifixion; and yet Moroni pretends to translate them again after the cross.

3. "Moroni informs us that the stone interpreters of the brother of Jared were sealed up with the plates; but the book of Mosiah makes no mention of finding stones with the plates, though Ammon talks to Limhi about stone interpreters possessed by Mosiah off in a distant land. What became of these sealed interpreters?

4. "Moroni tells us that Jared's brother's stone interpreters were sealed up with the plates that Limhi's people found, for the express purpose of enabling the finders to translate them; yet, according to the book of Mosiah, the finders could not translate them, not finding with the plates anything but swords and breast-plates; and finally, Ammon tells king Limhi that Mosiah 'hath wherewith he can translate,' called interpreters; and after a while the plates are carried over to Mosiah in Zarahemla, and Mosiah translates them with his own interpreters 'set in two rims of a bow.' But what became of the interpreters that were sealed up with those plates found by Limhi's people?

5. "Mosiah not only had interpreters before receiving the twenty-four plates found by the people of Limhi, but he had previously exercised his gift of interpreting languages, and his uncle before him, also, by which Ammon knew that he possessed this gift; and an instance is given of its exercise in a book written by Omni, before the book of Mosiah: 'And it came to pass in the days of Mosiah, there was a large stone brought unto him, with engravings on it; and he did interpret the engravings, by the gift and power of God.' So Mosiah did not need the interpreters of Jared's brother; but still the question continues to come up, since they were sealed at God's bidding, what became of them? And, as Moroni claims to have had them, where did he get them? After Moroni represents God as saying to Jared's brother, 'These two stones will I give unto thee, and ye shall seal them up also'—that is, with the plates—'wherefore I will cause in mine own due time that *these stones* shall magnify to the eyes of men these things which ye shall write.' Moroni adds, 'After Christ had truly showed himself unto his people, he commanded that they should be made manifest. * * * Behold I have written upon these plates the very things that the brother of Jared saw.' Again he adds, 'I am commanded that I should

hide them up again in the earth, * * * and he also hath commanded that I should seal up the interpretation thereof; wherefore I have sealed up *the interpreters*.' Where did he get them, seeing they were not found when the people of Limhi found the twenty-four plates, with which they were hid?

6. "Mosiah's stone-interpreters, 'set in two rims of a bow,' which he possessed previous to the finding of these twenty-four plates by the people of Limhi, 'were prepared from the beginning, and were handed down from generation to generation, for the purpose of interpreting languages' (Mosiah, 12th chapter); while the 'two stones' possessed by the brother of Jared were given to him by the Lord after confounding the language at the tower, without any 'rims of a bow.' But when Nephi came to America, he was very careful to tell us about bringing Laban's sword, Lehi's compass, and the brass plates taken from Laban, but not a word about these precious stone interpreters, which 'were prepared from the beginning, and were handed down from generation to generation.' Where did Mosiah get his interpreters, seeing they were not imported from Jerusalem, and seeing preceding generations on this continent were unknown to him till after he possessed those interpreters? Here is another puzzle, or crooked story."

Precisely, Mr. S. As you have rendered it, it is a "puzzle;" and as you have told it, it is a "crooked story." It is a fair specimen of your work. Your garbled quotations, your unfair inferences, and brazen misstatements, have perverted the facts and quite distorted the entire account.

Allowing that, possibly, there is a mistake in the person's *name* who is said to have kept the plates of Ether and the interpreters, (Ether 1:11), a matter of no historical moment as affecting the value of the record,—(Moroni claims to be writing only a small abridgment, Ether 1:1, and to write from *memory*, Ether 2:1, and no intimation is given that he writes in a way to preclude possibility of verbal errors, such as in names, etc.)—allowing that it should have been Mosiah, instead of Benjamin, your second statement is quite untrue, viz, that Moroni said "they [the plates] were not to be translated till after Christ was 'lifted up upon the cross.'" It was not the plates of Ether, as a whole, but the remarkable things *seen* and *heard* by the brother of Jared when in the presence of the Lord upon the mount:

"And the Lord commanded the brother of Jared to go down out of the mount from the presence of the Lord, and write the things which he had seen [in the mount]; and *they* were forbidden to come unto the children of men, until after that he should be lifted up upon the cross; and for this cause did King Benjamin keep them, that they should not come *unto the world*, until after Christ should shew himself unto his people."—Ether 1:11.

Your statement that, "Moroni pretends to translate them [the plates] again after the cross," is wholly without foundation. The account states that he *abridged* what he found on the plates of Ether; and he professed to give but a *part only* of what he there found:

"I [Moroni] give not the full account, but a part of the account I give, from the tower down until they [the Jaredites] were destroyed."—Ether 1 : 1. See also paragraph 9.

You next state that "the book of Mosiah makes no mention of finding stones [interpreters] with the plates." Suppose it does not, does that omission prove that they were not with the plates? It proves nothing of the kind. Matthew *omits* many things concerning Jesus which John and others mention. These *omissions* by Matthew disprove nothing written by John and others, nor do they invalidate either account. Paul, in the description of his remarkable conversion, as told to King Agrippa, (Acts, 26 : 12-19), omits some important items from the account which himself gives of it at another time before the Jews—(Acts, 22 : 6-16). He *omits* to tell King Agrippa the important fact, that he was blinded by "the glory of that light," and that he was "led by the hand of them that were with" him. He *omits* to tell how Ananias came and instructed him, and said unto him, "Brother Saul, receive thy sight;" and how Ananias commanded him, saying, "Arise, and be baptized, and wash away thy sins, calling on the name of the Lord." All these, and many more omissions are found in comparing the different accounts of Paul's conversion, but these do not invalidate each other, even though they are found in the same book, and written by one and the same person.

The Book of Mosiah is simply silent upon the point as to whether "the two stones" given to Jared's brother were found by the people of Limhi with the twenty-four gold plates of Ether, or not; yet it is implied, from Mosiah 12 : 3, that they were *with the plates when found*. For it is said:

"And now he [Mosiah] translated them by the means of *those two stones* which were fastened into the two rims of a bow."

This is the account that Mormon, the father of Moroni, gives. He is the one who translated and greatly abridged the records handed down to him; and he says: "I cannot write the hundredth part of the things of my people."—Words of Mormon 1 : 2. It is Mormon who says that Mosiah translated the plates found by the people of Limhi, by "means of those stones which were fastened into the rims of a bow."

STONE INTERPRETERS.

Your next statement that "Ammon talks to Limhi about stone interpreters possessed by Mosiah off in a distant land," is entirely untrue. Ammon does not mention "stone interpreters." What he said to Limhi, touching the matter of translation, reads as follows:

"Now Ammon said unto him, I can assuredly tell thee, O King, of a man that can translate the records: for he has wherewith he can look, and translate all records that are of ancient date; and this is a gift from God."

DIRECTORS.

Now Mosiah the *first*, as we may call him, who was a great prophet, and who lived some years before Mosiah the *second*, was possessed of the gift and *means* of interpretation. "He did interpret the engravings [found upon 'a large stone'] by the gift and power of God."—Omni 1:9. To *interpret* is to translate, to unfold, to explain, or reveal, to make known what before was hidden or mysterious. That *this means* was handed down with the records to Benjamin, and then to his son Mosiah, is highly probable, if not absolutely certain; for we read that "the sacred things," which included "the records which were engraven upon the plates of brass," [containing the five books of Moses, the records of the Jews down to the first of Zedekiah, also the prophecies of the prophets down to and including much of the prophecies of Jeremiah] (*d*). "And also the plates of Nephi, and also the sword of Laban, and the ball or director, which led our fathers through the wilderness, which was prepared by the hand of the Lord, that they thereby might be led, even according to the heed and diligence which they gave unto him" (*e*), were to be "handed down from one generation to another, or from one prophet to another" (*f*).

This may serve to explain why we find Mosiah the first (*g*), Mosiah the second (*h*), and Ameliki (*i*), all conversant with the fact, and possessing *the means* of interpreting languages. For it is certain that the wonderful "directors" given to Lehi, and "handed down from one prophet to another," was an important means of revelation and divine instruction to those prophets. In describing

(*d*) 1 Nephi 1:46.   (*e*) Mosiah 1:3.   (*f*) 1 Nephi 5:47.   (*g*) Omni 1:9.
(*h*) Mosiah 1:3.   (*i*) Omni 1:12.

their importance and utility, also the manner in which instruction, guidance and revelation were obtained by them, Nephi says:

"And there was also written upon them a new *writing*, which was plain to be read, which did give us understanding concerning the way of the Lord; and it was written and changed from time to time, according to the faith and diligence we gave unto it."—1 Nephi 5:12.

Here is *a means* of revelation given to Lehi, and handed down from one prophet to another, reaching Mosiah the second, by which we see that he had a means of interpretation besides the "two stones" mentioned in connection with the plates of Ether. Of the character of these "directors" we further learn by Alma's instruction to his son Helaman: "And now, my son, these directors were prepared that the word of God might be fulfilled, which he spake, saying, I will bring forth out of darkness unto light, all their secret works, and their abominations." Thus we see again that they were a means of revelation, so that, as Ammon said, Mosiah had "wherewith he can look, and translate all records that are of ancient date; and it is a gift of God."

"INTERPRETERS."—"TWO STONES."

But, further, it is not impossible that, in the providence of God, the very "two stones" given to the brother of Jared came into the possession of Mosiah the first, and so passed down to Mosiah the second; and that he had them prior to the time of his receiving the twenty-four plates of Ether. Coriantumr, the last of the Jaredites, was discovered by the people of Zarahemla, and "he dwelt with them for the space of nine moons."—Omni 1:10. By this we learn that some knowledge of the Jaredites was had by the people of Zarahemla. We further learn that something of the history of the Jaredites was obtained from "a large stone," the "engravings" on which were interpreted by Mosiah the first.—par. 9. Here are channels through which much was learned by them of Zarahemla, and finally by them of Nephi in regard to the Jaredites. And might it not be that "the two stones" given to Jared's brother found their way through the Zarahemlaites to Mosiah the first, and so to Mosiah the second? We see nothing improbable in this; certainly nothing impossible.

"INTERPRETERS" SEALED UP.

You next state that "Moroni tells us that Jared's brother's stone interpreters were sealed up with the plates that Limhi's people found, for *the express purpose* of enabling the finders to translate them." This statement is not true. The nearest to it is a saying of Moroni concerning the Lord's instructing the brother of Jared as follows:

"The language which ye shall write I have confounded; wherefore I will cause in my own due time that these stones shall magnify to the eyes of men, these things which ye shall write."—Ether 1:10.

Your next statement that "the finders [meaning, probably, the people of Limhi] could not translate them, not finding with the plates any thing but swords and breast-plates," is wholly unwarranted. They may have found many things which they failed to mention. As we have already seen, important items may be omitted in an account without vitiating that account.

Luke, in giving his account of the sermon on the mount, omits many important items in that sermon, when we compare it with Matthew. What folly it would be to say that Jesus really taught at that time only what Luke mentions! Also, Luke omits a part of the Lord's prayer. Matthew fails to mention the fact, time, and place of the ascension of Christ. Mark omits to mention the earthquake which occurred at the resurrection. Matthew, Luke, and John, omit to mention the "young man, sitting on the right side, [in the sepulchre], clothed in a white garment."—Mark 16:5. And all but John fail to mention the "two angels in white, sitting; the one at the head and the other at the feet, where the body of Jesus had lain." Now these omissions are just as important and just as damaging, as is that in regard to the stone interpreters. All you can say in truth is that Mosiah does not mention, directly, that the stone interpreters were found by the people of Limhi with the twenty-four plates of Ether. To say more than this is unwarrantable and unfair.

MR. S. PERVERTS HISTORY.

We pass by your fifth paragraph, as we have already answered and refuted what you there say. However, the latter part of that paragraph, where you say again that the interpreters "were not found when the people of Limhi found the twenty-four plates, with which they were hid," is so like your former self, that we will remind you that your statement is naked assumption. You, with characteristic effrontery, make the text state that which is not there. The text neither states, nor implies, that the interpreters were not found with the plates.

MOSIAH'S STONE INTERPRETERS.

You assume, as usual, that "Mosiah's stone interpreters," "set in two rims of a bow," which you say he possessed previously to the finding of these twenty-four plates by the people of Limhi, *were not the ones* given to the brother of Jared. This we have before shown is utterly groundless, as the probabilities are that they were the very ones given to the brother of Jared, and were either found with the plates by the people of Limhi, or came down to Mosiah, the second, and his predecessors, by way of the Zarahemlaites; for the Zarahemlaites knew of the history of the Jaredites through Coriantumr, the last Jaredite king, as also through their writings on stone, as we have already seen.

The "beginning" mentioned, is most probably the beginning of the Jaredite nation.

INTERPRETERS, HOW OBTAINED.

As to your question:

"Where did Mosiah get his interpreters, seeing they were not imported out of Jerusalem, and seeing that preceding generations on this continent were unknown to him till after he possessed the interpreters?"

We reply, first, he had two ways of obtaining the interpreters given to Jared's brother, as we have already seen; and, in the next place, it is *possible* he used the "directors" as interpreters, for we have seen that they were a prominent and efficient means of divine revelation. And as to your assumption that "preceding generations on this continent were unknown to him [Mosiah] till after he possessed these interpreters," (namely, those deposited with the plates found by the people of Limhi), we reply that it is simply false to the record, and you *ought* to know it. For, as we have seen before, the knowledge concerning the Jaredites came by the way of Coriantumr, the last Jaredite king, who lived for a time with the Zarahemlaites, who finally became identified with the Nephites; and, likewise, by means of the history translated by Mosiah, the first, from that "large stone."

CHAPTER II.

THE INSPIRED TRANSLATION.

Mr. S. devotes a large proportion of his second chapter to an endeavor to make a very marked contradiction between the Book of Mormon and the Inspired Translation of the Bible, in the teachings of Christ. He urges what is not true, that the Book of Mormon agrees precisely with our common version of the Bible, in respect to the teachings of Jesus; and he then argues that if the Book of Mormon and the Inspired Translation were both true, and divinely inspired, they would exactly agree in language and in fact.

Now it happens that in the Book of Mormon there are many things taught by Christ which are not taught in the New Testament at all. In the next place sentiments taught by our Savior in the New Testament are found in the Book of Mormon clothed in *quite different language*. For instance:

"Yea, blessed are the poor in spirit *who come unto me*, for theirs is the kingdom of heaven. * * * * And blessed are all they who do hunger and thirst after righteousness, for they shall be filled *with the Holy Ghost*."—Nephi 5: 9.

The words in italics are not found in the New Testament of the common version, but in both the Book of Mormon and the Inspired Translation. Again; in the Book of Mormon it is written:

"Ye have heard that it *hath been* said by them of old time, *and it is also written before you, that* thou shalt not kill; and whosoever shall kill shall be in danger of the judgment *of God*."—Nephi 5: 10.

Again:

"Therefore, if ye *shall come unto me, or shall desire to come unto me*, and rememberest that thy brother hath aught against thee, *go thy way unto thy brother, and* first be reconciled to thy brother, and then come *unto me with full purpose of heart, and I will receive you*."—*Ibid.*

As before, the words in italics are not found in the common version, nor does the text agree exactly with the Inspired Translation.

Now these quotations, with scores of others, in which there are striking verbal differences between the Book of Mormon and the common version in regard to the teachings of Christ, show conclusively that Joseph Smith did not copy from the common version, as Mr. S. boldly and impudently asserts. He says: "The fact is, when preparing the Book of Mormon our version was freely used, with all its defects." The reader can judge from the above how much of truth there is in this statement.

The Inspired Translation does not profess to be a translation of or from the Book of Mormon, but only to be a translation, in part, of the Bible; therefore we may not look for *verbal* agreement even where the same principles and sentiments are taught. In many instances in the Book of Mormon texts, professedly from Moses and the prophets, are found to differ, *verbally*, and sometimes in *sentiment*, widely, from the common version. For instance:

"*Hearken* and hear this, O house of Jacob, *who* are called by the name of Israel, and are come forth out of the waters of Judah, *who* swear by the name of the Lord, and make mention of the God of Israel, *yet they swear* not in truth nor in righteousness; *nevertheless* they call themselves of the holy city, *but they do not* stay themselves upon the God of Israel, *who is* the *Lord of Hosts: Yea*, the Lord of Hosts is his name. *Behold*, I have declared the former things from the beginning; and they went forth out of my mouth, and I shewed them. I did *show* them suddenly, *and I did it* because I knew thou *wert* obstinate, and thy neck *was* an iron sinew, and thy brow brass; *and* I have, even from the beginning, declared to thee, before it came to pass I shewed *them* thee; *and shewed* them *for fear* lest thou shouldst say, mine idol hath done them, and my graven image, and my molten image hath commanded them. Thou hast *seen and heard* all this; and will ye not declare *them?*"—1 Nephi 6: 1; with Isa. 48: 1-6.

Again:

"The word that Isaiah, the son of Amoz, saw concerning Judah and Jerusalem: And it shall come to pass in the last days, *when* the mountain of the Lord's house shall be established in the top of the mountains, and shall be exalted above the hills, and all nations shall flow unto it, and many people shall go and say, Come ye, and let us go up to the mountain of the Lord, to the house of the God of Jacob; and he will teach us of his ways, and we will walk in his paths; for out of Zion shall go forth the law, and the word of the Lord from Jerusalem. And he shall judge among the nations, and shall rebuke many people; and they shall beat their swords into plough-shares, and their spears into pruning hooks: nation shall not lift up sword against nation, neither shall they learn war any more. O house of Jacob, come ye, and let us walk in the light of the Lord; *yea, come, for ye have all gone astray, every one to his wicked ways.*

"Therefore, *O Lord*, thou hast forsaken thy people, the house of Jacob, because they be replenished from the east, and *hearken unto* soothsayers like the

Philistines, and they please themselves in the children of strangers. Their land also is full of silver and gold, neither is there any end of their treasures—their land is also full of horses, neither is there any end of their chariots: their land is *also* full of idols—they worship the work of their own hands, that which their own fingers have made: and the mean boweth *not* down, and the great man humbleth *not* himself, therefore, forgive *him* not.

"*O ye wicked ones*, enter into the rock, and hide thee in the dust, for *the* fear of the Lord, and * * the glory of his majesty *shall smile thee*. And *it shall come to pass that* the lofty looks of man shall be humbled, and the haughtiness of men shall be bowed down, and the Lord alone shall be exalted in that day. For the day of the Lord of Hosts *soon cometh upon all nations; yea, upon every one; yea*, upon the proud and lofty, and upon every one *who* is lifted up; and he shall be brought low."—2 Nephi 8: 4, 5, 6; with Isa. 2: 1-12.

The words in italics are wanting, or differ in connection, in the common version, while the asterisks indicate that in those places in the common version there is something more than in the Book of Mormon. It will be seen on careful reading that the sense is materially better, and clearer, in the texts from the Book of Mormon (*j*).

The extracts here given, and the texts cited, utterly disprove the statement of Mr. S. that the common "version was freely used, by Joseph, with all its defects," when "preparing the Book of Mormon."

The thought that the illiterate young man, Joseph Smith, did copy from the common version, making all these important changes in the texts,—and changes that greatly improve the texts,—is quite groundless and inconsistent. He did not copy from the common version. He was not qualified, naturally, for making those important changes. Nor will it do to say that he copied from Mr. Spaulding's manuscript; for no intelligent Presbyterian minister would *dare* change the text of the Bible, as it is everywhere changed in the Book of Mormon. In its language, and in much of its subject matter, it agrees with neither the common version nor the Book of Mormon, in respect to the teachings of Christ. The Book of Mormon does not *claim* to agree with either the Inspired Translation or the common version. It claims to be a record given to another people, under somewhat dissimilar circumstances, and having quite different surroundings. If the Book of Mormon claimed that the teachings of Jesus, as therein found, were identically the same as that which he gave to his disciples in Judea, then we might expect the Inspired Translation to agree with it, so far as facts and senti-

(*j*): See also 2 Nephi 5: 9, with Isa. 51: 17-20, &c.

ments are concerned; but not necessarily in regard to forms of language, for the language of the two peoples was manifestly different in some degree.

In translating the Book of Mormon it was evidently intended to transfer, so far as practicable, the forms of speech peculiar to the language in which it was found; while in the Inspired Translation the apparent object seems to be, (1), to restore essential parts that had been taken away, especially from the gospel, and, (2), to strike out what had been added by uninspired men, and, (3), to give the *sense*, rather than the *form* of speech, in those passages where the meaning was ambiguous and the sense obscure. Many of the forms of speech peculiar to the Israelites of eighteen hundred years ago, and well adapted to their modes of thought and expression, are quite unsuited to the people of the nineteenth century, so great has been the change in language. And it is not at all surprising, that in correcting and translating the Scriptures by inspiration, the *sense*, rather than the *forms* of the text should be given.

The Book of Mormon is a work quite distinct from the Inspired Translation; and, while we may expect that there will be no considerable differences between the two records, we may *not* expect to find precisely the same sentiments, no more and no less, taught in both of them; neither to find the same forms of speech even when the same sentiments are taught by the same person. The same truths may be and often are taught by the same person under different forms of language. Man, with prolific mind and facile tongue, is not a mere machine that he should always give to the same thought the same form of words, as Mr. S. would argue.

GRAMMAR.

Mr. S. next finds fault with the grammar of Joseph's Inspired Translation, and quotes Rev. 1:3, as a specimen of it. This is a specimen, not of "Joseph's grammar," but that of King James' translators'. "The Holy Scriptures, translated and corrected by the Spirit of Revelation, by Joseph Smith Jr., the Seer," was not a translation of the entire text of the common version, but only a translation of some parts of it, a "correction" of others, while many parts of it were left untouched. Corrections were made by striking from or adding to the text; as also by transferring the sense of certain texts into more correct and suitable forms of words, but the text quoted by Mr. S. is one of that very numerous class left as found in the text.

As for the matter of grammar, there is no little difference among grammarians of to-day in regard to it; while there is a very striking difference between those of the present and those of preceding times. The translators of the "common version" were very learned men, and, no doubt, good grammarians, for their times. We should not judge them hastily by our standards, lest coming generations, measuring us by theirs, pronounce us equally faulty. Grammar changes with the education and tastes of the people. But Mr. S., with characteristic assurance, tells us, that "Inspiration gives the language, as well as the thoughts." Hence he argues that Joseph's defective grammar (according to *his* standard) is evidence that he was not a prophet of God. If the logic of Mr. S. was valid, it would prove that the Bible, being defective in its grammatical construction, was not inspired, and that its inspiration would come and go according to its grammatical or ungrammatical construction or translation. This is worse than nonsense.

With the Germans, and other nations, it is a rule to put the noun before the adjective, thus—horse black; tree tall; woman beautiful; but with the English speaking nations it is just the reverse—black horse; tall tree; beautiful woman. That usage which is *a law* among the one people, is *a violation of law* with the others. If inspiration is subject to the laws of grammar will Mr. S. kindly tell us *which class* of laws, for they differ widely, as we see, among the different nations. Are they those of ZENODOTUS of Ephesus? or ARISTOPHANES of Byzantium? or are they those of MURRAY and KIRKHAM? or PINNEO and QUACKENBOSS? Pray tell us, Mr. S., for it is important to find the exact and only grammatical channel through which inspiration may come to us!

We apprehend that God may inspire persons to speak and write irrespective of men's notions as to what is or is not grammatical. The chief value of any communication depends, not upon its strictly grammatical qualities, but upon the quality and amount of intelligence it conveys. The loftiest principles, and the grandest truths, are often found in broken and unpolished sentences, even as the purest gold, and the most precious gems, are found with the confused quartz or the shifting sands. The *sense* of a sentence is the measure of its worth; its structure is of secondary importance. As the style of garment is to man, so is the form of language to sentiment—it is its *clothing*.

If Mr. S. persistently objects to the inspiration of a work on the grounds of defective grammar, we propose that he enters upon a criticism of the Old and New Testaments, which he professes to love so dearly, and to believe so firmly, and then inform us as to whether they are inspired records or not. As to inspiration giving "the language, as well as the thoughts," it is true in part, and only in part.

DEGREES OF INSPIRATION.

There are different degrees of inspiration, as one may readily see on reading the Scriptures, unless they are blinded by prejudice or be-fogged by the commentaries, creeds and catechisms of uninspired men. That degree of inspiration which gives the prophetic word, and the open vision, is greater than that which inspires a dream or moves to write current history. That degree that enabled Jesus to know what was in man, and to work his wondrous miracles, was far greater than that which inspired the council of "apostles and elders at Jerusalem," (Acts 15:29), or that which moved Paul to write the seventh chapter of First Corinthians. Paul says: "I think also that I have the Spirit of God." The degree of the Spirit which he then possessed was so small that there was no certainty that what he wrote at that time was inspired of God at all.

If inspiration always "gives the language, as well as the thoughts," why is there not an exact verbal agreement between the evangelists when they describe the same events, or rehearse the same teachings? And why is not the language of James, and John, and Jude, as precise and scholarly as that of Paul and Luke? And why is there as wide a difference between the style of language found in Ezekiel and that of David, or Isaiah, or Solomon, as there is between the terse sentences of Josephus, and the polished periods of Gibbon? The language of Habakkuk, and Job, and Nahum, and the Psalms is lofty and elegant, while that of Daniel, Hosea and Malachi, is plain, vigorous, and unpoetic in comparison.

Inspiration is:—

"The conveying of certain extraordinary and supernatural notions or motions into the soul; or it denotes any supernatural influence of God upon the mind of a rational creature, whereby he is formed to any degree of intellectual improvement."

These are the judicious remarks of Dr. Buck, and their propriety, we think, may not be questioned. He further aptly says in regard to the various measures of inspiration:

"1. An inspiration of *superintendency*, in which God does so influence and direct the mind of any person, as to keep him more secure from error in some various and complex discourse, than he would have been merely by the use of his natural faculties.

"2. *Plenary superintendent inspiration*, which excludes any mixture of error at all from the performance so superintended.

"3. *Inspiration of elevation*, where the faculties act in a regular, and, as it seems, in a common manner, yet are raised to an extraordinary degree, so that the composure shall, upon the whole, have more of the true sublime, or pathetic, than natural genius could have given.

"4. *Inspiration of suggestion*, where the use of the faculties is superceded, and God does, as it were, speak directly to the mind, making such discoveries to it as it could not otherwise have obtained, and dictating the very words in which such discoveries are to be communicated, if they are designed as a message to others."

INSPIRED TRANSLATION.

Mr. S. next undertakes to show a huge error in the promises made in the Book of Covenants relative to the Inspired Translation. He argues that the promise, "My Scriptures shall be given as I have appointed, and they shall be preserved in safety," means that *all* the Scripture ever inspired of God was to be given to the Church in the Inspired Translation. There is scarcely any occasion to reply to so stupid a statement. The promise was: "My Scripture shall be given *as I have appointed;*" and then comes the promise, "And they shall be preserved in safety;" and then follows the advice:

"And it is expedient that thou shouldst hold thy peace concerning them, and not teach them until ye have received them in full."—D. C. 42:15.

That is, the Church was not to teach those Scriptures which God had "appointed," ordained, or decreed, to give to the Church, until they had those "appointed" Scriptures "in full." It remained for the Church to wait and see what Scriptures God had "appointed" unto them, in what he should give in the Inspired Translation; for it was the Inspired Translation that was spoken of.

SPIRITUAL CREATION.

The next point that Mr. S. urges against the Inspired Translation is, in that it says:

"For I, the Lord God, created all things of which I have spoken, *spiritually, before* they were naturally upon the face of the earth. And I, the Lord God, *had created all the children of men*, and not yet a man to till the ground, for *in heaven* created I them, and there was not yet flesh upon the earth, neither in the water, neither in the air; but I, the Lord God, spake, and there went up a mist from the earth, and watered the whole face of the ground. And, I the Lord God, formed man from the dust of the ground, and breathed into his nostrils the breath of life; and man became a living soul; the first flesh upon the earth, the first man also; nevertheless, all things were *before* created, but *spiritually* were they created and made, according to my word."—Gen. 2 : 5–9.

Here is the full text, underlined as we find it in the article of Mr. S. He then quotes Gen. 6 : 52:

"And he called upon our father Adam, by his own voice, saying, 'I am God; I made the world, and *men before they were in the flesh.*"

Mr. S. thinks this is contradicted, directly, by Paul, 1 Cor. 15 : 44–49, where he says:

"The first man Adam, was made a living soul; the last Adam was made a quickening spirit. Howbeit that which was natural first, and not that which is spiritual; but afterwards that which is spiritual; the first man is of the earth earthy; the second man is the Lord from heaven."

Now, when the Lord says, "I made the world, and *men before they were in the flesh,*" it is easy to see that the creation of man here spoken of, is not the one alluded to by Paul, when he says, "The first man is of the earth, earthy." Paul clearly refers to the creation of the earthly tabernacle, the fleshly body of man, while Gen. 2 : 4, 5, 6, 9, and 6 : 52, as clearly relate to their spiritual creation. Mr. S. would deny that the spirits of all intelligent beings are, in any sense, pre-existent. Here is the main issue between him and the text quoted from Genesis.

Now the common version, with all the other versions that have fallen under our notice, teaches that, "In the day that the Lord God made the earth and the heavens," he made "every plant of the field *before it was in the earth*, and every herb of the field *before it grew.*"—Gen. 2 : 4, 5. Now, inasmuch as the Lord did so much for the vegetable world in its pre-existent state, is it at all surprising that he created and fashioned man's spirit before it took a tabernacle of flesh, and even before there was any kind of flesh, either in the air, or in the water, or upon the earth? We think not.

There are a great many texts that teach the pre-existence of spirits, a doctrine very fatal to the theories so fondly entertained by Mr. S. and his fellows. The Bible proclaims the Lord as "the God of *the spirits of all flesh.*"—Num. 16 : 22; 27 : 16. And Paul declares him to be "the father of spirits."—Heb. 12 : 9.

Now, that the spirit of at least *one man* pre-existed, is, we think quite evident; and if the spirit of one pre-existed, pray why not all? The law governing one case clearly governs all, for God is no respecter of persons. Of "the man Christ Jesus,"—that his spirit, as a conscious, active entity, did exist ages before he took an earthly body, a fleshly tabernacle from the womb of Mary, is placed beyond question by his own words, and by the words of prophets and apostles. Hear him:

"I came forth from the Father, and am come into the world: again, I leave the world, and go to the Father."—John 16:28.

And Jesus commends this belief in his pre-existence as *an important element in the true faith,* for he says:

"For the Father himself loveth you, because ye have loved me, *and have believed that I came out from God.*"—Verse 27.

Again he says:

"And now, O Father, glorify thou me with thine own self, with the glory which I had with thee *before the world was.*"—John 17:5.

Again:—

"The bread of God is he which cometh down from heaven, and giveth life to the world."—John 6:33.

John testifies of him:

"In the beginning was the Word, and the Word was with God, and the Word was God. * * * All things were made by him. * * * And the Word was made flesh, and dwelt among us."—John 1:1, 3, 14.

Paul says:

"By him were all things created, that are in heaven, and that are in earth, visible and invisible."—Col. 1:16.

And of his incarnation Paul says:

"When he [Christ] cometh into the world, he saith, Sacrifice and offering thou wouldst not, but *a body* hast thou prepared me."—Heb. 10:5.

This "body" was evidently "prepared" of God in the womb of the virgin Mary; and into this "body" at its birth, the pre-existent, intelligent spirit of Christ entered, and accomplished the work assigned of the Father for the redemption of man. Now Paul draws a parallel between Christ, who came into the world to save man, and man whom he came to save. He says:

"Forasmuch then as the children [whom he came to save] are *partakers of flesh and blood,* he also likewise took part of the same; that through death he might destroy him that had the power of death, that is, the devil."—Heb. 3:14.

When he says that "the children are partakers of flesh and blood," he says, in substance, that "the children" had an existence *before* they partook of "flesh and blood;" and especially when he says "he also, likewise [in like manner] took part of the same" [flesh and blood]; thus putting Christ and the children on the same grounds. This places the matter beyond refutation, that the spirits of all men, as well as the spirit of Christ pre-existed.

With this idea in the mind, we can easily reconcile and understand many passages in both Testaments, which otherwise would remain profoundly mysterious. Such, for instance, as the following:

"Master, who did sin, this man, or his parents, that he was born blind?"—John 9:2.

This question pre-supposes a conscious, responsible pre-existence; and Christ's disciples thought, no doubt, that the spirits of all men existed in a state intellectual consciousness and moral freedom, similar to that of "the angels which kept not their *first* estate," mentioned by Jude, (verse 6), and "the angels that sinned," mentioned by Peter, (2 Pet. 2:4), and the devil, who "abode not in the truth," mentioned by our Savior, (John 8:44). Again:—

"Where wast thou when I laid the foundations of the earth? Declare if thou hast understanding. * * * When the morning stars sang together, and all the sons of God shouted for joy."—Job 38:4, 7.

Christ was one of the morning stars, (Rev. 22:16), and is it improbable that those who are ministers of God with him were also morning stars? As for "the sons of God," Jesus was one, and Adam was another.—Luke 3:38. This being the case, it is conclusive that Adam's children, too, those whom Christ came to save and bless, were likewise, in their pre-existent state, "sons of God." Paul said to the Athenians, "We are also his offspring."—Acts 17:28. The sons of God could have "shouted for joy" at the founding of our earth only in a pre-existent state. So much for the pre-existence of the spirit of man; and yet but a small amount of the available proof has been adduced.

As to the pre-existence of the spirits of *all flesh*, one thing we think is clear, and that is that the *law of existence* that appertains to one class of spirits appertains to all. There certainly is nothing in the Scriptures nor in philosophy against this idea, but, on the contrary, very much to favor it. Of the condition of spirits in their pre-existent state but little, comparatively, is said. However, the doctrine of pre-existence is much more ancient than apostolic times, and it was extensively taught in the first centuries of the Christian era, as may be seen by consulting the early Christian Fathers. We have seen on page nineteen, that Eusebius held to the pre-existence of Christ. To this we refer the reader.

Mr. S. attempts to make the Inspired Translation contradict itself in regard to the creation, by confounding the two creations, spiritual and physical, in one. This is a genuine Infidel trick, and Mr. S. probably borrowed it from that class of critics. The first chapter in the Inspired Translation embraces an epitomized statement of the creation, while the chapters following contain a recapitulation, and more detailed account. The same thing is true of the common version. Reading the account of the creation with this view in the mind, as one evidently should do, there is then not the least appearance of contradiction. Here is a passage he uses with evident satisfaction to prove a conflict:

"And I, the Lord God, had created all the children of men, and not yet a man to till the ground."—Gen. 2:6.

And then opposes to it the following:

"Let us make man in our own image."—Gen. 1:27.'

Now Mr. S. knew when he wrote the statement, that the quotation from Gen. 2 : 6, was qualified and explained by its contexts, so as to make it relate to the creation of spirits, or the spiritual creation, for they read:

"For I, the Lord God, created all things of which I have spoken, spiritually, before they were naturally upon the face of the earth. * * * And I, the Lord God, had created all the children of men, and not yet [at the time when he created the spirits] a man to till the ground, for in heaven created I them, and there was not yet [at the time the spirits were created] flesh upon the earth, neither in the water, neither in the air."—Gen. 2:5, 6.

Nothing can be plainer than that these texts relate to the creation of pre-existent spirits *before* there was any kind of flesh on the earth. At the eighth verse of the same chapter begins the account of man's physical creation:

"And I, the Lord God, formed man from the dust of the ground, and breathed into his nostrils the breath of life; and man became a living soul; the first flesh upon the earth, the first man also."

That this relates to man's physical creation is further apparent from what follows in the next verse:

"Nevertheless, all things were before created, but spiritually were they created and made according to my word."—Verse 9.!

Mr. S. then charges that there is a conflict between the account (in chapter 1 : 22–26) of the creation of the lower orders of animal life, and the account of the creation of man which follows, (in verses 27–30), and the statement in chapter 2 : 8, where it says that man was the first flesh "upon the earth," as though it was a question only and merely of *time*, whereas, it is clearly one of rank, position, and dignity. Man was the "first flesh upon the earth," from the fact that God placed them in the first rank in dominion, and made them first in physical excellence, and gave them dominion over all the earth, and over every living thing.—Gen. 1 : 28–31.

JOSEPH, HIS TWO FATHERS.

Mr. S. next avers that

"Joseph's inspired version clashes with itself and with reason, by giving two natural fathers to Joseph, the husband of Mary, * * * in rendering Matt. 1:4, 'Jacob begat Joseph,' and in translating Luke 3:30, Joseph 'was from the loins of Heli.' Certainly he could not have been begotten by Jacob, and also come from the loins of Heli."

We think that he could, Mr. S., just as well as that Jesus could come of the "loins" of David, and at the same time be *begotten* by the Holy Ghost. Peter, on the day of Pentecost, when under the inspiration of the Holy Spirit, declared that God had sworn unto David

"That of the fruit of his *loins*, according to the flesh, he would raise up Christ to sit on his throne."—Acts 2:30.

Now, Joseph was only the *putative* father of Jesus, and in this manner did Jesus descend from the *loins* of David. It was a custom of the ancient Hebrews, (Gen. 38 : 8), and a *law* under the Mosaic polity, for a man to marry his brother's widow and raise up seed unto his brother. And it was especially provided

"That the firstborn which she beareth shall succeed in the name of his brother which is dead, that his name be not put out of Israel."—Deut. 25 : 6.

Now Joseph, the husband of Mary, was the *natural* son of Jacob, but, under the law we have cited, he was reckoned from "the loins" of Heli; for Joseph's mother was first married to Heli, and, as he died without seed, Jacob took her to wife and their first born was Joseph, who by *the law* was reckoned as Heli's son, and as being "from the loins of Heli." It will be seen on comparing Matt. 1 : 15 with Luke 3 : 23, 24, that Matthan (Matthat, *Greek*) was the father of both Jacob and Heli, and that Heli was not the father of Mary, as Mr. S. asserts; for the lineage is reckoned in the male line and not in the female, as claimed by Mr. S. Of this matter Eusebius, a competent authority, says:

"Thus, then, we shall find the two [Jacob and Heli] of different families, [Jacob, through Matthan, his natural father, is of the family of Solomon; while Heli, his brother, had the same mother, his father *under the law* being Matthan, while his natural father was Melchi, who was of the family of Nathan], Jacob and Heli, brothers by the same mother. Of these, the one, Jacob, on the death of his brother, marrying his widow, became the father of a third, viz., Joseph; his son both by nature and calculation. Wherefore it is written, Jacob begat Joseph. But according to *the law* he was the son of Heli; for Jacob being his brother raised up seed to him. Wherefore, the genealogy traced also through him, will not be rendered void."—Eccl. Hist. 33.

The Son of God was "made of a woman, made under the law," (Gal. 4 : 4); yet his genealogy, as provided for by the law, and as we have seen in the history of the case, is traced in the male line, through his supposed father, back through "the loins of David;" so, under that same law, and according to the same custom, is Joseph reckoned "of the loins of Heli. Mr. S. has the same grounds for saying that Peter's statement makes David the *natural* progenitor of Jesus, that he has for saying that Joseph Smith's translation makes Heli the *natural* father of Joseph. The cases are parallel. Jesus was not the *natural* son of David, though he was reckoned, under the law governing genealogies, as proceeding from his "loins;" and Joseph was not the *natural* son of Heli, yet under the law he was reckoned as descending from his "loins."

BAPTISM.

Mr. S. next finds fault with the Inspired Translation because it introduces *baptism* in the days of Adam. It is not so much with the fact of baptism as it is for using the term *baptism*, which he tells us is "a Greek word with an English termination." *Baptism* is not a Greek word. It is purely an English word, though derived from the Greek, as are thousands of other English words. *Baptism* is the name of a religious ceremony; and, so far as its *mode* is concerned, is performed by immersion. Immersion is not always baptism; for a person may be immersed in a variety of ways, as by accident, or force, without the least reference to religion. Now, in translating a word from the original that signified the religious ceremony of baptism, why not call it *baptism* as Mr. Smith has done? The duty of a translator is to transfer the sense and import of words found in one language into words having the same sense and import in another language. This Mr. Smith has done.

Mr. S. next says:

"If Adam's baptism, as recorded by Joseph, was a true pattern, all subsequent baptisms are faulty: 'Adam cried unto the Lord, and he was caught away by the Spirit of the Lord, and was carried down into the water, and was laid under the water, and was brought forth out of the water; and thus he was baptized.'—(Gen. 6:67). Why, [says Mr. S.] was not baptism subsequently administered on the same principle, if this was really God's work?"

Simply, we reply, because there was no occasion for it, God having, after the baptism of Adam, provided suitable administrators. Will Mr. S. deny that God may, and often does, accomplish the same ends in different ways? God bestowed the Holy Ghost "through laying on of the apostles hands" in "the city of Samaria," (Acts 8:18), and then bestowed it upon Cornelius and his household while they were listening to the discourse of Peter, (Acts 10:44). Christ's ministry usually traveled as men generally do, when they went forth to preach, yet we read of an extraordinary case of journeying wherein the Lord stepped out of his usual way of doing things:

"The Spirit of the Lord caught away Philip, that the eunuch saw him no more; and he went on his way rejoicing. But Philip was found at Azotus."—Acts 8:39, 40.

A crafty critic might claim that Philip's case was "a pattern," and urge that all Christ's ministers, in all ages, should be "caught away" by the Spirit, as Philip was; and then we would be equally as reasonable as Mr. S. There are ordinary methods for curing the sick, for making bread, for raising fish, for making oil, for feeding the hungry, and for making wine, yet this does not preclude the Lord's accomplishing the same things in an unusual manner. And when the Lord, in an extraordinary way, performs any work, professed Bible believers are scarcely justified in assuming that as "a pattern" for all coming time.

BAPTISM, OF ANCIENT DATE.

As for baptism being a very ancient rite, there is much evidence to prove it. Baptism was clearly no new thing to the Jews, for when John came preaching "the baptism of repentance for the remission of sins," "all the land of Judea, and they of Jerusalem," responded to the call, (Mark 1:4, 5); which they would not have done if that distinguishing ordinance had been new and strange to them, either in fact, or in the mode of its administration. Again, the question addressed by the Priests and Levites to John: "Why baptizest thou then, if thou be not that Christ, nor Elias, neither that Prophet?'' (Jno. 1 : 25), is conclusive that they understood well concerning baptism, and that the ministration of Christ, Elias, and "that Prophet," in the looked for dispensation, would be eminently distinguished by that ordinance. Anciently, when a Gentile was converted to the Hebrew faith, he was baptized. Baptism was practiced to a great extent among the Pagan nations of the East, both before and since the Christian era. Whence did this ancient practice, whether among Hebrews or Pagan nations, originate? Evidently from the religious ceremony of baptism given of God to his people in the beginning.

The idea of the One God; of the virgin-born Redeemer; paradise; the fall of man; the temptation through the serpent; the cross and its wondrous saving power; sacrificial offerings, and the atonement for sin; the incarnation of the Creator; the crucifixion; the resurrection; the pre-existence and immortality of man's spirit; the reign of the Holy One in peace and glory; preaching to the spirits in prison; the New Jerusalem; the renewal of the earth, and the final restitution, etc., etc,—ideas held in part or in whole by many of the ancient Pagan nations of the East, as also in part by the ancient Peruvians and Mexicans—are all referable to the one source, viz., *an early revelation given to God's people;* of which these ideas, corrupted though they be, are the remaining traditions, brought down from Adam and the antediluvian patriarchs to Noah; and from Noah, through his posterity, to the Tower; and from the Tower, at the confounding of languages, they were borne out with the various streams of emigration to all the different parts of the world.

These traditions and practices bear the unmistakable impress of those grand truths that distinguish original Christianity, as taught by the prophets, and by Christ and his apostles; and which, as taught in the Inspired Translation, the Book of Mormon, and the Book of Doctrine and Covenants, were revealed of God to the first patriarchs and prophets, from Adam to Noah, and from Noah to Moses.

As the limpid and refreshing streams of the mountains, springing from the bosom of eternal snow, go down and are defiled and darkened by mingling with the turbid river of the valleys, sweeping on, and on, to the great sea, so these wondrous, heaven-born truths, given to man in the morn of time, and coming down through the ages, have become obscured and polluted as they have been mingled with the corrupting systems and creeds of men, till, at length, but a dim shadow, a faint likeness, of their former character and excellence remains.

CHAPTER III.

Mr. S. next attacks Joseph's account of the baptism of O. Cowdery and himself, after their first ordination by the angel; also the statement of the angel concerning "baptism by immersion for the remission of sins."

BAPTISM, ITS MODE.

"If baptism is immersion, [says Mr. S.], then this angel really talks about immersion by immersion. * * Such an angel ought to go to school before discoursing on baptism."

Baptism, as a Christian rite, a religious ceremony, (and that is what the angel was talking about), is more than mere immersion, as we have said before. Baptism, as that term has been used in the true Christian Church, is a religious ordinance, and is designed both for *the remission of sins* and as a means of initiation into the fold and Church of Christ—the family of God. To this agree both the Scriptures and the primitive church history. Now, it was eminently proper that the angel should explain both the *object* of baptism, and the *mode* of administering the rite, especially when we consider that Joseph and Oliver had been reared in the midst of a people who held that baptism by sprinkling or pouring was valid. The angel, like a true minister for Christ, addressed himself to the manifest wants of the case, speaking to the understanding of the young men, and making his instruction plain to their comprehension and conclusive to their judgment. If his manner had been mysterious, and his instructions ambiguous, then there would have been good ground for questioning his mission. A true teacher, whether angel or otherwise, will suit his instruction to the needs, and to the understanding of those whom he addresses.

BAPTISM FOR REMISSION OF SINS.

Mr. S. next objects:

"If baptism is 'for the remission of sins,' in the Mormon sense of the statement, instead of the Bible sense, why need Joseph have been baptized, seeing that his sins previously had been forgiven him?"

On similar grounds, Mr. S., that Cornelius and his household, whom "God hath cleansed," (Acts 10 : 15), needed to be baptized. Peter said:

"Forasmuch as God gave them the like gift as he did unto us, who believed on the Lord Jesus Christ, what was I, that I could withstand God?"—Acts 11: 17.

"Can any man forbid water that these should not be baptized, which have received the Holy Ghost as well as we? And he commanded them to be baptized in the name of the Lord,"—Acts 10: 47, 48.

This case is directly in point, as showing that the Lord may forgive an unbaptized person their sins, under extraordinary circumstances, and yet the person be a proper subject for future baptism. Mr. S. further says:

"Here was a divinely inspired man engaged in translating ancient records, and still a sinner, not having been baptized for the remission of sins, which implies, according to Mormon interpretation, the forgiveness of sins."

Mr. Smith, like Cornelius and his household, whose case we have just cited, had been graciously "cleansed," or forgiven his sins, as Joseph's record states; and for the matter of God's using him as an instrument to do his work, and to promote his glory without previous baptism, there is nothing either unreasonable or unscriptural in it. Caiaphas, the Jewish high priest, who was neither a Christian nor friendly to the gospel, was moved of God to prophesy concerning the death and mission of Christ, (Jno. 11 : 49-52); Balaam was used of God as an instrument through whom to foretell the future history of Israel, and the coming of Christ, (Num. chapters 22, 23, 24); Pharaoh, (Gen. 41 : 1); Abimelech, (Gen. 20 : 3-7); Nebuchadnezzar, (Dan. 2); and others not identified with God's people, were used of God in revealing his marvelous purposes and doings to man. So also Josephus, the Jewish general and historian, (Wars, B. 3, ch. 8, sec. 9). With these precedents before us, it is not at all strange to Bible believers that the Lord should call and use Joseph in the divine work of either prophesying, baptizing, ordaining, or translating records, prior to his baptism, in laying the foundation of the Latter Day Work.

ORDINATION OF JOSEPH AND OLIVER.

Mr. S. professes to see something very unreasonable in Joseph and Oliver mutually ordaining each other after having been ordained by the angel. He says the angel "virtually repudiates his own act of ordination by commanding them to ordain each other." We are not aware of there being any Bible precedent by which to prove the scripturalness of this procedure, yet there is an act of our Savior in which the same principle is involved:

"And, behold, there came a leper and worshipped him, saying, Lord, if thou wilt, thou canst make me clean. And Jesus put forth his hand, and touched him, saying, I will; be thou clean. And immediately his leprosy was cleansed. And Jesus saith unto him, See thou tell no man; but go thy way, show thyself to the priest, and offer the gift that Moses commanded, for a testimony unto them."—Matt. 8: 2–4.

Jesus did not "repudiate his own act," by commanding the leper to comply with the law provided for cleansing leprosy, (Lev. 13 3–10); nor did the angel repudiate *his* own act of ordination by commanding Joseph and Oliver to comply with the law governing ordinations. The command was highly proper, and in perfect harmony with the teachings and doings of Christ and the apostles, who always paid respect to the law and order of God. Though the leper was "immediately" cleansed by Jesus, yet he was commanded to "offer the gift that Moses had commanded, *for a testimony unto them*," (meaning, evidently, the priest and the people who chanced to know his leprosy); so Joseph and Oliver, though ordained by the angel, yet were commanded to ordain each other, upon vote of the Saints, "for a testimony to them," and to all interested, and in respect to the law and order of God.

SONS OF LEVI.

Again Mr. S. objects, that

"This same angel intimates that the sons of Levi are *again* to offer an offering unto the Lord, which would be a repudiation of Christ, the great anti-typical sacrifice, by again introducing the shadow."

Their making in the future an offering unto the Lord would be no more a repudiation of Christ, than Christ's eating the passover, in the future, in the kingdom of God, (Luke 22: 16), would be a repudiation of Christ himself. It is not improbable that in the world to come, when Christ reigns as King of kings and Lord of lords, many ceremonies will be performed, not as types pointing to the future, but as memorials commemorative of the past, such as the passover once was, and such as the sacrament now is. On this hypothesis we can explain and reconcile the prophetic visions of Ezekiel, chapters 40 to 48; Zech. 14:16–21; Isa. 66:21–23, etc. Ceremonies may be, and sometimes are, both typical and commemorative at the same time. Such was the passover. It pointed back to that terrible night in Egypt when the Lord destroyed Egypt's first-born and passed over faithful Israel, and also pointed forward to the Lord Jesus, "our passover" lamb.

God has promised by Isaiah, that, in the final gathering of Israel from all lands, and from the "isles of the sea," (Isa. 66:19, 20), he will "take of them for priests and Levites." He has also promised that

"He shall purify the sons of Levi, and purge them as gold and silver, that they may offer unto the Lord an offering in righteousness. *Then* shall the offering of Judah and Jerusalem be pleasant unto the Lord, as in the days of old, and as in former years."—Mal. 3:3, 4.

It would not be an easy task to prove that these promises were conditional, or that they have been already fulfilled, yet some will even undertake to do one, or both. The texts, with their contexts, show that they are not conditional; and further, that they remain to be fulfilled in the future.

JOHN, A PRIEST.

Mr. S. says:

"There is no proof that John was ever ordained a priest. This point needs proof—not conjecture. If he was not an officiating priest, how could he hold the keys of the Aaronic priesthood?"

John was the only son of an officiating priest, (Luke 1:5), and had a right to the priesthood of his father,—(Lev. 7:35, 36; Mal. 2:5). Of the chief and most important duties of a priest, the Lord says by Malachi, chapter 2:6, 7:

"The law of truth was in his mouth, and iniquity was not found in his lips; he walked with me in peace and equity, and did turn many away from iniquity. For the priest's lips should keep knowledge, and they should seek the law at his mouth; for he is *the messenger of the Lord of hosts.*"

John filled this description of a priest in a very eminent degree. And Jesus testifies of him:

"This is he of whom it is written, Behold I send *my messenger* before thy face, who shall prepare thy way before thee."—Matt. 11:10.

Besides this, while the Jews questioned the *authority* of Jesus, they never questioned the priesthood authority of John, which they evidently would have done if they had known that he did not hold the priesthood. The masses recognized his priestly authority to teach and reprove them, as may be seen in the fact that "all Judea and Jerusalem" answered to his call, and were baptized of him in the river Jordan.—(Mark 1). The mere fact of *the ordination* of Zacharias, or Caiaphas, or Annas, as well as John is not mentioned in Scripture, but it would be folly to deny their ordination simply because the Scriptures are silent upon that point. Such reasoning, which is quite common to Mr. S., would deny that the apostles of Christ were baptized, simply because no mention is made, in direct terms, of that fact. The Jews, as well as all the Israel of God, well knew that no person could minister in matters of religion without proper priesthood authority. They, as well as Pagan worshippers, had too much sound, practical sense to accept the religious ministrations of any person unless they were satisfied that they held proper, lawful authority.

MORE TRUTH THAN FOUND IN THE BIBLE.

The reader will have noticed ere this, that Mr. S. argues upon the assumption that all questions relative to matters of religion must be settled by *direct* proofs from the Bible. Direct evidence from that source is very excellent, but there are many superior proofs that can only be *inferred;* and there are thousands of valid proofs in matters of religion outside of the Bible. To claim that all the facts and proofs peculiar to the Christian religion are embraced within the Old and New Testaments is preposterous. If we had all the teachings of Jesus, and all the teachings of his apostles, and all the writings of the prophets, yet that, great as it would be, would not compass *all* that relates to matters of religion in Christ Jesus. The apostles had the "law and the prophets." And, without doubt, they had many more sacred writings than what we now have in the Old Testament, for both the Savior and the apostles quote scriptures not found in the common version; and besides this, many quotations are made by Josephus, professedly from the old prophets, which are not now to be found in the Old Testament, as may be seen by consulting *Whiston's Josephus,* pp. 38, 66, 67, 126, 277, etc., etc. They had also the teachings of Jesus, the thousandth part of which we probably have not, (Jno. 21:25); and then they had the constant revelations of the Comforter, (Jno. 14:26; 16:

13, 14, 15). Now, if we had all this, still we would not be justified in claiming that we had *all* the truths of God.

If we had the books of all the ancient prophets and seers mentioned in the Bible, some 'twenty or more in number; also all the writings of the early Christian Church for the first three centuries, especially the first epistle which Paul wrote to the Corinthians, (1 Cor. 5 : 9); likewise "the epistle from Laodicea," (Col. 4 : 16); the epistle of Jude on the common salvation, (Jude 4); and the "many" gospels mentioned by Luke, (Luke 1 : 1), we, no doubt, would be furnished with evidences on doctrine and history which would be of use in solving questions of importance in respect to the Christian religion. The idea that nothing relative to doctrine, ceremony, or practice, in church affairs can be true except there can be found for it in the Bible a direct *verbal* proof, or an unquestionable precedent, is highly absurd. If the early Christians had been subjected to such an iron rule the gospel would have been fettered, and the Church manacled. All the truths of Christ's religion are harmonious. There must be no conflict, no contradiction, no confusion; and there *is* none in the revelations of the past or the present, and surely there will be none in the future.

PRIESTHOOD.

Now, in respect to the subject of the priesthood, Mr. S. seems painfully sensitive. It would seem that he cannot say enough against the idea that there is an authorized priesthood in the Church of Christ. He attacks it again and again, conscious that if the idea proves true, his labors in the ministry, and that of many others, would be found of no authority in Christ, and of no gospel power or value. God is Judge of all, and we will have no controversy as to whether Mr. S. holds authority from Christ or not; but we shall attempt to prove that there is in the Church of Christ an authorized, ordained priesthood, whatever may be the conclusions of Mr. S. and his fellows.

NECESSITY FOR PRIESTHOOD.

That any religious system could exist without an authorized priesthood to teach its doctrines, administer its rites, govern its membership, and have the lawful and special watch-care of all its interests, is an idea quite foreign to all ancient forms, whether Christian, Jewish, or Pagan. The ancient Jewish religion, authorized of God, was of far less importance and value than the religion of Christ, and yet it was of so much importance in the sight of God that none were permitted to minister the laws and ceremonies appertaining to it but those who were legally and properly called to those sacred offices. There was authoritative power given to those ministers, and the power and grace of God attended their faithful ministrations. There was also a specific order provided by which ministerial authority was both delegated and transmitted, so that there need be no mistake in regard to the matter of priesthood authority. This was eminently wise and just, as order and good government are indispensibly essential. Inasmuch, then, as the religion of Christ, and the Church of Christ, are of far greater importance, for time and eternity, than that of the Jews, why is it not at least equally important, to have an authorized priesthood, and well defined rules in regard to delegating and transmitting authority in the Church of Christ?

But some will say, "Where are those rules? we do not discover them in the New Testament." Very true, we do not discover them there in their completeness, and there is good reason for it. The New Testament contains but a portion of the writings given to the primitive Church. When we consider how the early Christians were persecuted and driven from place to place by Jew and Gentile, we may wonder only that so much has been preserved to us. Bingham, in his *Antiquities of the Christian Church*, when speaking of the writings of the primitive church, says:

"An exact and authentic catalogue of these first foundations, would be a very useful and entertaining thing; but at this distance of time, it is impossible to gratify the world with any such curiosity, whatever pains should be taken about it. Yet there are *some scattered remains and fragments* to be collected out of the ancient writers."—p. 57.

In view of the foregoing facts, we may not look to find in the writings of the primitive Church anything beyond fragmentary evidences in regard to the subject of priesthood, and to those we appeal.

WHAT IS PRIESTHOOD?

We may first enquire as to what the priesthood really is. Webster gives a fair definition when he says it is "The order of men set apart for sacred offices; the order composed of priests." Buck informs us that a priest is "a person set apart for the performance of sacrifice, *and other offices and ceremonies of religion.*" Both Buck and Webster tell us that "the word *priest* is a contraction" of the word *presbyter*, and "of the same import with *Elder*." Smith, in his Dictionary of the Bible, says, "Its root-meaning uncertain as far as Hebrew itself is concerned, is referred by Gesenius to the idea of *prophecy*." He further says that Saalschutz considers the primary meaning of the word as equivalent to *minister*.

ORIGIN OF PRIESTHOOD.

Of the origin of the priesthood Smith remarks:

"The idea of a priesthood connects itself, in all its forms, pure or corrupted, with the consciousness, more or less distinct, of sin. Men feel that they have broken a law. The power above them is holier than they are, and they dare not approach it. They crave for the intervention of some one of whom they can think as likely to be more acceptable than themselves. He must offer up their prayers, thanksgivings, sacrifices. He becomes their representative 'in things pertaining to God.' He may become also (though this does not always follow) the representative of God to man. The functions of priest and prophet may exist in the same man."

The foregoing may serve to place the subject properly in the mind of the reader, and dispel any prejudice he may have against the idea of a real, genuine priesthood in Christ's Church, and to forever explode the doctrine held by some that a priest must necessarily offer bloody sacrifices.

ALL CHRISTIANS NOT PRIESTS.

Now, Mr. S. claims that there was no priesthood *in* the primitive Church, but that the entire body of Christians, old and young, male and female, ministers and members, constituted the priesthood. To prove this, he quotes 1 Pet. 2 : 9, Rev. 1 : 6, etc. Peter says, "But ye are a chosen generation, a royal priesthood."

Now this is clearly to be understood in a qualified and restricted sense, evidently meaning that the Church as "a chosen generation," and, as the people of God, possessed within their midst this "royal priesthood."

A KINGDOM OF PRIESTS.

A passage precisely the parallel of that in Peter is found in Ex. 19 : 6; and its interpretation is furnished in the subsequent facts of Jewish history, so that there can be no cavil as to what was intended in the promise there made. It reads, "And ye [Israel] shall be unto me a *kingdom of priests*, and a holy nation." Now this certainly did not mean that each individual Israelite, male and female, should be a priest; if it did, then the promise has failed. It is clear that no such thing was intended, but only that as a nation and people they should possess the distinguished privilege of having among them heavenly appointed priests, a priesthood appointed of God. Israel was "a kingdom of priests," yet the priestly office was restricted and confined to probably less than one in thirty of their number. The primitive church was "a royal priesthood," yet the priestly office was exercised by the few, and not by all.

The learned Bingham says:—

"But when his [God's] ministers are to be distinguished from the rest of his people in the church, then the name *clerici*, or clergy, was their appropriate title, and the name of the other, laymen. And this observation will help to set another sort of persons right, who confound not only the names, but the *offices* of laity and clergy together; and plead that originally there was no distinction between them. The name of *priesthood*, indeed, is sometimes given in common to the whole body of Christian people; 1 Pet. 2: 9; Rev. 1: 6; but so it was to the Jewish people, Ex. 19: 6: 'Ye shall be unto me a kingdom of priests, and an holy nation;' yet every one knows, that the offices of priests and Levites among the Jews, were very distinct from those of the common people, not by usurpation, but by God's appointment. And so it was among the Christians, from the foundation of the church."—*Ant. Chris. Church*, p. 40.

Bingham further remarks:

"Tertullian says it was customary *among heretics* to confound the offices of the clergy and laity together."

The reader will make special note of this. Again:

"St. Jerome observes, They [the early Christians] reckoned that to be *no church*, which had *no priests*."

Again Bingham says:

"St. Jerome, who will be allowed to speak the sense of the ancients * * * says that both in the *Old and New Testament* the high priests are an order, the priests another, and the Levites another."—p. 50.

"Tertullian, in his book *De Baptismo*, says, The *right* of baptizing belongs to the chief priests."

Says Bingham:

"These allegations, are sufficient evidences, as to matter of fact, and the practice of the church in the first three ages, that there was then an order of chief priests, or bishops, superior to the presbyters, settled and allowed in the Christian Church."

Of the "chief priests" he further says:

"It was no human invention, but an original settlement of the apostles themselves, which they made by divine appointment."—p. 54.

Again Bingham:—

"Now this is most expressly said by Theodoret, that he [Ignatius] received the gift of the *high priesthood* from the hand of the great Peter."—p. 60.

Again:—

"If it be enquired, as it is very natural to ask the question, why Optatus gives all three order of Bishops, Presbyters [Elders] and Deacons, the title of *priesthood*, answer is plain and obvious; because according to him every *order* had its share though in different *degrees*, in the *Christian priesthood*. Which is not, as some imagine, a power to offer Christ's body and blood really upon the altar, as a propitiatory sacrifice for the quick and dead, (which is such a notion of the Christian priesthood, as no ancient author or ritual ever mentions); but it consists in a *power* and *authority* to minister publicly according to God's apointment in holy things, or things pertaining to God. And there are *several parts* to this *power*, according to the different participation of which, in the opinion of Optatus, Bishops, Presbyters, and Deacons had each their respective share in the *priesthood*. Thus it was one act of the priest's office to offer up the sacrifice of the people's prayers, praises, and thanksgiving to God, as their mouth and orator, and to make intercession to God for them. Another part of the office was in God's name to bless the people, particularly by admitting them to the benefit and privilege of *remission of sins by spiritual regeneration or baptism*. And thus far Deacons were anciently allowed to minister in holy things, as mediators between God and the people. Upon which account a late learned writer joins entirely with Optatus, in declaring Deacons to be sharers in this *lowest degree* of the *Christian priesthood*. Above this was the power of offering up to God the people's sacrifices at the altar; that is, as Mr. Mede and others explain them, first the eucharistical oblations of bread and wine, to agnize or acknowledge God to be the Lord of the creatures; then the sacrifice of prayer and thanksgiving in commemoration of Christ's bloody sacrifice upon the cross, mystically represented in the creatures of bread and wine; which whole sacred action was commonly called the Christians' reasonable, unbloody sacrifice, or the sacrifice of the altar. Now the Deacons (as we shall see in another chapter) were never allowed to offer these oblations at the altar, but it was always a peculiar act of the Presbyter's [Elder's] office, which was therefore reckoned a superior degree of the priesthood. Another act of the priestly office was to interpret the mind and will of God to the people; as also to bless them solemnly in his name."—pps. 246, 247, 248.

JOHN, THE APOSTLE, A PRIEST.

We now turn to Eusebius, from whose writings we obtain further evidence that there was a priesthood *in* the primitive Christian Church. First, "Polycrates, who was Bishop of the church of Ephesus," says:

"John, that rested on the bosom of our Lord, who was a *priest* that bore the sacerdotal [priestly] plate."

This plate was thought by some to be similar too, if not identical with the ephod of the high priest.

ORIGEN, A PRIEST.

Eusebius says of Origen, "He had not yet obtained the *priesthood* by the laying on of hands."—p. 240. Again:

"At this time Origen, being compelled by some necessary affairs of the church, went to Greece by way of Palestine, where he received the ordination to the *priesthood*, at Cesarea, from the bishops of that country."—p. 243.

Much more evidence might be given from this source, but this may suffice, as we establish the fact by Eusebius that there was a priesthood in the primitive church, and that it could be obtained only by legal ordination, and not by virtue of being merely a member, as Mr. S. claims. We further see that the Apostle John "was a priest that bore the sacerdotal plate,"—the insignia of the high priest. From Bingham we learn, by abundant proofs, not only that there was in the primitive church an ordained priesthood, but one of degrees, and that it was "no invention" of man, but ordained of God, and that none but heretics opposed the idea. We also learn that there were "chief priests," "high priests," "priests," and "Levites." We also learn from him of the distinction of their respective offices, and of their degrees of authority and spiritual power. We also learn how the early Christians interpreted 1 Pet. 2 : 5 and Rev. 1 : 6, that they interpreted them as meaning the same as the promise in Ex. 19 : 6, viz., that there was *in* the church "a royal priesthood," and not that every member was an officiating priest, as Mr. S. and his kind would hold. Such a claim is the height of absurdity, and savors much of "Mystery Babylon."

TRANSMISSION OF PRIESTHOOD.

Not only was there a priesthood in the primitive church, but there were strict rules in regard to its transmission. As it was important under the law that "no man taketh this honor unto himself, but he that is called of God as was Aaron," so under the gospel, it was, and is, essential that no man takes the ministry or priesthood upon himself, except he be called of God and ordained according to the divine rule. Persons taking part in the ministry must be ordained by those having authority, otherwise their ministrations are valueless. To act "in the name of the Father, and of the Son, and of the Holy Ghost," is to act by their authority. This authority no one can get from the Bible, but only by being divinely called and set apart to minister in that name. It would be far more safe and proper for persons to read the statutes of our land, and then, without being duly called to, and legally qualified in an office, to undertake to officiate therein, than to read the Bible and then, without divine calling and consecration, undertake to officiate in the things of God. Are the things of God less important than those of human governments? And should they not be more carefully guarded? Should the offices in Christ's church be less protected from encroachment, from lawlessness, abuse and confusion, than the offices in human governments? To state these questions is to answer them, with any thoughtful, unprejudiced mind.

Mr. S. claims that the Aaronic priesthood was not in the primitive Church. He says, "It never had a place there." Possibly it did not, so far as *name* is concerned, and yet be in it *in fact*, so far as *authority* is concerned. This authority, or priesthood, was not denominated *Aaronic* or *Levitical*, until, in Israel, it was given to Aaron and the family of Levi, yet the same priesthood in kind existed before.—Ex. 38 : 1-3, 41; Num. 3 : 12.

MELCHIZEDEK PRIESTHOOD.

Mr. S. also tells us that the Melchizedek priesthood was not in the Church; and further, that Christ was not a priest till he reached heaven! If no one can hold the Melchizedek priesthood on earth, how did it happen that Melchizedek was so favored as to hold and exercise it in the times of Abraham? If Christ did not hold priesthood on earth, by what authority did he baptize, ordain others, preach the gospel, and administer the sacrament of bread and wine? He was very particular to comply with the law of baptism, and is it presumable that he would be less particular in respect to priestly prerogatives? He verily performed the functions of a priest, even to the offering of a bloody sacrifice, which he offered upon the cross; and shall we say that he did all this without holding priesthood authority? Nay, verily. The idea is as false as it is derogatory to the character of our Great High Priest. He was priest when he offered himself upon Calvary for a ruined race; and he was a priest before that—he was manifestly one from the beginning of his ministry.

"But," says Mr. S., "Paul says, 'If he were on earth he should not be a priest, seeing that there are priests that offer gifts according to the law.'" Precisely; he would not be *that kind* of a priest of which Paul is speaking—an Aaronic priest, but this is not to say but what he would be a Melchizedek priest.

CHRIST WAS A MELCHIZEDEK PRIEST.

Christ was a priest while on earth, for it was here that he began the work of sacrifice and offering. None could administer in that respect unless he was a priest. The sacrifices and offerings of

Christ and his ministry differ *in kind* from those of the Aaronic priests under the law, yet both orders of priests ministered before the Lord. And that Christ was a Melchizedek priest while on earth, is seen in the fact that "the high priest entereth into the holy place;" so Christ must be a high priest *before* he could enter into the antitypical "holy place," even heaven, (Heb. 9 : 23–25).

OTHER MELCHIZEDEK PRIESTS.

We have shown, on pages 13 and 14, that Moses held higher priesthood than Aaron; and that Jethro was a priest of God, though not of the order of Aaron; also that many of the patriarchs, including Melchizedek, were priests; and we have also shown the probabilities of some of them having been of the higher order with Melchizedek. And we are not alone in concluding that they were Melchizedek priests. Smith, in his *Dictionary of the Bible*, says that the New Testament writers "recognize in Christ, the First-born, the King, the Anointed, the Representative of *the true primeval priesthood* after the order of Melchizedek, from which that of Aaron, however necessary for the time, is now seen to have been a deflection." —Art. Priest. This is the very sensible result of his profound researches upon this subject; and it is in harmony with the statements made by Joseph Smith, the young prophet and seer, in *Doctrine and Covenants* 104 : 3 :

"There are, in the Church, two priesthoods, namely: the Melchizedek, and the Aaronic, including the Levitical priesthood. Why the first is called the Melchizedek priesthood is because Melchizedek was such a great high priest: before his day it was called *the holy priesthood after the order of the Son of God;* but out of respect or reverence to the name of the Supreme Being, to avoid the too frequent repetition of his name, they, the church, in ancient days, called that priesthood after Melchizedek, or the Melchizedek priesthood. All other authorities, or offices in the church are appendages to this priesthood; but there are two divisions, or grand heads—one is the Melchizedek priesthood, and the other is the Aaronic, or Levitical priesthood. * * * The second priesthood is called the priesthood of Aaron, because it was conferred upon Aaron and his seed, throughout all their generations. Why it is called the lesser priesthood is, because it is an appendage to the greater, or the Melchizedek priesthood."

Here is furnished a reasonable solution of what would otherwise be a very complicated and troublesome question. That there were various priestly offices before the law, under the law, and under the gospel, is manifest from the Scriptures and church history; but their respective degrees of authority, their duties, rights, and privileges, as also the manner in which they were conferred and transmitted, are matters not so clearly and definitely stated as could be desired. If we had all the sacred writings given before the law, under the law, and under the gospel, with the full history of the church for the first three centuries, then, no doubt, much if not all of the difficulty that now surrounds this subject would be removed.

BOTH PRIESTHOODS BUT ONE.

It would seem that before the law, all the priestly offices were held as belonging to one priesthood; and that also under the gospel they were so held, though the same priestly authority that was conferred upon Aaron and his seed existed *before* the times of the law, and was likewise in the church after the law, as a code, was abrogated. Both priesthoods are but one priesthood, and are two only in the sense of there being two divisions.

"All other authorities, or offices in the church [including the Aaronic priesthood] are appendages [something added] to this [Melchizedek] priesthood." D. & C. 104; 3.

This may account for there being more offices in the early Christian Church than there appears to have been among God's people in the times of the patriarchs, though both peoples held to the same priesthood. And it may also explain any real or seeming difference in the arrangement of the priesthood in the church now, from what there was in any former time.

OFFICES OF PRIESTHOOD.

"When he [Christ] ascended up on high, he led captivity captive, and gave gifts unto men. * * * And he gave some, apostles; and some, prophets; and some, evangelists; and some, pastors and teachers."—Eph. 4: 8–11.

These were different officers, yet all and each possessed authority in the priesthood of the Christian Church. And it is a fact to be borne in mind, that all these were not called and ordained at once, but only as the Master saw that there was *need for them;* and this principal applies with equal propriety in these latter times.

JOHN BAPTIST RESURRECTED.

We had almost forgotten to reply to another marvelous objection of Mr. S. He claims that it should be *proven* if John the Baptist "was raised from the dead before ordaining Joseph." The Scriptures teach that

"Many bodies of the saints which slept arose, and came out of the graves after his resurrection, and went into the holy city, and appeared unto many." —Matt. 27: 52, 53.

Is there anything incredible in the idea that John was one of that number? We think not. It is probable that all the bodies of the Saints who were found worthy came forth at that time; and none, we trust, will question the worthiness of John.

JOSEPH AND OLIVER ORDAINED BY JOHN BAPTIST.

"How [says Mr. S.] did Joseph know that it was John that ordained him?"

Probably in a similar manner as Daniel knew that it was "the man Gabriel" whom *he* had seen in a vision, (Dan. 9 : 21); or that Mary knew that it was "the angel Gabriel" that ministered to her, (Luke 1 : 26); or that Paul knew that it was Jesus that appeared unto him in the way to Damascus. These parties were fully satisfied that the ministrations in their cases were genuine and really divine. All the surrounding condition were such as to forbid imposture. So in regard to the ordination of Joseph and Oliver by the angel, John the Baptist. We herewith subjoin portions of their account of that very remarkable event. Joseph says:

"We still continued the work of translation, when, in the ensuing month, (May, 1829), we on a certain day went into the woods to pray and inquire of the Lord respecting baptism for the remission of sins, as we found mentioned in the translation of the plates. While we were thus employed, praying and calling upon the Lord, a messenger from heaven descended in a cloud of light and having laid his hands upon us, he ordained us, saying unto us, 'Upon you, my fellow servants, in the name of Messiah, I confer the Priesthood of Aaron, which holds the keys of the ministering of angels, and of the gospel of repentance, and of baptism by immersion for the remission of sins; and this shall never be taken again from the earth, until the sons of Levi do offer again an offering unto the Lord in righteousnes.'"—*Times & Seasons, vol.* 3, *p.* 726.

Oliver's testimony is as follows:

"After writing the account given of the Savior's ministry to the remnant of the seed of Jacob, upon this continent, it was easily to be seen, as the prophet said would be, that darkness covered the earth and gross darkness the minds of the people. On reflecting further, it was easily to be seen, that amid the great strife and noise concerning religion, none had authority from God to administer the ordinances of the gospel. For, the question might be asked, have men authority to administer in the name of Christ, who deny revelation? when *his* testimony is no less than the spirit of prophecy? and his religion based, built, and sustained by immediate revelations in all ages of the world, when he has had a people on earth? If these facts were buried, and carefully concealed by men whose craft would have been in danger, if once permitted to shine in the faces of men, they were no longer to us; and we only waited for the commandment to be given, 'Arise and be baptized.'

"This was not long desired before it was realized. The Lord, who is rich in mercy, and ever willing to answer the consistent prayer of the humble, after we had called upon him in a fervent manner, aside from the abodes of men, condescended to manifest to us his will. On a sudden, as from the midst of eternity, the voice of the Redeemer spake peace to us, while the veil was parted, and the angel of God came down clothed with glory, and delivered the anxiously ooked for message, and the keys of the gospel of repentance! What joy! What wonder! What amazement! While the world was racked and distracted—while the millions were groping as the blind for the wall, and while all men were resting upon uncertainty, as a general mass, our eyes beheld—our ears heard. As in the 'blaze of day;' yes, more—above the glitter of the May sunbeam, which then shed its brilliancy over the face of nature! Then his voice, though mild, pierced to the centre, and his words, 'I am thy fellow-servant,' dispelled every fear. We listened—we gazed—we admired! 'Twas the voice of the angel from glory—'twas a message from the Most High! and as we heard we rejoiced, while his love enkindled upon our souls, and we were rapt in the vision of the Almighty! Where was room for doubt? No where: uncertainty had fled, doubt had sunk, no more to rise, while fiction and deception had fled forever!

"But, dear brother, think, further think for a moment, what joy filled our hearts, and with what surprise we must have bowed (for who would not have bowed the knee for such a blessing?) when we received under his hand the holy priesthood, as he said, 'Upon you, my fellow servants, in the name of Messiah, I confer this priesthood, and this authority, which shall remain upon earth, that the sons of Levi may yet offer an offering unto the Lord in righteousness."

"I shall not attempt to paint to you the feelings of this heart, nor the majestic beauty and glory which surrounded us on this occasion; but you will believe me when I say, that earth, nor men, with the eloquence of time, cannot begin to clothe language in as interesting and sublime a manner as this holy personage. No: nor has this earth power to give the joy, to bestow the peace, or comprehend the wisdom which was contained in each sentence as they were delivered by the power of the Holy Spirit! Man may deceive his fellow man; deception may follow deception, and the children of the wicked one may have power to seduce the foolish and untaught, till nought but fiction feeds the many, and the fruit of falsehood carries in its current the giddy to the grave; but one touch with the finger of his love, yes, one ray of glory from the upper world, or one word from the mouth of the Savior, from the bosom of eternity, strikes it *all* into insignificance, and blots it forever from the mind! The assurance that we were in the presence of an angel; the certainty that we heard the voice of Jesus, and the truth unsullied as it flowed from a pure personage, dictated by the will of God, is to me past description, and I shall ever look upon this expression of the Savior's goodness with wonder and thanksgiving while I am permitted to tarry, and in those mansions where perfection dwells, and sin never comes, I hope to adore in that DAY which shall never cease!"—*Messenger and Advocate, October,* 1834.

Where was there a chance for these men to be deceived? Their hearts were set to do the will of God; and at the time of the vision they had gone "aside from the abodes of men," and called upon the Lord in a fervent manner, or, as Joseph puts it, "We, on a certain day, went into the woods to pray and inquire of the Lord;" and here, under these circumstances, they heard "the voice of the Lord," and, "The vail was parted and the angel of the Lord came down clothed with glory; * * * then his voice, though mild, pierced to the center, and his words, 'I am thy fellow servant' dispelled every fear." Surely, we may say with Oliver, "Where was room for doubt?" It is preposterous to claim that they were deceived. The whole of the surroundings of the case, as they give it, utterly forbid such an idea. They saw the vision, and received the ordination, as they claim, under the hands of the angel, or else they were the vilest impostors known to history. They could not have been deceived in the matter. These men lived and died bearing this testimony, Joseph Smith at Carthage Jail, Illinois, and Oliver Cowdery at or near Far West, Caldwell county, Missouri.

We have occupied more space in considering this question of the priesthood, and its restoration in the latter days, than we had intended. The only apology that we offer, is, that the subject seems to demand it.

CHAPTER IV.

LEHI'S PLATES OF BRASS.

Mr. S. thinks he has discovered another error in the prophecy of Lehi respecting the brass plates, where he says that

"These plates of brass should go forth unto all nations, kindreds, tongues, and people, who were of his seed."—1 Nephi 1:48.

Mr. S. says:

"Whether this language be applied to the material of the brass plates, or to the record contained upon them, the statement has proven untrue. These plates of brass are represented as having been carefully preserved by the Nephites, and to have been handed down by them till the days of Mormon, being carefully kept from the Lamanites, who were of Lehi's seed."

This is a technical quibble at most, and Mr. S. might with equal propriety question the prophecy of Jesus, in Luke 21:24. But how does Mr. S. know that the Lamanites were reckoned as the "seed" mentioned in Lehi's prophecy? The prophecy implies that the plates would go only to the righteous; and subsequent history shows that they did go only to them, while the contents of the plates went to many of Lehi's posterity who were not righteous. The plates and other sacred things, were to be handed down "from one prophet to another," (1 Nephi 5 : 47), and so they were, until they reached Mormon, who hid them up unto the Lord, and wrote as follows:

"Having been commanded of the Lord that I should not suffer that the records which had been handed down by our fathers, which were sacred, to fall into the hands of the Lamanites, (for the Lamanites would destroy them), therefore I made this record out of the plates of Nephi, and hid up in the hill Cumorah, all the records which had been entrusted to me by the hand of the Lord, save it were these few plates which I gave unto my son Moroni."— Mormon 3: 2.

This confirms the supposition that the plates of brass were designed to go to none others than the righteous of Lehi's posterity; and the recorded facts of history in the Book of Mormon show its accomplishment. In 1 Nephi 1: 23, 35, 46, 47, we first learn of the plates of brass, and something of their contents; and in paragraphs 25, 49, we learn the purpose for which they were taken from Laban; and in chapter 6 : 1, we find them in the hands of the prophet Nephi, as the teacher of his people; and in chapter 5 : 47, we further learn that the Lord purposed that these records, with other "sacred things," should "be kept for the knowledge" of Nephi's people.

From Nephi they passed on down among the righteous, "from one prophet to another," going first to Jacob (*k*); Jacob to Enos (*l*); Enos to Jarom (*m*); Jarom to Omni (*n*); Omni to Amaron (*o*) Amaron to Chemish (*p*); Chemish to Abinadom (*q*); Abinadom to Amaleki (*r*); Amaleki to Benjamin (*s*); Benjamin to Mosiah (*t*); Mosiah 2nd to Alma (*u*); Alma to Helaman (*v*); Helaman to Shiblon (*w*); Shiblon to Helaman 2nd (*x*) Helaman to Nephi (*y*); Nephi to Nephi 2nd (*z*); Nephi to Amos (*a*); Amos to Amos 2nd (*b*); Amos 2nd to Amaron (*c*); Amaron to Mormon (*d*); Mormon hides them up in Cumorah, except those given to Moroni (*e*), and Moroni hides up the balance (*f*).

In this long line of transmission, we see that the sacred things, in-

(*k*) Jacob 1:1; (*l*) Jacob 5:9; (*m*) Jarom 1:1; (*n*) Jarom 1:6; (*o*) Omni 1:2; (*p*) Omni 7:3; (*q*) Omni 1:5; (*r*) Omni 1:6; (*s*) Omni 1:12; (*t*) Mosiah 1:3; (*u*) Mosiah 13:1; (*v*) Alma 17:5; (*w*) Alma 30:1; (*x*) Alma 30:5; (*y*) Helaman 2:6; (*z*) Nephi 1:1; (*a*) Nephi 1:6; (*b*) Nephi 1:7; (*c*) Nephi 1:11; (*d*) Mormon 1:1; 2:3; (*e*) Mormon 3:2; (*f*) Moroni 10:1.

cluding the brass plates, were kept among the righteous of Lehi's posterity, thus establishing the idea that only the righteous of Lehi's posterity were the promised "seed." Nor is this method of interpretation peculiar:

"They which be *of faith* are blessed with faithful Abraham."—Gal. 3: 9. "And if ye be Christ's then are ye Abraham's *seed*, and heirs according to the promise."—v. 29. "They which are the children of the flesh, these are not the children of God; but the children of promise are counted for *the seed*."—Rom. 9: 8.

The principle applying in the case of Abraham, applies equally well in the case of Lehi. The Lord said that it was not meet for him, Lehi, that he should take his family into the wilderness alone; but that his sons should take daughters to wife, that they might "raise up *seed unto the Lord* in the land of promise." Those who by righteousness proved themselves to be the Lord's "seed," were the seed of righteous Lehi, and the ones to whom the promise was made.

WHO SHOULD SEE PLATES OF MORMON.

And now comes one of the characteristic perversions of Mr. S. He says:

"The plates of the Book of Mormon were to be seen by three witnesses, and 'none else;' yet they were shown to eight others."

And to prove his assertion, he quotes D. C. 4: 3:

"This generation shall have my word through you; and in addition to your testimony, the testimony of three of my servants, whom I shall call and ordain, unto whom I [will] show these things, and they shall go forth with my words that are given through you; yea, they shall know of a surety that these things are true; for from heaven will I declare it unto them; I will give them power that they may behold and view these things as they are; and to none else will I grant this power to receive this [same] testimony, among this generation."

In the first place Mr. S. has not quoted correctly, and in the next place he has utterly perverted the sense and intention of the text. The word *will* enclosed in brackets, he has quoted *shall;* the word *same*, enclosed in brackets, he has left entirely out. In this we see recklessness and unreliability, whether for want of honest purpose, or through lack of mental calibre, we shall not undertake to decide. The word *same* is very essential to the passage, as it points to the identity and quality of the *testimony* spoken of. No one but the *three*, in connection with Joseph, should have "this *same* testimony" relative to the plates; which testimony was, (1) the hearing the voice of God out of heaven concerning the plates, and their translation by Joseph; and (2) that the Lord, (not man), would show the plates unto them:

"They shall know of a surety that these things are true, for *from heaven will I* [God] declare it unto them; I [God] will give them power that they may behold and view these things as they are; and to none else will I grant this power to receive *this same testimony*, among this generation."—D. & C. 4: 3.

Nothing is here said or intimated that no others were to see the plates, but only that no others were to *see* and *hear*, and *know* of them *in the same manner*. The testimony of the Book of Mormon relative to the plates being shown is as follows:

"And behold, ye [Joseph] may be privileged that ye may show the plates unto those who shall assist to bring forth this work: and unto *three shall they be shown by the power of God:* wherefore *they* shall know of a surety that these things are true."—Ether 2: 1.

By this we learn that *Joseph* was privileged to show the plates unto those who should assist to bring forth the Book of Mormon; and then that "unto three shall they be shown by the power of God." Again:

"Wherefore, at that day when the book shall be delivered unto the man of whom I have spoken, the book shall be hid from the eyes of the world, that the eyes of none shall behold it, save it be that *three witnesses shall behold it by the power of God*, besides him to whom the book shall be delivered, and they shall testify to the truth of the book and the things therein. And there is none other which shall view it, save it be *a few*, according to the will of God, to bear testimony of his word unto the children of men."—2 Nephi 11: 17.

PLATES, BREAST-PLATE, ETC.

Mr. S. next says:

"These three witnesses were not only to see the plates, but also other things mentioned in a revelation to Joseph for the three. 'Behold, I say unto you, that you must rely upon my word, which if you do, with full purpose of heart, you shall have a view of the plates, and also of the breast-plate, the sword of Laban, the Urim and Thummim, which was given to the brother of Jared upon the mount, when he talked with the Lord face to face, and the miraculous directors which were given to Lehi while in the wilderness, on the borders of the Red Sea; and it is by your faith that you shall obtain a view of them, even by that faith which was had by the prophets of old. And after that you have obtained faith, and have seen them with your eyes, you shall testify of them.' But they never testified of them; hence the revelation is unreliable."

How does Mr. S. know that they never testified to seeing them? Hundreds of people are now living who will bear witness that they *did* testify that they saw them. And besides, if they had never seen them, it would not prove that "the revelation is unreliable," as Mr. S. affirms, unless it could be shown that they, on their part, complied with the *conditions* of the promise. Mr. S. says, impliedly, that they were to testify to seeing them by *a written statement*. This he is not warranted in doing. It is neither expressed, nor implied, that they were to give *a written statement* of seeing the breastplate, Urim and Thummim, etc.

O. COWDERY'S TESTIMONY.

As to seeing the "Urim and Thummim," O. Cowdery, in a letter to W. W. Phelps, Sept. 7th, 1834, writes:

"Near the time of the setting of the sun, Sabbath evening, April 5, 1829, my natural eyes, for the first time beheld this brother, [Joseph Smith]. He then resided in Harmony, Susquehanna county, Pennsylvania. On Monday, the 6th, I assisted him in arranging some business of a temporal nature, and on Tuesday the 7th, commenced to write the Book of Mormon.

"These were days never to be forgotten—to sit under the sound of a voice dictated by the *inspiration* of Heaven, awakened the utmost gratitude of this bosom! Day after day I continued, uninterrupted, to write from his mouth, as he translated with the Urim and Thummim, or, as the Nephites would have said, 'Interpreters,' the history, or record, called 'the Book of Mormon.'"— *Messenger and Advocate*, Vol. 1, No. 1: also *Latter Day Saints' Herald*, Vol. 2. No. 3.

D. WHITMER'S TESTIMONY.

David Whitmer, now living at Richmond, Mo., one of "the three witnesses," recently said to a reporter of the *Chicago Times*, that he had free access to the room where the translation was going on, at the time Joseph and Oliver were at his father's house, (for they went there from Harmony),

"And was an eye-witness to the method of procedure. The plates were not before Joseph while he translated. * * * The method pursued was commonplace, but nevertheless effective. Having placed the Urim and Thummim in his hat, Joseph placed the hat over his face, and with prophetic eyes read the invisible symbols, syllable by syllable and word by word, while Cowdery or Harris acted as recorders. * * So illiterate was Joseph at that time, that he didn't even know that Jerusalem was a walled city, and he was utterly unable to pronounce many of the names which the magic power of the Urim and Thummim revealed, and therefore spelled them out in syllables, and the more erudite scribe put them together. The stone was the same used by the Jaredites at [from?] Babel. I have frequently placed it to my eyes, but could see nothing through it. I have seen Joseph, however, place it to his eyes and instantly read signs one hundred and sixty miles distant, and tell exactly what was transpiring there. When I went to Harmony after him, he told me the name of every hotel at which I had stopped on the road, read the signs, and described various scenes without having ever received any information from me."

Of "the stone," or "interpreters," Mr. Whitmer is represented as saying:

"But a stone had been found with the plates, shaped like a pair of ordinary spectacles, though much larger, and at least half an inch in thickness, and perfectly opaque, save to the prophetic vision of Joseph Smith. On the tablets or plates were engraven the records of the tribe of Nephites, and the stone was the Urim and Thummim, by which the seers of old had deciphered the mysteries of the universe."—*Chicago Times*, Aug. 7, 1875.

Here are definite testimonies, by O. Cowdery and D. Whitmer, that they not only saw the plates, but also the Urim and Thummim. If they and Martin Harris omitted mentioning in writing, that they saw the breast-plate, sword of Laban and directors, that would be no evidence at all that they had not seen them. They frequently testified, orally, to the fact, and O. Cowdery and D. Whitmer, have testified freely and pointedly, as we see, in writing, that they saw the Urim and Thummim, or "stone interpreters."

MR. S. THINKS THE PLATES MAY HAVE BEEN COLORED TIN!

"Perhaps they saw some plates which might have been tin, colored in some dye that would give them a golden complexion, to those not familiar with that metal; they might have heard a ventriloquist affirm they were translated by divine power, or they might merely have heard the voice of God *through Joseph;* they testify that an angel came down from heaven and brought the plates, *perhaps on the strength of Joseph's statement,* for they do not affirm that *they saw the angel*; but whether they saw the plates thus prepared or some other kind, they *failed to see the rest of the furniture promised.*"

The latter clause is a groundless assumption, and by what we have already seen we know it is false; and by the testimony of many witnesses now living we know the conjectures to be wholly false, as they testified to seeing "the furniture promised," as Mr. S. is pleased to call them. As for their seeing "plates which might have been tin, colored in some dye that would give them a golden complexion;" and that "they might have heard a ventriloquist affirm they were translated by divine power;" and that "they might merely have heard the voice of God *through Joseph;*" and, further, the probability that "they testify on the strength of Joseph's statement that an angel came down from heaven and brought the plates;" and lastly, that "they *do not* affirm that *they saw the angel*," is so weak, so preposterous and puerile, and so false to the written record, that we should not consider a reply called for, did not the article in which it appears fill a large space in the leading organ of the society of which Mr. S. is a prominent minister and champion.

DOES MR. S. THINK THAT COWDERY, WHITMER, AND HARRIS WERE IDIOTS?

Mr. Martin Harris was aged near forty-five years at the time of the translation, was a well-to-do farmer, and a sensible, intelligent man, and an honored member of society. Oliver Cowdery was a school teacher before he began to write the translation of the plates, and was a highly intellectual man, a good citizen, and possessed a fair education. After breaking off his active connection with the Church he practiced law at Elkhorn, Wis., after which he went to Missouri, where he died sometime after 1847. We have been informed by credible witnesses that in 1846, or 1847, he attended a conference at Carterville, a hamlet near Council Bluffs, Iowa, and was there re-baptized, and re-ordained to the office of an elder, at which time, from the public stand, he bore testimony to the truth of the Book of Mormon and the prophetic mission of Joseph Smith. After this he returned to Missouri, soon after which he died. He recognized the fact, seemingly, of the priesthood being, in part, with that people who were following under the leadership of Brigham and a portion of the Twelve, though he did not endorse that leadership; and he also felt the necessity of doing his "first works" over again, before passing into the presence of that God whose voice he had heard, whose Spirit he had enjoyed, and in whose work he had been for many years actively and prominently engaged. While in the practice of law at Elkhorn, many of the Saints questioned him in regard to his former testimonies in respect to the Book of Mormon, Joseph, and the Church, and he constantly affirmed those testimonies to be true. Of this we have been told by Brn. Wm. Aldrich, John C. Gaylord, James M. Adams, and others. As for David Whitmer, he still lives, and his reputation for intelligence and probity, as a man among men, is most excellent. Of him the reporter of the *Chicago Times*, who interviewed him, says:

"He is now seventy years of age, but as hale and hearty as most men of fifty. In person he is above the medium hight, stoutly built though not corpulent, his shoulders inclining to stoop as if from so long supporting his massive head rather than from the weight of years; his frank, manly, and benevolent face closely shaven, and his whole exterior betokening him to be one of nature's gentlemen. The rudiments of education he learned in school, and a life-time of thought and research have served to expand and store his mind with a vast fund of information. The *Times* reporter found him at his pleasant, two-story, white frame residence, near the centre of the town of Richmond, Mo., and in company with Hon. J. T. Child, editor of the *Conservator*, was admitted, introduced, and received a cordial greeting. When the object of the call was made known, Mr. Whitmer smilingly and meditatively remarked that it was true he had in his possession the original records, [manuscripts?], and was conversant with the history of the Church of Christ from the beginning, but was under sacred obligations to hold both history and records sacred until such time as the interests of truth and true religion might demand their aid to combat error. Presently he became quite animated, arose to his feet and with great earnestness and good nature spoke for half an hour on the harmony between the Bible the original Book of Mormon, showing how the finding of the plates had been predicted, referring to the innumerable evidences, in the shape of ruins of great cities existing on this continent, of its former occupation by a highly civilized race, reverently declaring his solemn conviction of the authenticity of the records in his possession, and closed by denouncing the Latter Day Saints of Utah as an abomination in the sight of the Lord. * * * When the question of polygamy was broached, and it was asked if the original Book of Mormon justified the practice, Mr. Whitmer most emphatically replied: 'No! it is even much more antagonistic to both polygamy and concubinage than is the Bible. Joseph Smith never to my knowledge advocated it, though I have *heard* that he virtually sanctioned it at Nauvoo. However, as I cut loose from him in 1837, I can't speak intelligently of what transpired thereafter.' David Whitmer believes in the Bible as implicitly as any devotee alive; and he believes in the Book of Mormon as much as he does in the Bible. The one is but a supplement to the other, according to his idea, and neither would be complete were the other lacking. And no man can look at David Whitmer's face for a half hour, while he charily and modestly speaks of what he has seen, and then boldly and earnestly confesses the faith that is in him, and say that he is a bigot or an enthusiast. While he shrinks from unnecessary public promulgation of creed, and feels that the Brighamites and Danites and numerous other 'ites' have disgraced it, yet he would not hesitate, in emergency to stake his honor and even his life upon its reliability. * * * Neither does he believe that the Book of Mormon is the only record of the lost tribes hidden in the earth, but, on the contrary, that the caves hold other records, that will not come forth till all is peace, and the lion shall eat straw with the lamb. *Three times* has he been at the hill Cumorah and seen the casket that contained the tablets and the seer-stone."—*Chicago Times*, Aug. 7, 1875.

The foregoing description of Mr. Whitmer is probably correct, as also the statement of his testimony, in the main.

Now we ask, Is it at all probable, nay is it *possible*, for these three intelligent men to have been deceived in regard to the *quality* of the plates, or the fact of *seeing the angel* come "down from heaven," bringing the plates and laying them before their eyes, so that they "saw the plates and the engravings thereon;" and the further fact that they were shown unto them "by the power of God and not of man," and that "the voice of the Lord commanded" them that they should bear record of it; and, finally, that the voice of the Lord declared to them that the plates had "been translated by the gift and power of God," all of which is set forth in their joint testimony in the prefatory pages of the Book of Mormon? Is it possible, we again inquire, for these men to have been deceived in all or any of these things? We think all right-minded people will say, No; they saw and heard what they testify of, or they were vile deceivers. The dye-colored-tin-plate-ventriloquist-second-hand-testimony- "through-Joseph-Smith" theory is as foolish as it is false, and is useful only as showing to what absurd extremes some men will go in order to shield themselves and their theories from the force of true, direct, and unimpeachable testimony. These men *saw*, and *heard*, and *knew*, when in the full vigor of life, when free from excitement, and when all the conditions forbade deception; and they in cool and sober moments testify, and testify the same things all their lives, and the dying go down to their graves with their words of testimony on their lips, while the living, bending under the weight of accumulated years, boldly, yet meekly and joyfully, affirm the truth of their former testimony. They were not deceived.

THE NEW JERUSALEM.

Passing over one or two unimportant points, and the trifling remarks of Mr. S. concerning them, we next notice his effort to prove Joseph Smith a false prophet because the New Jerusalem has not yet been built. He says:

"Over forty-two years ago Joseph Smith prophesied that the new Jerusalem should be built in Western Missouri, and that the temple should be reared in this generation: 'Verily this is the word of the Lord, that the city New Jerusalem shall be built by the gathering of the Saints, beginning at this place, even the place of the temple, which temple shall be reared in this generation; for verily this generation shall not all pass away, until an house shall be built unto the Lord, and a cloud shall rest upon it, which cloud shall be even the glory of the Lord, which shall fill the house.'—D. C. 83:2. This revelation was given in September, 1832, over forty-two years ago, and yet there is no sign of a temple in Western Missouri; and not a trace can be found of the New Jerusalem there; so the prophecy limiting the building of the temple to 'this generation' is a failure."

Not exactly, Mr. S. The conclusion to which you jump with such eagerness is not a very sensible one, and does great injustice to the text. The text says "this generation shall not *all* pass away, until an house shall be built," etc. This implies that the most or greater part of it would pass away; *i. e.,* that the house would not be built *until the closing times of this generation.* The word "generation," as here used, plainly signifies the life or age of man, and not the *average* age of man, as is urged by Mr. S. The Lord said to Abraham, concerning the deliverance of his posterity from Egypt: "In *the fourth generation* they shall come hither again."—Gen. 15:16. Now, if Mr. S. had lived in the times of Abraham, and had reasoned as he now does, he doubtless would have said that the above revelation to Abraham was false, because Israel did not "come hither again" in just four of *his* generations of thirty years each—or one hundred and twenty years. The "fourth generation" from the time of promise, measured, as we see, four generation of almost *one hundred and eight years each.*

That the gathering of the Saints to the center stake, (Independence, Mo.), and the building of the temple, was to take place after *many* years from the giving of the revelation in question, is apparent from another revelation, one given thirteen months *before* the former one; it reads:

"Ye can not behold with your natural eyes, for the present time, the design of your God concerning those things which shall come hereafter, and the glory which shall follow, after much tribulation. For *after much tribulation* cometh the blessing. Wherefore the day cometh that ye shall be *crowned with much glory.*"—D. C 58:2.

The Church has been passing through "much tribulation" ever since the times in which the foregoing was given, but especially since November, 1833, when most violent persecutions began to come upon them. Men were whipped, tarred and feathered, imprisoned, brutally beaten, and many were killed at different periods from 1833 to 1845, whilst women and children suffered for food and shelter, and all manner of indignities, and even death, and worse than death. Then there came the great latter-day "departing from the faith, giving heed to seducing spirits and doctrines of devils, teaching lies in hypocrisy, having their conscience seared with a hot iron;" and this has caused untold and immeasurable "tribulation," and the end is not yet. It was not until after all this that the Saints were to be "crowned with much glory," a condition of things that can be fully realized only in the final restoration and gathering of the Saints, and the building up of Zion and the temple of the Lord. From all this we learn that the speedy building up of "the center stake" and "the temple, was not contemplated in the revelations of Joseph, yet "this generation shall not *all* pass away, until an house shall be built unto the Lord."

MR. S. AS A MATHEMATICIAN.

We can not close on this point until we give the reader a specimen both of the profound skill of Mr. S. as an arithmetician, and of his remarkable zeal in pointing out the errors(?)of his fellowmen. In his anxiety to make out his case he undertakes, in a very elaborate manner, to enlighten us with respect to "the length of a generation in Mormon literature," and he says "it is easily learned." His first term in the proposition is:

"His [Moroni's] word shall hiss forth from *generation to generation.*

That is after the Book of Mormon came forth. His next is:

"Joseph, my son, if thou livest till thou art eighty-five years old, thou shalt see the face of the Son of Man."

And now comes his statement:

"As Joseph was born in 1805, his eighty-fifth year would be in 1890, when Christ's coming is due according to this revelation."

And now his conclusion:

"So if the generations, during which the words of God written by Moroni were to 'hiss forth,' began with the publication of the Book of Mormon in 1830, and end at the coming of the Son of Man in 1890, there are only sixty years given for two generations, and only thirty years for one generation; and taking this measurement for a generation, that temple should have been built over twelve years ago."

And now the final result:

"The truth is, the prophecy is a failure."

There are too many *ifs* in this proposition to make it even interesting, to say nothing about its inaccuracies. Archimedes, *if* he possessed the needed fulcrum, could have raised the earth. In the first place, it is not strictly authentic with the Reorganized Church that Joseph had a revelation locating the time of the coming of the Son of man. We do not admit the one quoted in evidence, as it came from the Brighamite publications. It may or may not be genuine. In the next place, the Book of Mormon may "hiss forth" to many generations *after* Christ comes, and no doubt will; so we are not, necessarily, compelled to locate the "two generations" claimed by Mr. S. on this side of his coming. And, finally, Mr. S. errs egregiously, in interpreting the promise, "His word shall hiss forth from generation to generation." If his words "hiss forth" to parents, and then to their children, it fulfills the promise. If it goes to parents, children, grand-children, and great grand-children, then they "hiss forth from generation to generation" just as truly, only on a more extended scale.

"I the Lord thy God am a jealous God, visiting the iniquity of the fathers upon the children unto *the third and fourth generation* of them that hate me."—Ex. 20: 5.

In this passage the word *generation* is used to convey the same idea or meaning as that from Moroni. It relates to successive generations of posterity, and has no direct reference to mere periods of time. Mr. S. and his fellows seem very partial to all questions of time, and mathematical calculation; but their past history admonishes us that they are not always, if ever, accurate, and therefore need close watching. There are too many *ifs* and *buts* in their methods, for profit.

BOOK OF LEHI.

Mr. S. next finds fault because the book of Lehi was not published. He quotes:—

"The Lord God hath said, that the words of the faithful should speak as it were from the dead. Wherefore, the Lord God will proceed to bring forth the words of the book; and in the mouth of as many witnesses as seemeth him good, will he establish his word."—2 Nephi 11: 17.

"But a part of the words, (118 pages), called the book of Lehi," [says Mr. S.], "were never published, the manuscript having been stolen, as we learn from the ninth section of the Book of Covenants."

Yes, they were stolen; we learn this from the section cited, and also from the lips of the late Martin Harris, Sen. He told the writer, in 1860, all about the leading circumstances connected with the theft. Mr. Harris, by much persuasion, obtained them from Joseph in order to read to his wife, and to some very pious (?) friends who were at the time visiting at his house, whom he hoped to benefit by showing them the manuscript. Before retiring for the night he took the manuscript and put it in a bureau drawer, and locked the drawer; he then locked the parlor in which the bureau was, putting both keys in his pocket. This was the last he ever saw of the manuscript. But this did not prevent "the words of the faithful" Lehi from going forth in the Book of Mormon. Let us see:—

"And now, verily I say unto you, that an account of those things that you have written, which have gone out of your hands, are engraven upon the plates of Nephi. Yea, and you remember, it was said in those writings, that a more particular account was given of these things upon the plates of Nephi."—D. & C. 9:8.

From "the plates of Nephi" then, we get not only what was in the book of Lehi, but "a more particular account." Nephi's plates contained in part, "an abridgement of the record" of his father, Lehi.—1 Nephi 1 : 7. Messrs. Cowdery, Harris, D. Whitmer, and probably others, were most likely knowing to the fact, from observation, that the writings from "the plates of Nephi" contained "a more particular account" of those matters found in the book of Lehi; so there was no possible room for deception on that score. Mr. S. inquires, "Is it not strange that inspiration could not have forseen all this?" (that is the theft of the manuscript). And we may with equal propriety inquire, Was it not strange that inspiration could not have forseen "the loss of the book entitled the Common Salvation?" (Jude 3); and of the many gospels? (Luke 1 : 1); and of the prophecy of Enoch? (Jude 14); "the book of Nathan the prophet?" and "the book of Gad the Seer?" (1 Chron. 29 : 29), with twenty-five or more books, either cited or quoted in the Bible, but now lost? And "Is it not strange that inspiration could not have forseen" that King Jehoiakim would *burn* the prophetic roll of Jeremiah? (Jer. 36 : 23); or that the Philistines would capture "the ark of the covenant of God?" (1 Sam. 4 : 4, 11).

THE INSPIRED TRANSLATION AGAIN.

Mr. S. affirms that,

"The inspired version betrays itself in first rejecting certain names given in our version, as being incorrect, and subsequently adopting the same names as being correct. We present a few samples. Our version of Matt. 24:37, reads, 'But as the days of *Noe* were,' etc.; but Joseph's inspired version repudiates 'Noe,' and substitutes 'Noah.'"

We have before said that much of the "Inspired Translation" was simply a *revision* and *correction* of the most essential parts of the text, and not a complete translation of the entire Bible. This may account, in a measure, for many seeming irregularities in both the *letter*, and historical statements, of the Inspired Translation. We remark again, that the evident object in giving what is called the Inspired Translation, was to relieve the Scriptures of gross and harmful errors, whether of doctrine, morals, history, etc., and to restore valuable portions that had been taken away. Now, as for the difference in spelling a name, "Noe," or "Noah;" "Sion," or

"Zion;" "Jeremy," or "Jeremiah," there is no evidence but that "inspiration" may use both forms, as they both signify precisely the same thing. The *spirit* and *substance* of a matter is of chief importance. And this may be clearly seen in the quotations of Jesus and the apostles from the various prophets. They seldom quote letter for letter, but mainly the substance; from which we may learn that "inspiration" is concerned most entirely, if not quite, about the *sense* and *meaning*, and *application* of things. Again, says Mr. S:

"The inspired translation, is made to address Joseph thousands of years before he was born, in the following two verses: 'These are the words which I spake unto my servant Moses. And they are true even as I will. And I have spoken them unto you. See thou show them unto no man, until I command you, except they that believe.'—Gen. 3: 32, 33."

This statement is utterly untrue. All of the words quoted are in *parenthesis*, at the close of a chapter, and were given to Joseph in explanation of the origin of the preceding revelation, and are words of instruction to Joseph. If Mr. S. had put them in parenthesis, as he found them, he would only have done his bounden duty. To leave out the parenthesis in his quotation, is just as vicious as to have mutilated the text by leaving out or adding words. It is a gross perversion, and utterly beneath a fair-dealing controversialist. Mr. S. says: "This putting two verses into the book of Genesis addressed to Joseph was certainly a wonderful blunder on his part." But they were not intended as a part, neither are they a part of the narrative of the Book of Genesis. We find in John 7: 39, and Acts 22: 2, that John and Luke introduce, in parenthesis, explanations touching the teachings of Jesus; and Paul, in a similar manner as Joseph, in the verses in question, introduces an explanation respecting the revelation to Moses. The cases are exactly parallel. And, by the way, those two verses are of great value, as settling the authorship of Genesis, and the perplexing question as to how Moses, if he wrote the book, (which some question), obtained the information contained therein, especially that which relates to the creation, the fall of man, and other kindred matters. Some think that as "Moses was learned in all the wisdom of the Egyptians," and probably had access to the ancient documents in the archives of the priesthood, he, by the aid of the Holy Spirit, was enabled to collate important facts, and make such extracts as were essential, and that he embodied them in what is now the book of Genesis.

"Ewald, the keenest of critics, and the most learned of skeptics, concerning the authorship of the Pentateuch as a whole, does not hesitate to ascribe to Moses the tables of the law, and the substantial groundwork of the system that bears his name."—*Genesis and Geology*, by Prof. Thompson, D. D., LL. D.

Yet Professor Thompson thinks that Genesis was made up, largely, of oral traditions and written documents, and further says:

"The composer of Genesis, as we possess it, may have worked up materials already extant in the form either of oral traditions or of written documents before him."

Yet he believes that those portions relating to the creation were in a direct manner displayed by God to man. He writes:

"A probable conjecture is, that what here is given in narrative passed before the mind of the original narrator in a series of retrospective visions; that it was a panoramic optical presentation, as, in a prophetic vision, future events are made to pass before the mind in a scenic form."

But he does not claim that *Moses* had this vision. Smith, in his Dictionary of the Bible, Art. Pentateuch, says:

"We can hardly escape the conviction that it [Genesis] partakes of the nature of a compilation. It has indeed a unity of plan, a coherence of parts, a shapeliness and an order, which satisfy us that as it stands it is the creation of a single mind. But it bears also manifest traces of having been based upon an earlier work; and that earlier work itself seems to have had embedded in it fragments of still more ancient documents. * * * The history contained in Genesis could not have been narrated by Moses from personal knowledge; but whether he was taught it by immediate divine suggestion, or was directed by the Holy Spirit to the use of earlier documents, is immaterial in reference to the inspiration of the work."

These quotations may serve to illustrate the mystery and uncertainty among learned men, as to who wrote the Book of Genesis; and as to whether, if Moses wrote it at all, he wrote the whole or any part of it by revelation direct from God. Now, the verses in question decide this important matter, when it is said, "These are the words which I spake unto my servant Moses."

BAPTISM UNDER THE LAW.

Mr. S. continues:

"In the Book Mormon, baptism is enjoined in connection with the law of Moses, and numerous instances are recorded where it is said to have been administered."

He points to this as proof that Joseph Smith was not inspired of God, and that the Book of Mormon is not a divine record. This mode of reasoning would condemn the four gospels, for each of them informs us of the administration of baptism by John the Baptist, and by Christ and his disciples, for some years before the abrogation of the law. Such logic would impeach the divine mission of Jesus and John the Baptist. If baptism could be administered in Judea for many years in connection with the law, and by those who were so very exact in keeping the law as was John and Jesus, and the Jewish disciples, then it might be administered by a branch of Israel in America, under similar circumstances. It was not "a requirement under the law," as Mr. S. would claim that the Book of Mormon teaches, but it was a requirement *superior to the law*, as is taught in the Book of Mormon, and as is seen in the case of Jesus, John, and their disciples. That baptism was an ancient rite among many different nations is now generally conceded. Smith, in his Dict. Bible, Art. Baptism, says:

"It is well known that ablution, or bathing, was common in ancient countries as a preparation for prayers and sacrifices, or *as expiatory of sin*. * * * There is an *universal agreement* among later Jewish writers that all the Israelites were brought into covenant with God by circumcision, *baptism*, and sacrifice, and that the same ceremonies were necessary in admitting *proselytes*. These usages of the Jews will account for the readiness with which all men flocked to the baptism of John the Baptist."

By this we learn, what we have hitherto remarked, that baptism was not new and peculiar to the times of John, Jesus, and the primitive Christians, but was an ordinance dating back to a very early antiquity.

BAPTISM OF CHILDREN.

And now comes an effort of Mr. S. which exhibits most clearly, intentional perversity. We regret it deeply, as it is a most unpleasant thing to think that any person would purposely misrepresent the views and statements of others. He says:

"The Book of Mormon clashes with Joseph's revelation concerning the baptism of children. In the eighth chapter of Moroni we find the following remarks: 'For I have learned the truth, that there have been disputations among you concerning the *baptism of your little children*. And now, my son, I desire that you should labor diligently, that *this gross error* should be removed from among you.' Again: 'I know that it is solemn mockery before God that yo should baptize little children.' And again: 'He that saith little children need baptism, denieth the mercies of Christ, and setteth at naught the atonement.' Yet on page page 225 of the Book of Covenants, Joseph thus speaks of John the Baptist: 'For he was *baptized* while he was yet in his childhood, and was ordained by the angel of God at the time he was eight days old.'"

Mr. S. knows that "childhood" has its different stages, and reaches up as high as twelve or fifteen years. He furthermore knows that the interdictory texts from Moroni relate to "little children," and not to children of advanced age, for the texts read so, literally. And he also knows that the text, "For he was baptized while he was *yet* in his childhood," implies that he was in the advanced stages of his childhood, bordering upon that period denominated *youth*. His quotation from "Apostle Pratt," that "baptism always precedes ordination," is not legitimate in his effort to make the Book of Mormon and the revelations of Joseph "clash." That quotation has nothing to do with the texts which he falsely claims are contradictory, and he is aware of it.

Ishmael was a "child" when he was fourteen years old, Gen. 21: 14; Samuel was a "child" when he was old enough to minister before the Lord, 1 Sam. 2: 18; Jesus was a *little* child, or "young child," at his birth, Matt. 2: 11, 18; and he was still a "child" when twelve years old, Luke 2: 40, 42. It was "little children" those who were not capable of believing intelligently on Christ, and of repenting of actual sins, that Mormon was writing about to Moroni, and Mr. S. was not ignorant of the fact. As for the early ordination of John the Baptist, that of Jeremiah was at a still younger age:

"Before thou camest forth out of the womb I sanctified thee, and I ordained thee a prophet unto the nations."—Jer. 1: 5.

PRINTING HOUSE.

He next denounces the revelations of Joseph as spurious, because a *commandment* to build a printing house at Kirtland, O., for the printing of the Scriptures was not accomplished, and because the Inspired Translation was "published at Plano, Ill.," instead of at Kirtland, and in the house spoken of. If a failure on the part of men to keep a *commandment* was proof that the command was not of God, then farewell to the Bible—both Old and New Testaments—farewell to the inspiration of Jesus, and Moses, and all the prophets and apostles; for, from Adam and Eve in Eden, to John upon Patmos, commandments have been received from God and not kept; and the fact is so patent to all Bible readers that quotations, or even citations, in proof, are not needed. The history of the race is the history of man's disobedience to the commands of God. If it was not manifest that our critic was crafty, we might think him crazy.

WORD "MORMON."

He next complains that Joseph did not "study and learn, and become acquainted with all good books, and with languages, tongues, and people," as he was commanded to do, D. C. 87:5. And he does not approve of Joseph's analysis of the word *Mormon*, and of his statement that in its root-meaning it signifies "more good." Well, from the manner in which Mr. S. handles the English, his mother-tongue, it would hardly be safe to accept him as a competent critic, nor his opinions as proper criterions. Mr. Smith studied the English branches, especially grammar, under Dr. McLellin, after the date of this revelation, March, 1833, with remarkable success, as the writer had it from Mr. McLellin in 1873. He afterwards studied Hebrew, making wonderful proficiency, under Messrs. Peixotto and Noah. He likewise studied other languages with some success. He also studied history, etc., etc. But suppose he studied none of the above, that would not prove the revelation commanding him to study, false, as any one of fair common sense may see. As to whether Mr. Smith's explanation of the word *Mormon* is good or not, the matter lies so far above the reach of Mr. S. that we may not trouble ourselves in regard to his opinion about it for at least one millenium.

APOCRYPHA.

Again says Mr. S.:

"In March, 1833, a revelation was given to Joseph, assigning reasons why he need not translate the Apocrypha, which reasons render his translation of the Bible equally needless. 'Verily, thus saith the Lord unto you, concerning the Apocrypha, there are many things contained therein that are true, and it is mostly translated correctly; there are *many things* contained therein that are *not true*, which are interpolations by the hands of men. Verily, I say unto you, that it is not needful that the Apocrypha should be translated. Therefore, whoso readeth it let him understand, for the Spirit manifesteth truth, and whoso is enlightened by the Spirit shall obtain benefit therefrom; and whoso receiveth not the Spirit cannot be benefitted; therefore it is not needful that it should be translated.'—D. C. 88:1. If the possession of the Spirit will lead to a discrimination between truth and error in the Apocrypha, so that a translation is needless, the same would be true with the Bible, and consequently render Joseph's work in translating it needless."

That the Spirit of God will enable its possessor to judge between good and evil, truth and error, is just as true as the words of Jesus and the Apostles.—Heb. 10:15; John 14:26; 16:13; and 1 Cor. 2:15. "He that is spiritual judgeth all things." But there is this notable difference between the Apocrypha and the Bible: the latter is "Holy Scriptures" while the former is not; and not being so, although it contained many truths which might be gleaned out from its errors by the spiritually minded, there was no need of its translation. The revelation under consideration does not even intimate that the Apocrypha was in any sense Holy Scriptures but only that it contained many truths and many errors; and they were of no vital importance beyond what may be found in Josephus, Philo, or similar works.

JOSEPH vs. HIS TRANSLATION (?)

Mr. S. says:

"Joseph had no faith in his own translation, unless he was a dishonest man, for our version of Heb. 11:40, which reads, 'That they without us should not be made perfect,' is rendered by Joseph's version thus: 'Without suffering they should not be made perfect.' Yet nine years after finishing this translation, Joseph falls back on to the common version to prove baptism for the dead in these words: 'For their salvation is necessary and essential to our salvation, as Paul says concerning the fathers,' 'that they without us cannot be made perfect; neither can we without our dead be made perfect.'—D. C. 110:15. If Joseph was an honest man, he never would have quoted *spurious scripture* to prove any doctrine."

To this we reply, (1) that the Inspired Translation was not yet published, and was not in common use; hence the propriety of not quoting it in discussing, popularly, any doctrine. And, (2) Joseph quotes the passage, (Heb. 11:40), not because baptism for the dead was in fulfillment of it, but because the *idea, or principle*, embraced in those words fitly applied in illustrating his argument. Paul, when at Athens (Acts 17:28) quoted the Greek poet, Aratus, not because the quotation was genuine Holy Scripture, but because the ideas embraced in it were true, as Paul used it, and suitable to the occasion; so with Joseph, and neither were dishonest. And, lastly, the passage, though improperly translated, was *not spurious*. Coin issued at the United States Mint, though it contain more alloy than is legal, yet it is not *spurious*. A legal document, whether deed, bond, mortgage, bill of sale, license, power of attorney or whatever it may be, if it be improperly worded, yet it is not, therefore, *spurious*. That which is spurious is *counterfeit, illegitimate, not of genuine origin, intentionally false or corrupt*.

INTERPRETERS.

Mr. S. has, for the want of a better subject, taken another bout at the "interpreters." He would like to make the Book of Mormon cross itself in its history of their origin or transmission. But this he cannot do. He says:

"Joseph tells us that the stone-interpreters, which he claims to have found, 'were given to the brother of Jared;' (D. C. 15:1); and Moroni, who claims to have found the same interpreters, says in the first chapter of Ether, 'I have sealed up the interpreters,' that is with the plates. So far they agree; but upon examining the Book of Mormon we find that Mosiah's stone-interpreters are the ones handed down with the records, and not those given to Jared's brother."

We have shown, hitherto, that all the probabilities favor the idea that the interpreters with which Mosiah translated the "twenty-four plates found by the people of Limhi," were *found with the plates;* for, though the record is silent, directly, as to the finding the interpreters with the plates, yet the stone-interpreters are first mentioned *after finding the plates,* and in immediate connection with the translation, "by means of those two stones which were fastened into the two rims of a bow."—Mosiah 12 : 3. The silence of the record as to finding the interpreters with the plates, directly, is no evidence at all against their having been found with them. The silence of Matthew, Luke, and John as to Jesus saying, "these signs shall follow them that believe," is no evidence that he did not say so; and the silence of Matthew, Mark and John is no proof that Jesus did not say to the penitent thief, "To-day shalt thou be with me in paradise." So the silence of Mosiah as to finding the "interpreters" with the plates, is not evidence that they were not found with them. Joseph testifies that the angel told him that with the plates "there were two stones in silver bows." (*g*).

David Whitmer, one of the three witnesses to the Book of Mormon, now living at Richmond, Mo., described the "interpreters" to a *Chicago Times* reporter, in August, 1875, as follows:

"But a stone had been found with the plates, *shaped like a pair of ordinary spectacles*, though much larger, and at least half an inch in thickness, and perfectly opaque save to the prophetic vision of Joseph Smith."

O. Cowdery testifies that Joseph translated the plates by means of "the Urim and Thummim, or, as the Nephites would have said, 'interpreters.'" (*h*). Now all these testimonies are substantially the same, and fix the identity of the "interpreters," or "two stones which were fastened into the two rims of a bow," (Mosiah 12 : 3) as being the same as the two stones (Ether 1 : 18, 11) given to the brother of Jared. We have shown in another place the possibility of Mosiah's having obtained the stone interpreters by the way of Coriantumr, the last Jaredite king, or in connection with other important discoveries, (among them Jaredite engravings), made by the people of Zarahemla, (Omni 1 : 9, 10), many years before the

---

(*g*) Times and Seasons; Mil. Star; also Pearl of Great Price, 41.
(*h*) Times and Seasons, page 201.

times of Mosiah 2d. Here are two valid solutions of the question as to how Mosiah became possessed of the "two stones"—"interpreters"—given to the brother of Jared. And he might have obtained them in either of these ways.

Mr. S., by a technical criticism, strives to make the Book of Mormon say that the "interpreters" of Mosiah were handed down from Jerusalem. He says, "Mosiah conferred his interpreters upon Alma, together with the plates:"

"Now after Mosiah had finished translating these records * * * he took the plates of brass, and all the things he had kept, and conferred them upon Alma, who was the son of Alma; yea, all the records, and also the *interpreters*, and conferred them upon him, and commanded him that he should keep and preserve them, and also a record of the people, handing them down from one generation to another, even as they had been handed down *from the time Lehi left Jerusalem.*"—Mosiah 13:1.

Now, the chief object in this passage is that of "the records;" and it is of these, and not, necessarily, of the interpreters that Mosiah speaks, when he says, "as *they* had been handed down *from the time Lehi left Jerusalem.*"

"And these records [thus handed down] did contain the five books of Moses, which gave an account of the creation of the world, and also of Adam and Eve, who were our first parents; and also a record of the Jews from the beginning, even down to the commencement of the reign of Zedekiah king of Judah; and also the prophecies of the holy prophets from the beginning, even down to the commencement of the reign of Zedekiah; and also many prophecies which have been spoken by the mouth of Jeremiah."—1 Nephi 1:46.

To these were added the records of succeeding Nephite prophets, and, finally, in the times of Mosiah 2nd, the "twenty-four plates" found by the people of king Limhi. It is manifestly *the records* that Mosiah alludes to as having "been handed down *from the time that Lehi left Jerusalem.*" This is evidently the *sense* and *intention* of the passage. Our common version says:

"Joseph also went up from Galilee, out of the city of Nazareth, into Judea, unto the city of David, which is called Bethlehem, * * to be taxed with Mary his wife, being great with child."—Luke 2:4, 5.

Yet none would question but what it was intended to say that it was Mary, and NOT *Joseph* who was "great with child." It also says:

"But as they [the disciples] sailed, he [Christ] fell asleep; and there came down a storm of wind on the lake, and *they were filled with water.*"—Luke 8:23.

Though there are verbal defects in these passages, the *meaning of* them is quite apparent; and yet they afford ample grounds for a crafty critic to build up a flimsy argument upon.

FEET WASHING.

Mr. S. says:

"Feet washing is pronounced an ordinance, and restricted to the priesthood, (D. C. 85: 45, 46). We will not argue the question as to whether feet washing was ever an ordinance in the church, or not; but it certainly was not restricted to the ministry in its administration, if Paul's testimony has any weight: 'If she has washed the saints' feet.'"

Oh, no! feet washing "was not restricted to the ministry in its administration," not by any means; and it is good that it is not. Persons could wash their own feet; and both men and women could "wash the saints' feet." But feet washing *as an* "*ordinance*," that of which the *Doctrine and Covenants* speaks, is a very different thing. Partaking of bread and wine, anointing with oil, and being immersed, are "not restricted to the ministry" in their administration, except when used as *ordinances* of the Church, and then, like feet washing, *they are*. Feet washing was appointed to his ministry by the Savior, (John 13: 4-15).

PRIESTHOOD COVENANT.

Mr. S. says:

"The breaking of the priesthood covenant is pronounced an unpardonable sin: 'But whoso breaketh this covenant, after he hath received it, and altogether turneth therefrom shall not have forgiveness of sins in this world nor in the world to come.' (D. C. 83: 6). Covenant-breaking is poor business, if the covenant is a good one; but Christ restricts the unpardonable sin to one thing— blasphemy against the Holy Ghost. After Peter had lied, and cursed, and swore, and had thus broken his ministerial covenant, he found pardon, and subsequently spent long years in the ministry."

That Peter sinned, and sinned greviously, none can deny; but to say that he broke his priesthood covenant, is to say what is evidently not true. If he had broken that covenant, and "altogether" turned "away therefrom," his case would have been vastly different. That would have involved his knowingly, willingly, and willfully turning away from God; which would have embraced, substantially, his sinning against the Holy Ghost. It is he who not only breaks "this covenant after he hath received it," but also "altogether turneth therefrom," "that shall not have forgiveness of sins in this world nor in the world to come." Mr. S. has a peculiar faculty of cutting a sentence in two, as above, and then arguing against a detached and incomplete part.

ST. JOHN TO TARRY.

He next finds fault with the revelations of Joseph, because it is claimed that Christ said unto John: "Thou shalt tarry until I come in my glory, and shall prophesy before many nations, kindreds, tongues, and people."—D. & C. 6:1. Mr. S. says:

"History affirms that John died at Ephesus. But if history is false, as John never disguised himself when alive, why does he not come out like a man and show himself, and settle some of these theological disputes in the land, and also let us know whether he helped ordain Joseph? Why sneak around in this way?"

If Mr. S. had lived in the days of the first Christian disciples, he probably would have reasoned in a similar strain concerning Jesus. The Pharisees of *those* times said, "Master, we would see a sign from thee," (Matt. 12:38); and some said, "If he be the king of Israel, let him now come down from the cross, and we will believe him," (Matt. 27:42). And no doubt many said, If Jesus is actually risen from the dead, why does he not come out like a man and show himself, and settle some of these theological disputes in the land, and also let us know whether he had raised up many of the bodies of the saints,—why skulk around in this way? The heavens were not bound to gratify the morbid curiosity of the sign-seekers in those days, nor are they now. Jesus was not shown openly to the world after his resurrection, "but unto witnesses chosen before of God," (Acts 10:41). God's wisdom, anciently, and modernly, is very different from that of man's.

As to John's death, history is conflicting and unsatisfactory. Smith, in his *Dictionary of the Bible*, says:

"The very time of his death lies within the region of conjecture rather than of history, and the dates that have been assigned for it range from A. D. 89 to A. D. 120."

That the early Christians, with John, understood that he was not to die, but remain till the second coming of Christ, is apparent from John 21:22, 23:

"Jesus saith unto him, If I will that he tarry till I come, what is that to thee? Follow thou me. Then went this saying abroad among the brethren, that that disciple should not die; yet Jesus said not unto him, He shall not die; but, If I will that he tarry till I come what is that to thee?"

ADAM—MICHAEL AN ANGEL.

Mr. S. objects further to the revelations of Joseph, because one, in D. C. 104:28, calls Adam "Michael, the Prince, the Archangel." He says:

"The Bible never represents saints as turning into angels at any past or future time."

Well, the Bible does not contain all the truths there are, either in heaven, or on earth; and yet the Bible *does* teach that men become angels. In the Hebrew, in Isa. 42::19; Hag. 1:13; Mal. 3:1, what in the common English version is "messenger," is there "angel." In Revelations 1:20; 2:1, 8, 12, etc., the elders in charge of the seven churches of Asia, are called by the Holy Spirit, *angels*. And in Rev. 19:10, the angel who ministers to John says:

"I am thy fellow servant, and *of thy brethren* that have the testimony of Jesus."

Of here signifies, clearly, *from among*. He was, therefore, "from among" those, John's "brethren that have the testimony of Jesus, * * * for the testimony of Jesus is the Spirit of prophecy." Again, "The Lord came from Sinai, and rose up from Seir unto them; he shined forth from Paran, and he came with ten thousand of *saints*; from his right hand went forth a fiery law," (Deut. 33:2). Now David calls these "saints" "angels."—"The chariots of God are twenty thousand, even thousands of *angels;* the Lord is among them as in Sinai in the holy place," (Ps. 68:17). This identifies these "saints," as being the "angels" of God. These may have been of that company of saints composed of Enoch and others, who were translated.

Bingham, in his *Antiquities of the Christian Church*, p. 75, states that the Bishops were called the "angels of the churches; a name which some authors suppose to be used by St. Paul, 1 Cor. 11:10."

Now, inasmuch as the ministers of God, under the Old Testament, and the New Testament, were called angels, why may not Adam be be also called an angel? And inasmuch as the personage who ministered to John, and who was "of" John's brethren, was called an angel, and *was* an angel, why may not others of John's faithful brethren, and Adam pre-eminent among them, become "angels?" Jesus says:

"They which shall be accounted worthy to obtain that world, and the resurrection from the dead, neither marry nor are given in marriage; neither can they die any more; for they are *equal* unto the angels."—Luke 20:35, 36. "But are *as* the angels of God in heaven."—Matt. 22:30.

Being then "*as* the angels of God in heaven," and "*equal* unto the angels," will Mr. S. tell us wherein they differ from them. And inasmuch as they are changed into the condition, and nature, of "the angels of God in heaven," are they not, substantially, angels? It is true that man was made "a little lower than the angels," (of heaven), being made liable to death, possessing less power, and having a more limited sphere than they, but that is not to say that men may not become angels, in a limited sense, while in this life, and "*as* the angels of God in heaven" in a world to come. Christ, before his incarnation, ministered as the "angel of the Lord." Gen. 22:15; Ex. 3:2, 6, 14; Acts 7:30-35; Gen. 48:15, 16, with Heb. 1:2, 3, 8, 10; 1 Cor. 15:47. And he is now "a quickening Spirit."—1 Cor. 15:45.

Inasmuch as resurrected holy men are made "*equal unto the angels,*" and "*as* the angels of God in heaven," why not those who are translated—Enoch, Elijah, and probably others—why not they be "equal unto," and "*as* the angels of God in heaven?" This is further seen in the fact that the Lord promised to send "Elijah the prophet" (Mal. 4:5, 6) "to minister to them who shall be heirs of salvation," Heb. 1:14. In Luke 9:30, 31, Moses and Elias (Elijah) appear in *the capacity* of angels, though not in *the name* of angels.

"There talked with him [Christ] two *men*, which were Moses and Elias; who appeared in glory, and spake of his decease, which he should accomplish at Jerusalem."

Angels were frequently called *men* (Gen. 18:2; Josh. 5:13, 15; Luke 24:4; Acts 1:10; Heb. 13:2, etc., etc.). Now, all these proofs place the matter beyond question: (1) that men in this life are sometimes called angels; and (2) that translated persons, and resurrected persons, become "equal unto," and "*as* the angels of God in heaven;" and (3) that some of them have ministered in that capacity.

THREE FUTURE WORLDS.

Mr. S. next opposes the idea that there are "three future worlds —celestial, terrestial, and *telestial.*" He says:

"Celestial means heavenly; terrestial means earthly; but what does telestial mean?"

Why, Mr. S., it means "the glory of the stars," (1 Cor. 15:21), the last and least "order" of glory in the resurrection, (1 Cor. 15:21, 23, 24), and is to be possessed by those worthy of it, when the Lord judges all men "according to *their works,*" (Rev. 20:13; Rom. 2:6; Matt. 16:27; Rom. 14:11, 12). It is not "the Restorationist's hell," as you flippantly assert; but it is that condition of future being and glory into which "they who are thrust down to hell *.* who are not redeemed from the devil until the last resurrection, until the Lord, even Christ the Lamb shall have finished his work," (D. C. 76:7), shall finally be brought. "The wicked shall be turned into hell, and all the nations that *forget* God," (Ps. 9:17); yet "death and hell" shall deliver up the dead which are in them, and they shall be "judged every man according to his works," (Rev. 20:13). Jonah says: "Out of the belly of hell [a place of God's punishment] cried I, and thou heardest my voice," (Jonah 2:2). So from these, and other Bible testimonies, we learn, that although the wicked may, and do, go down to hell, it is for their punishment, and reform, and that it is not the purpose of God that they should eternally remain there; nor is it his purpose that they should become unconscious at death and remain so till they are resurrected and judged, and then be annihilated; for that would defeat justice and pervert equity, and render forever impossible the just judgment of God, "who without respect to persons judgeth according to every man's *work*," (1 Pet. 1:17).

That all the race (with one class as an exception—they who sin against the Holy Ghost), will be subdued unto God, and will finally *know* and *confess* Christ, is evident from the Scriptures. Paul says:

"That at the name of Jesus every knee should bow, of things in heaven, and things in earth, and things under the earth; and that every tongue should confess that Jesus Christ is Lord to the glory of God the Father."—Phil. 2:10, 11.

John says:

"And every creature which is in heaven, and on the earth, and under the earth, and such as are in the sea, and *all that are in them*, heard I saying, Blessing and honor, and glory and power, be unto him that sitteth upon the throne, and unto the Lamb forever and ever,"—Rev. 5:13.

There is a wide difference in men's works, and consequently there will be a wide difference in the degrees of their condemnation and rewards, and in their future conditions.

They of the telestial glory dwell outside of the city New Jerusalem, and where God and Christ are they cannot come:

"For without [the city] are dogs, and sorcerers, and whoremongers, and murderers, and idolators, and whosoever loveth and maketh a lie."—Rev. 22:15.

"And the glory of the telestial is one, even as the glory of the stars is one, for as one star differs from another star in glory, even so differ one from another in glory in the telestial world; for these are they who are of Paul and of Apollos, and of Cephas; these are they who say they are some of one and some of another, some of Christ and some of John, and some of Moses, and some of Elias; and some of Esaias, and some of Isaiah, and some of Enoch, *but received not the gospel, neither the testimony of Jesus, neither the prophets; neither the everlasting covenant:* last of all, these all are they who will not be gathered with the saints, to be caught up unto the church of the first born, and received into the cloud; these are they who are liars, and sorcerers, and adulterers, and whoremongers, and whosoever loves and makes a lie; these are they who suffer the vengeance of eternal fire; these are they who are cast down to hell and suffer the wrath of Almighty God until the fullness of times, when Christ shall have subdued all enemies under his feet, and shall have perfected his work, when he shall deliver up the kingdom and present it unto the Father spotless saying: I have overcome and have trodden the wine-press of the fierceness of the wrath of Almighty God: then shall he be crowned with the crown of his glory to sit on the throne of his power to reign forever and ever. But, behold, and lo, we saw the glory and the inhabitants of the telestial world, that they were as innumerable as the stars in the firmament, or as the sand upon the sea shore, and heard the voice of the Lord saying: These all shall bow the knee, and every tongue shall confess to him who sits upon the throne forever and ever; for they shall be judged according to their works; and every man shall receive according to his own works, and his own dominion, in the mansions which are prepared, and they shall be servants of the Most High, but where God and Christ dwell they cannot come, worlds without end."—D. C. 76: 7.

The foregoing is a brief explanation of what the *telestial* glory is, or *means*. In it we see the benevolent provisions of an All-wise God for the future conditions of erring man.

The terrestial glory is greatly in advance of that of the telestial world, while the celestial is vastly superior to the terrestial, it being the glory of the Father and the Son, where they who enjoy it are made possessors of all things—those things that "eye hath not seen, nor ear heard, nor hath entered into the heart of man," except as revealed unto some by the Spirit of God. With "the second death" and eternal perdition for those only who become like the devil and his angels.

The teachings of the Scriptures and the verdict of all right-minded people, is, that all mankind, without respect of persons, should be judged *according to their works;* and this provision of the three glories, or "three future worlds," as Mr. S. is pleased to call them, meets all the demands of the case, manifesting alike the justice, the equity, and the love of God.

That doctrine is neither sensible nor Scriptural, however popular it may be, that reckons all sinners *alike* in the sight of God—that ranks the midnight assassin, the red-handed murderer, and those of the viler sort, with the Sabbath-breaker, the common liar, or the petty thief, in the same class. All are transgressors, *but not to the same degree;* and therefore justice, equity, and mercy demand that there should be a difference in their judgment. Jesus teaches in plain terms that "it shall be more tolerable" for one class of sinners in the day of judgment than for others, (Matt. 11 : 22, 24; 10 : 15; 12 : 41, 42). But this could not be true if all kinds and classes of sinners went down to hell at death and remained there worlds without end, as some teach; or if the wicked were unconscious after death till their resurrection, and were then simply judged and *annihilated*, as others teach. God is just, and his tender mercies are over all his works, to do right by them.

THE SOUL OF MAN.

Mr. S. next enters into a profitless quibble in regard to what is said in the revelations about the soul of man,—"And the spirit and the body is the soul of man. And the resurrection from the dead is the redemption of the soul," (D. C. 85 : 4). "O God, receive my soul," (Mosiah 9 : 5). Mr. S. says:

"Did he mean receive my spirit and body?"

To this we reply, that the meaning of a word is to be determined by the office it performs in a sentence. This is an essential law of language. Consequently, when I speak of *a door*, I may speak of an aperture or passage-way into a room or building, or, of that which fills the aperture, or shuts up the passage. When we speak of a *gate*, we may mean the opening, or entrance, or we may mean that which closes up the entrance. When we use the word *cleave*, it may signify *adhere, unite;* or it may mean, *to part, separate, divide.* The meaning of these words and thousands of others, *soul* included, has various meanings, which can be determined only by the office they perform in their connection with other words.

The *soul*, in Gen. 2 : 7—"man became a living soul,"—relates to man as a living being composed of *body* and *spirit*, (Eccl. 12 : 7; Jas. 2 : 26. So Lev. 23 : 30; Acts 27 : 37; 1 Pet. 3 : 20, etc.). But in Gen. 35 ; 18,—"as her soul was in departing," and 1 Kings 17 : 21,—"let this child's soul come into him again; and Prov. 16 : 24, —"Pleasant words are sweet to the soul;" and Matt. 10 : 28,—"Fear not them which kill the body, but are not able to kill the soul;" and Acts 14 : 22,—"confirming the souls of the disciples;" and Rev. 6 : 9,—"I saw under the altar the souls of them that were slain for the word of God, and for the testimony which they held," with scores of other passages which might be quoted, the word *soul* clearly relates, not to the *body*, but to the spirit of man. So then, the *spirit* of man is the *soul* as taught in Mosiah, and the *spirit and body* is also the soul, as taught in D. C. 85:4; and there is no contradiction, though Mr. S. would love to make it appear so.

NON-ENGLISH WORDS.

Mr. S. complains that:

"In translating the Book of Mormon, words are often used not contained in the English language. The following is a sample: 'a fifth part of their ziff.'—Mos. 7:1."

These words were transferred, probably, because there were no English equivalents for them. If "ziff" was some kind of metal, as is rather likely, it is not at all strange that there was not, at the time of the translation, an English equivalent for it. A number of new metals have been discovered since then, and there may yet be many more discovered, and possibly the very kind in question.

GIFT TO TRANSLATE.

Mr. S. wishes to know:

"(1) Was the gift [to translate] in the stone-interpreters, or in Joseph? (2) If Joseph himself had the gift, what need of the stones? (3) If the gift was in the stones, how could Joseph lose it, without losing the stones?"

To the first question we reply: the gift was in both,—in the stones as *a means*, and in Joseph as an *agent* to use that means. To the second we reply: Though Joseph was the agent to translate, yet the stones were necessary as *a means* by which to work. In reply to the third we have to say,—that Joseph might have lost *his* power as *a seer*, and in this sense lost his gift to translate; or he might have lost the stone, which was *a means* in translating. An astronomer may lose the telescope by which he traces the pathway of the stars, and discovers and visits those beautiful islands of light in the limitless expanse of the heavens, or he may lose his natural sight—the power to *use* that wonderful instrument.

URIM AND THUMMIM.

Mr. S. now proceeds to enlighten us in regard to the Urim and Thummim. He says:

"The Jewish High Priest never read languages by this means, but wore them upon his breast-plate,—they were not used to read through, but were outward emblems of divine illumination upon the heart of the wearer."

Brown, in his *Dict. of Bible*, art. Urim and Thummim, says, "What they were cannot be determined." Smith, in his *Dict. Bible*, says:

"In what way the Urim and Thummim were consulted is quite uncertain.

Josephus and the rabbins supposed that the stones gave out *the oracular answer* by preternatural illumination. But it seems to be far simplest, and most in agreement with the different accounts of inquiries made by Urim and Thummim, (1 Sam. 3:18, 19; 23:3, 12; 28:6; Judg. 20:28; 2 Sam. 5:23, &c.), to suppose that the answer was given simply by the word of the Lord to the high priest (compare John 11:51), when he had inquired of the Lord, clothed with the Ephod and breast-plate."

Who should better understand than "Josephus and the rabbins?" None, we think, but those who are favored with a divine revelation, or with experimental knowledge, as Joseph and the first Elders and members of the church. The opinions of "Josephus and the rabbins" are in essential accord with the statements of Joseph, O. Cowdery, M. Harris, D. Whitmer, and others, and quite adverse to the opinion volunteered by Mr. S. The Septuagint Bible renders the signification of Urim and Thummim, as *"revelation and truth."* Whiston, in a note, on p. 94, *Josephus*, says that the "shining stones" were used in revealing the will of God, after a *perfect* and *true* manner to his people Israel. Of these stones Josephus, Ant. Jews, B. 3, ch. 9, par. 9, says, "Now this breast-plate, and *sardonyx* left off shining two hundred years before I composed this book." With the information we have before us, one thing is certain, and that is, that the Urim and Thummim, as Joseph claims, was a divine means of *revelation from God*, "after a perfect and true manner;" and that it was through the "preternatural illumination" of the stones. That it was a means of obtaining revelation and instruction directly from God is seen in the fact that Joshua "shall stand before Eleazer the priest, who shall ask counsel for him after the judgment [decision, revelation] of Urim before the Lord," (Num. 27:21); and that, "When Saul inquired of the Lord, the Lord answered him not, neither by dreams, *nor by Urim*, nor by prophets," (1 Sam. 28:6). In all these evidences we see that it was a means of revelation from God, enabling those gifted with the power to use it to *read* and learn in regard to hidden matters, and *know* what was otherwise secret and unrevealed.

FIRST GIFT.

Mr. S. thinks he has found "a direct collision" in the fact of Joseph's having the gift of prophecy, in connection with O. Cowdery, May, 1829, when they baptized each other, whereas a commandment was given in March, 1829, two months before, saying to Joseph:

"And you have a gift to translate the plates, and this is the first gift that I bestowed upon you; and I have commanded that you pretend to no other gift until my purpose is fulfilled in this, for I will grant unto you no other gift until it is finished."—D. C. 4:1.

That this could have no direct reference to spiritual gifts, such as discerning of spirits, visions, angelic ministrations, revelations, etc., etc., is evident from the fact that Joseph possessed all these for months, and years, prior to the revelation. It referred, no doubt, to matters of translation, the chief topic of the clause quoted, and to showing the plates to others. Joseph had "the gift" to translate only the unsealed part of the plates, and he was not privileged to show the plates to any until the translation was completed; for Joseph says;

"The same heavenly messenger delivered them up to me with this charge: that I should be responsible for them: and that if I should let them go carelessly, or through any neglect of mine, I should be cut off; but that if I would use my endeavors to preserve them, until he, the messenger should call for them, they should be protected."—*Millennial Star*, vol. 14, Supplement, page 6.

And it was further said to Joseph:

"I have caused you that you should enter into a covenant with me, that you should not show them [the plates] except to those persons whom I commanded you, and you have no power over them except *I grant it* unto you."—D. C. 4:1.

Now this was said to Joseph because Martin Harris "desired a witness [at the hand of the Lord] that you, my servant Joseph Smith, Jr., have got the plates of which you have testified and borne record that you have received of me," (D. C. 4:1). In June of 1829, Martin Harris obtained from the desired witness, in connection with D. Whitmer and O. Cowdery. Now Joseph had the gift to *translate* the plates, but not to *show* them until the translation was finished. This is the easy and natural solution of what Mr. S. has labored hard to make "a puzzle," and a contradiction.

IMITATING BIBLE.

Mr. S. says:

"The Book of Mormon betrays its weakness in imitating the style of Bible phraseology—a style in common use at the time our Bible was first translated into the English language, but which has long since ceased to be used, except as it is retained in our version of the Bible."

All critics do not agree with Mr. S. on this point. Some hold that the *dissimilarity* in the style of the two books, in respect to their phraseology, is evidence that the Book of Mormon is spurious. That the style of speech in the Book of Mormon is somewhat like that of the Bible, especially the Old Testament, is true; but that it is *strikingly* so, is not true, as any one who carefully reads the two books can see. That the diction, or manner of expression, peculiar to both the Bible and the Book of Mormon is largely and mainly due to *the style of the originals*, is, we think, a well attested fact; though of the Bible Mr. S. asserts to the contrary, holding that its style of phraseology is due to that which was common to *its translators*. Max Müller, one of England's most eminent scholars, in one of his *Essays on the Science of Religion*, holds the very opposite of Mr. S. Prof. Müller, in his admirable and successful effort to prove that the Hebrew original of *created*—"bara," (Gen. 1 : 1, etc.), signifies "to create out of pre-existing matter," says:

"In the minds of those whom Moses addressed, and whose language he spoke, it [the *phrase*, or form of expression, by which he speaks of God's creating heaven and earth] could only have called forth the simple conception of fashioning or arranging. * * * To find out how *the words* of the Old Testament were understood by those to whom they were originally addressed is a task attempted by a very few interpreters of the Bible. The great majority of readers transfer without hesitation the ideas which they connect with words as used in the nineteenth century to the mind of Moses or his cotemporaries, forgetting altogether the distance which divides their *language* and their thoughts from the thoughts and *language* of the wandering tribes of Israel."

Again:

"It is well known that we have in the *language* of the New Testament the clear vestiges of Greek and Roman influences, and if we knew nothing of the historical intercourse between those two nations and the writers of the New Testament, the very *expressions* [phraseology] used by them, not only their *language*, but their thoughts, their *allusions*, *illustrations* and *similes*, would enable us to say that some historical contact had taken place between the philosophers of Greece, the lawgivers of Rome, and the people of Judea. * * * Why should there be any hesitation in pointing out in the Old Testament an Egyptian *custom*, or a Greek *word*, or a Persian *conception*. If Moses was learned in all the wisdom of the Egyptians, nothing surely would stamp his writings as more truly historical than traces of Egyptian *influences* that might be discovered in his laws."

Now all this teaches that the *style* of expression—*the phraseology*—as well as the *ideas*, of God's ancient people are sought to be preserved in the common version of the Bible. And it is not at all strange that there should be *some* similarity between the writings of the ancient Nephites in America and the ancient Israelites in Judea; for both sprang from the same nation, having the *same language* in the main, and the same Scriptures up to the time of

Jeremiah, and were taught by the same Spirit from one and the same God, and the same Lord Jesus Christ.

ELIAS—GABRIEL.

Mr. S. objects to the revelations of Joseph because that in D. C. 26:2, it is said: "Which Zachariah he [Elias] visited, and gave promise that he should have a son, and his name should be John," whereas in Luke 1:19, the angel's name is said to be "Gabriel."

Angels, as well as others, may have different names. Peter was sometimes called Cephas and sometimes Simon. Jesus had many titles—Christ, the Lord, the Holy One, Messiah, Immanuel, etc., etc. Mr. S. says "it is a trick of rogues," to change ones name. Was it a "trick of rogues" for Peter, and Jesus, and Jacob, and Abraham, and Saul of Tarsus, and hosts of other Bible worthies, to change their names? Are you not rather sweeping in your denunciations, Mr. S? In your effort to thus strike down "Mormonism," are you not fighting against the facts of the Bible? Men of God, as also Christ, have various names, which are alike honored of God by their being used by the Spirit of God. Why then should it be thought unreasonable that angels should have different names, and that the angel who announced to Zacharias the birth of John should be called both Elias and Gabriel? Presumptive evidence that the angel "Gabriel" was none other than "Elias" lies in the peculiarity of the promise: "And he [John] shall go before him in the *spirit* and *power* of Elias," (Luke 1:17), from which it may be easily inferred that "Elias" (Elijah, Heb.) would be "his angel," to watch over, direct, and aid him, in his life and ministry. Further evidence lies in the promise made through Malachi, 4:5, "Behold, I will send you Elijah [Elias, Gr.], the prophet before the coming of the great and dreadful day of the Lord," which Jesus applies to John the Baptist; (Matt. 11:14; 17:12); and yet which John denies, (John 1:21), when he said he was not the Elias. John was the Elias to that generation, inasmuch as he acted under the ministration of Elias (Elijah, Heb.), his angel; yet *personally* he was not the Elias, but only John the Baptist. In this we have a rational solution of a seeming contradiction between the testimony of John and Christ; and by this we also obtain a clue to the idea that the angel Gabriel was none other than the prophet Elijah, who was translated without seeing death, (2 Kings 2:1, 11). Inasmuch as John was to go before Christ "in the spirit and power of Elias,"

[Elijah], what more proper than that this translated prophet should announce to Zacharias the birth and mission of John? And what more proper than that this translated prophet, now that his condition was so changed toward God, should, like Abram, Jacob, Saul, Peter, and others, have "a new name," and be called "Gabriel," as well as "Elias?" These ideas are in exact accordance with Bible facts; and the thought that the angel Gabriel is the translated prophet Elijah, is good evidence of the divinity of that revelation of the young Seer in which it is found.

THE PLATES, AND THE WITNESSES.

We now come to another link in the lengthy chain of objections urged by Mr. S., and to the weakest and most unreasonable so far. It is in regard to the testimony of the three and the eight witnesses to the Book of Mormon. Mr. S. admits what no reasonable and informed person can well deny, that "Joseph might have had plates of some kind, either found or prepared to imitate gold;" yet he claims that the witnesses, all of them, the three and the eight, were mistaken—that is, deceived—and that their testimony is contradictory; and that many of its essential parts are based on second-hand testimony—"on the strength of Joseph's word." Mr. S , in his method of argument, reaches the very climax of absurdity, and exposes himself on every hand to contempt for his wit, and to painful distrust of the piety of his intentions. He inquires,—

"How did the three witnesses see the plates? In a revelation made to them 'previous to their viewing the plates' it was said to them: 'It is by your faith that you shall obtain a view of them, even by that faith which was had by the prophets of old.'—D. C. 15: 1. How much faith would it require to see a piece of gold where it really existed? Not much; but where it did not exist, it might need considerable faith to view it. Doubtless this might have been so with these sacred plates; they believed that what they saw was gold; that an angel brought them; and that the voice of God endorsed the translation, being told all this by Joseph."

The eight witnesses (not the three), claim that the plates "have the appearance of gold;" and claim also to have handled them with their hands, and to have hefted them likewise. Mr. S. questions the propriety of their faith having anything to do with their seeing the plates, and argues substantially, that they only imagined that they saw them. It is not at all strange that most implicit faith (not imaginings) should be required of the three witnesses, who saw the plates in the hands of the angel of God, in an open vision.

"Without faith it is impossible to please God."—Heb. 11:6.

"Go thy way; and as thou hast believed, so be it done unto thee. And his servant was healed from that hour."—Matt. 8:13.

"But the word preached did not profit them, [Israel], not being mixed with faith in them that heard it."—Heb. 4:2.

"For whatsoever is not of faith is sin."—Rom. 14:23.

"Having then gifts differing according to the grace that is given to us, whether prophecy, let us prophesy according to the proportion of faith."—Rom. 12:6.

"Then came the disciples to Jesus apart, and said, Why could not we cast him out? And Jesus said unto them, Because of your unbelief."—Matt. 17:20.

"And he did not many mighty works there [in his own country] because of their unbelief."—Matt. 13:58.

"Jesus said unto him, If thou canst believe, all things are possible to him that believeth."—Mark 9:23.

"If ye will not believe, surely ye shall not be established."—Isa. 7:9.

Time would fail us to cite the innumerable evidences that God works among his people according to their faith. Why should a professor of the religion of the Bible scoff at the idea that these three witnesses must have faith in God in order to be worthy to behold the wonderful vision by the power of God, of these sacred plates? Has he forgotten the scriptures? Or is he so unfair, so partisan, as to allow that *faith* was essential in the service of God in ancient times, but not necessary now!

As to his insinuation that the witnesses merely *imagined* that what they saw was gold, its folly is so self-evident that a reply is scarcely needed. The eleven witnesses,—O. Cowdery, M. Harris, D. Whitmer, Hiram Page, Joseph Smith, sen., Jacob Whitmer, Christian Whitmer, Peter Whitmer, jun., John Whitmer, Hyrum Smith, and Samuel H. Smith,—were men of at least ordinary natural abilities, while many of them had a fair English education, and a moderate acquaintance with the common affairs of business. Now it is highly improbable, if not quite impossible, for an illiterate young man of from twenty-three to twenty-five years of age, as was Joseph Smith, with whom they were most intimately acquainted, and with whom they were frequently associated, to have deceived these eleven witnesses in the manner claimed by Mr. S. The idea is absolutely preposterous, and reflects but little credit upon the sagacity of the one who originated it. Gold, as a medium of exchange, was then in common use, so that persons doing any business at all would have some actual knowledge as to what was gold, and what was not. To think that Joseph Smith could have prepared a large book of plates, "having the appearance of ancient work, and of curious workmanship, which have the appearance of gold," and could have imposed them upon eleven sensible, intelligent men, some of whom were skilled in all the common affairs of life, may do for idiots, for men without brains, but not for those who have an ordinary measure of common sense.

Says Mr. S., "They *believed* that what they saw was gold;" and he thinks "tin plates, dipped in a dye that would give them a golden color to superficial observers, would suffice in the hands of Joseph to get such a certificate," as is given by the eight witnesses. If they could be so easily duped in respect to *color*, how then in respect to the great *number* of the plates, and how in respect to their being "of ancient work, and of curious workmanship?" If there had been but *one* plate, and that without engravings, it would have been next to impossible for the young and inexperienced Joseph to have deceived the eleven witnesses, or even the eight, in respect to its material, and general character. But for him to prepare a large book of plates, and those plates elaborately engraved with characters that had "the appearance of ancient work, and of curious workmanship"—a work requiring great labor and most consummate skill—and then palm them upon eleven rational men as genuine records, records of very remote ages, and *sacred* at that, is quite past belief. The facts are, their testimony is true, and valid for the purposes for which it was given, or else these witnesses are deceivers of the basest class. The eight witnesses say:

"We did handle with our hands * * * as many of the leaves as the said Smith has translated; * * * we have *seen* and hefted, [*i.e.* lifted, for the purpose of judging of their weight], and know of a surety that the said Smith has got the plates of which we have spoken."

Mr. S. affirms.

"The testimony of the eight witnesses disagrees with the three. They do not claim that an angel brought the plates from heaven for them to view, and they deny that they were in the possession of the angel."

It *is* true that "*They* do not claim that an angel brought the plates from heaven for them to view;" but it is *not* true that "they *deny* that they were in the possession of the angel." They simply testify that when they saw them, handled them, and hefted them, that *then Joseph Smith did have the plates.* As to the fact of the angel's having them both before and after, that time, they do not testify, and this was very proper. In regard to the testimony of the three witnesses, in particular, Mr. S. says:

"They believed that what they saw was *gold;* that an angel brought them; and that the voice of God endorsed the translation, being told all this by Joseph."

In the first place *the three* do not testify as to the plates being gold, or as to their believing they were gold, as before seen. In the next place, these are not very judicious comments upon the intelligence and shrewdness of the three witnesses, of whom, Mr. S. knows nothing personally, and but little of their history; and, to our mind, his view of the case is very damaging to his judgment. For Mr. S. to assume that three such intelligent and experienced men as O. Cowdery, D. Whitmer, and M. Harris were, would give to the world a certificate so definite in its details, and so highly important and consequential in its claims, *and all based on the say so of Joseph Smith,* is to exhibit on the part of Mr. S. a sorry want of mental acumen. And for them to testify, "we also know that they [the plates] have been translated by the *gift* and *power* of God, for *his voice* hath declared it *unto us;*" and also testify, "we have seen the engravings which are upon the plates, and they have been shown unto us by the *power of God* and *not of man;*" and further, "we declare with words of soberness, that *an angel* of God came down from heaven, and *he* brought and laid before *our* eyes, that we beheld and *saw the plates,* and the engravings thereon;" and still further, "the *voice of the Lord commanded us* that we should bear record of it;" and for them to do all this upon the mere word or representation of Joseph to them—"being told all this by Joseph," as Mr. S. puts it, is for them to do a most improbable thing.

They testify that "the voice of the Lord" commanded them to bear record of the witness that God gave them concerning the Book of Mormon. They testify that "an angel of God came down from heaven, and HE brought and laid before our eyes, that we beheld and *saw the plates,* and the engravings thereon." They testify that the plates "have been translated by the gift and power of God, for his voice hath declared it unto us." And yet Mr. S. has the hardihood to state that

"These witnesses do not say that they saw the angel come down; they were doubtless told so by Joseph. Nor do they affirm that they *heard* the voice of God; it doubtless came through Joseph's revelation, commanding them to testify. Thus they *saw* no angel, and *heard* no voice; they simply affirmed on the strength of Joseph's word. If they really had *seen* an angel, they would have said so. If they had *heard* a voice from heaven, they would have said so. Nor is it sure that they saw the plates, except by faith *through Joseph*."

This is the extreme of nonsense. It is more—it is basely false, as Mr. S. well knows. If they, *personally*, saw not the plates, and the engravings thereon; and if they saw not "an angel of God" come down from heaven; and if the angel of God did not bring the plates and lay them before their eyes; and if they did not hear the voice of God to themselves; and if the plates were not shown to them "by the power of God and not of man," then they were base and willful impostors, for they unequivocally affirm as much. The disgraceful prevarications imputed to them by Mr. S., have not the slightest foundation in fact; and they would have been heartily spurned by those men of God, and hurled back with scorn upon those who might have suggested them.

O. Cowdery, who became an attorney of pronounced ability, always bore an undeviating testimony of the Book of Mormon till the cold waves of death swept him from the shores of time into the world of spirits. And he, after years of reflection and profound thought upon the matter, never marred his testimony by such quibbles as are presented in the criticisms of Mr. S.

Martin Harris, now passed within the vail, whose years reached more than fourscore and ten, reaffirmed his testimony, time after time, for all these forty-five years, and would have scorned the thought of having it explained after the manner of Mr. S.

David Whitmer, now aged over seventy years, a man who, by his upright life, commands the respect and esteem of all who know him, a man of high intellectual attainments, as noticed in the former part of our article, he, too, unflinchingly and unqualifiedly, maintains his former testimony concerning the Book of Mormon. He would despise the thought of his testimony being based upon such grounds as are assumed by Mr. S., or of explaining away its point and force, as Mr. S. has sought to do.

Joseph, in his History of the Church, gives an account of the manner in which the three witnesses obtained the evidences upon which their special testimony is based. He says:

"Not many days after the above commandment [D. C. 15] was given, we four, viz., Martin Harris, David Whitmer, Oliver Cowdery, and myself, agreed to retire into the woods, and try to obtain, by fervent and humble prayer, the fulfillment of the promise given in the revelation—that they should have a view of the plates, &c. We accordingly made choice of a piece of woods convenient to Mr. Whitmer's house, to which we retired, and having knelt down, we began to pray in much faith to Almighty God to bestow upon us a realization of these promises. According to previous arrangements I commenced by vocal prayer to our heavenly Father, and was followed by each of the rest in succession. We did not, however, obtain any answer or manifestation of the divine favor in our behalf. We again observed the same order of prayer, each calling on and praying fervently to God in rotation, but with the same result as before. Upon this, our second failure, Martin Harris proposed that he should withdraw himself from us, believing, as he expressed himself, that his presence was the cause of our not obtaining what we wished for; he accordingly withdrew from us, and we knelt down again, and had not been many minutes engaged in prayer, when presently we beheld a light above us in the air, of exceeding brightness: and behold, an angel stood before us; in his hands he held the plates which we had been praying for these to have a view of; he turned over the leaves one by one, so that we could see them, and discover the engravings thereon distinctly. He then addressed himself to David Whitmer, and said, 'David, blessed is the Lord and he that keeps his commandments.' When, immediately afterwards, we heard a voice from out of the bright light above us, saying, 'These plates have been revealed by the power of God, and they have been translated by the power of God. The *translation* of them which you have seen *is correct* and I command you to bear record of what you now see and hear.' I now left David and Oliver, and went in pursuit of Martin Harris, whom I found at a considerable distance, fervently engaged in prayer. He soon told me, however, that he had not yet prevailed with the Lord, and earnestly requested me to join him in prayer, that he also might realize the same blessings which we had just received. We accordingly joined in prayer, and ultimately obtained our desires, for, before we had yet finished, the same vision was opened to our view, at least it was again to me, and I once more beheld and heard the same things, whilst at the same moment, Martin Harris cried out, apparently in ecstacy of joy, ''Tis enough; mine eyes have beheld,' and jumping up, he shouted 'Hosannah,' blessing God, and otherwise rejoiced exceedingly.

"Having thus, through the mercy of God, obtained these manifestations, it now remained for these three individuals to fulfill the commandment which they had received, viz., to bear record of these things; in order to accomplish which, they drew up and described [subscribed] the following document."

Here follows the testimony of the three witnesses as found on the first leaves of the Book of Mormon. It will be observed that "they" (the "three witnesses") "drew up and described [subscribed] the following document" (their testimony).

To the question, "Did you go to England to lecture against Mormonism?"—a question propounded by Sr. H. B. Emerson, of New Richmond, O., in 1870, Martin Harris replied: (See *True Latter Day Saints' Herald*, for October 15, 1875):

"I answer emphatically, No, I did not; no man ever heard me in any way deny the Book of Mormon, the administration of the angel that showed me the plates; nor the organization of the Church of Jesus Christ of Latter Day Saints under the administration of Joseph Smith, Jr., the prophet, whom the Lord raised up for that purpose in these latter days, that he might show forth his power and glory. The Lord has shown me these things by his Spirit, by the administration of holy angels, and confirmed the same with signs following, step by step, as the work has progressed, for the space of fifty-three years."

He further said:

¶ "I do say that the angel did show to me the plates containing the Book of Mormon. Further, the translation that I carried to Prof. Anthon was copied from those plates." "I do firmly believe and do know that Joseph Smith was a prophet of God."—*Herald*, vol. 22, p. 630.

Before us is a letter just received, written by Elder Charles Derry who for many years was an active minister in the Church in England; and this letter contains important information as to the attitude of Martin Harris toward the Book of Mormon, when he was lecturing in England against the evils of Brighamism. It reads:

"In the *Herald* of October 15, 1875, I find a communication from Martin Harris, one of the three witnesses to the Book of Mormon, in which he declares that he did not go to England to lecture against Mormonism. That declaration is true; but it may be interesting to know *what he went there for*. Not having a *Millenial Star* by me of that date, I cannot tell exactly the time, but think it was in 1846. My first wife, (then Anna Stokes), told me that she saw him in Birmingham, in the Saints' Meeting House. He had gone there from this land to oppose the pretentions of Brigham Young and the Twelve, who were then laying the foundations for polygamy and the Brighamite rule. A young man of her acquaintance, in the presence of the assembly, presented to him his testimony with his name in connection with the other two witnesses' names, and asked him if that was his name, Martin replied, 'It is.' 'Did you put your name to that testimony?' Martin answered, 'I did; and that Book of Mormon is the Book of God. I know more about that book than any man living.'"

It should be borne in mind that these three witnesses withdrew from active fellowship in the Church as early as 1838; but not for want of faith in the Book of Mormon, or in the prophetic mission of Joseph. Some if not all of them, thought the Church was swerving from the right, and was tending to apostasy. And it is probable that personal grievances and personal interests had much to do with them in shaping their course toward the Church. But amid all their trials and afflictions, and though separated in their associations from the Church, and having many strong inducements to abandon their faith in the Book of Mormon, they nevertheless have steadfastly maintained, with cheerful and earnest zeal, and with a loving hope in God, their marvelous and highly important testimony. If they had remained in full and active fellowship with the Church and in the ministry, it might have been argued that all their interests and surrounding influences were of such a character as to forbid their turning from, or retracting their testimony. But these reasons cannot now be assigned for their steadfastness. There were many causes to prompt them to deny the work, and many surroundings well calculated to draw them away from the faith; but their love of God and his truth, their sincerity of heart, their honesty of purpose, and their exceeding great knowledge by the ministry of angels, by the gifts of the Holy Spirit, by the voice of the Lord, and by the many wonderful dealings of God within their observation and experience, all united to render it morally impossible for them to recant and turn away.

Joseph, Oliver, and Martin—their united testimony lives to-day, though they have passed away to that God who gave them being. They were competent and credible witnesses; and their joint testimony is now in force. And David Whitmer, spared of God for some wise and important end we trust, is still a witness for God, and for his strange and marvelous work. Men of intelligence, men of integrity, fearless and unflinching men, their testimony and their memory will live and be honored, when their defamers and traducers will have gone down into oblivion, or are remembered only with pity and with shame.

CHAPTER V.

Mr. S. nexts claims that Joseph Smith was a false prophet, and the Book of Mormon untrue, because they teach that the spirit or soul of man is a conscious being, a living, active entity, and remains such after the death of man. He says:

"While the Bible represents death as reducing man to a state of unconsciousness till the resurrection, the Book of Mormon affirms 'that there is a space between death and the resurrection of the body, and a state of the soul in happiness or in misery.'—Alma, ch. 18."

Joseph Smith and the Book of Mormon do teach that the soul of man survives the death of man, and that it exists in the intermediate state as an intelligent, active agent, possessing all the faculties and powers peculiar to the intellectual, spiritual part of man in this life. It is an exalted and cheering doctrine; one in harmony with the wisdom and love of God, while its opposite, the soul-killing doctrine, is cheerless, degrading, repulsive, and utterly dishonorable toward God and man.

The sleep, or mortality of the soul or spirit, is utterly repugnant to the natural sense, the common sentiment, and the universal God-given instincts of the race. For proof of this we consult the history, poetry, painting and sculpture of all nations and ages, and they all teach us, that man, everywhere, during all past time, believed the soul was a real substantive being, and possessed of intense consciousness and activity when no longer "in the flesh." The ruins of ancient Babylon, and Nineveh, and Thebes, and Memphis—with their temples, tombs, and monuments—open their stony lips and proclaim to us in their glyphs and sculpturings, how prominent was this sentiment in those times so near the tower of Babel and the flood. And when we examine the antiquities of America, the same kinds of evidence meet us.

All minds, from the gifted and cultured Plato, to the rude savage of the forest, have been thoroughly possessed with this elevating and ennobling thought, a thought so important and effectual in restraining evil, and inciting to that which is good—an incalculable power in lifting up the race into better conditions of life and being. We trace this instinctive sentiment in man as readily as we can trace in the lower orders of creation the instinctive traits peculiar to them. The works of the honey-bee, the spider, the ant, the beaver, the swallow, and a thousand others of the lower orders, teach us that the Creator has for wise and benevolent purposes, endowed these creatures with knowledge, wisdom, and skill suited to their wants and conditions. This instinct is in some sense, prophetic—revealing to the inner consciousness facts and conditions not known by actual experience. Man and the lower orders are alike, to a degree, in this respect.

A wise and loving God would never have implanted in man the belief—instinctively—of a conscious existence after death unless such a belief had a basis of fact in the divine economy and was proper, and unless such a state of existence was real. As soon would he endow the lower orders of creation with instincts, and then not provide them with those things, circumstances, and conditions to which those instincts invariably point or lead. Inasmuch, then, as the race is universally possessed with this sentiment, (except in cases of extreme barbarism, moral degredation, or perverted education), it is conclusive that the sentiment is a true one, and that it is ordained of God.

Our experiences in life are such as to prove that the soul or spirit of man is a living entity, a being distinct from the physical body, superior to the body, and not dependent upon it for its existence. The soul retains its perfect identity, its force and capacity, though the body be wasted with disease, or deprived of many of its members.

"The emaciated, consumptive patient, with only snatches of sleep, toils at his *intellectual* labors, even after reduced to a slender diet of bread and water, and with a vigor of Mind unsurpassed in days of health and refreshing enjoyments. The whole history of the malignant epidemic cholera presents the Mind as sparkling as ever in the midst of the *ruins of organic life*, in which are included *the brain* as well as the almost pulseless heart, and the expiring functions of every other organ, closely representing the disembodied soul."—*The Soul and Instinct*, 115.

The late Speaker of the House of Representatives, Michael Kerr, retained great strength of intellect, and force of spirit, until the immediate hours of death, though he had wasted slowly away in his physical powers to a mere skeleton. Of the late Hon. Wm. G. Brownlow, of Tennessee, it is said, "Latterly he was decrepit to the verge of utter helplessness, but his *mind* and *temper* remained unweakened." And now comes the Hon. A. H. Stephens, who "has been dying for the last twenty years," and who is as thin as a ghost, and, physically, as helpless as a child, who, being wheeled into the United States Court Room in his invalid chair, in which he sits, electrifies and astonishes his hearers with a lengthy, "clear, strong," and eloquent argument, without the aid of manuscript or brief, following all the intricate windings of "the case with a hawk-like alertness that showed his intense intellectual activity." All this shows both the superiority of the soul above the body, and the fact of the soul being a separate entity and independent of the body in its faculties and powers.

"Though our outward man perish, yet the inward man is renewed day by day."—2 Cor. 4:16.

"For when the body oft expiring lies,
Its limbs quite senseless, and half closed its eyes,
The *mind* new force and eloquence acquires,
And with prophetic voice the dying lips inspires."

Man is, in some sense, an animal machine. The soul is that which thinks, perceives, reasons, imagines, wills, hates, loves, rejoices and sorrows, hopes and worships—and all this while residing within, and having intelligent control of the body. The soul sustains a similar relation to the body that the intelligent engineer does to his engine. As the engineer, to control his engine, must be in contact with it, so the soul, to control the body, must dwell within it. As the engine represents the body, so the steam represents the blood, and the intelligent engineer the soul. And as the engineer may live and have active being while his engine is wrecked and destroyed, so the soul of man may live when free from the body—when "dust returns to dust as it was before, and the spirit returns to God who gave it."

Intelligence, and volition, are not the inherent properties of matter, but they are of the soul, and this demonstrates that the soul is above and superior to matter. Mind controls matter, and is capable of self-action and self-determination. The brain, is the *seat* of the mind, but it is not the mind itself, as some would claim. It is simply the *organ* of the mind, *the instrument* through which the mind operates, and manifests itself. The brain, in its mental operations, acts only as it is acted upon by the intelligent soul. The brain is the soul's chief instrument; the body with all its parts rendering subordinate service.

"In his lecture on 'Does Death End All?' in Boston, recently, Joseph Cook used this illustration of the immortality of the soul: 'As, therefore, from the structure of the eye we may infer the existence of a wholly external agent, light; or from that of the ear, the existence of a wholly external agent, sound; so from the absolute inertness of the cerebral structure in itself, we must attribute its activities to an agent as external to it as sound is to the ear or light to the eye. That agent is invisible to the external vision, and intangible to the external touch. It is positively known to consciousness, or the internal vision and touch. That agent is the soul. As the dissolution of the eye does not destroy the light, the external agent which acts upon it, and as the dissolution of the ear does not destroy the pulsation of the air, the external agent which acts upon it, so the dissolution of the brain does not destroy the soul, the external agent which sets it in motion.'"

We demonstrate the existence of the soul by the ideas it originates, and the work it performs. We see its work in music, poetry, painting, language, invention, mechanic arts, and in many other ways. While the body attains perfection in about from twenty to twenty-five years, or earlier, the intelligent soul continues to improve, and enlarge its capabilities and powers, till seventy, eighty, or more years pass away, and this, too, while the body is wasting, and failing in its natural powers.

The human mind, or soul, is evidently constituted after the pattern of the Divine mind, or soul. The Infinite Mind, which designed, originated, and constructed the universe in all its parts, has its counterpart (in its constitutions, though not in greatness and excellence) in the mind of man which designs, originates, and achieves the wonderful works of art seen in the world's history. Inasmuch as the works of the former proclaim His *personal being* as a spirit, so the works of the latter prove that the spirit or soul of man is a personal being. And if the works of God prove the immortality of the Mind of God, why shall not the *intellectual* works of man prove the immortality of the mind of man? Does not the spirit, the intellectual part of man, exist on the *same plan* with that of the "Father of spirits?" Who dare say it does not? That the spirit or soul of man is a real being, a separate entity, a self-acting agent when in the body of flesh or out of it, is, we think, just as reasonable, and demonstrable, as that the "Father of spirits" is a separate entity, a self-acting Being.

Lest some should think us irreverent in comparing the soul of man with the Divine Soul, we will give them our scriptural grounds for doing so:

"Your new moons and your appointed feasts *my soul* hateth."—Isa. 1:14. "Behold mine elect in whom *my soul* delighteth."—Isa. 42:1. "Be thou instructed, O Jerusalem, lest *my soul* depart from thee."—Jer. 6:8.

Thus far of God. Of man God says:

"Love the Lord your God with all your *soul*."—Deut. 11:13. "Come unto me, and hear, and your *soul* shall live."—Isa. 55:3.

As relates to both God and man, the term refers, we see, to the intelligent, conscious nature. The immortality of the soul may be clearly inferred in its *desires* for immortality; its *hopes* of immortality; its instinctive convictions of immortality; its adaptability for immortality; and, finally, in its essential likeness to God.

Who that has traced the development of the intelligent soul from the cradle to the grave, that has seen it battle with the ills and the obstacles of life, until it has won triumphant victories throughout the realms of mind and matter, in every department of life, and finally, in its explorations, planted its conquering standards upon the starry plains of infinitude—who that has seen this can believe in the mortality of the soul, or that it sleeps in unconsciousness at death? Such a belief degrades man, and dishonors God, his Maker.

As such doctrine is irrational, and unphilosophical, so it is unscriptural and utterly contrary to the belief of the chosen people of

God—first the Jews and after them the early Christians. Wherever, in the Old Testament, the spirit, or soul of man is spoken of, it is treated as something distinct and separate from the body of man. A few instances shall suffice:

"And it came to pass, as *her soul* was in *departing*, (for she died) that she called his named Ben-oni."—Gen. 35: 18.

Dr. Clarke renders the Hebrew text of this: "in the *going away* of her soul." In either case the soul did not *die* with the body, nor *sleep* with the body. The conscious activity of the soul is here plainly taught, in its "departing," "going away."

Elijah prayed:—

"O Lord my God, I pray thee, let this child's *soul* come into him again. And the Lord heard the voice of Elijah; and the *soul of the child came into him* again, and he revived."—1 Kings 17: 21, 22.

In this case, the child's soul left, or "departed" away, and at the prayer of the man of God it *returned* and "came into him." The soul is here spoken of as existing for a time, at least, out of the body; and then, the *same* soul, returning "into him." Now, if the soul could exist outside of the body from the time of the child's death till it was restored, why not exist for a longer time? Aye, forever? Again:

"Behold, all souls are mine; as the soul of the father, so also the soul of the son is mine; the soul that sinneth, it shall die."—Ezek. 18: 4.

Here we see the father, and the son—*living men*—are each possessed of a *soul*, and that soul an intelligent, responsible agent—capable of *sinning*, and of becoming dead in sin—"in trespasses and sins."

The inherent nature of a spirit is life, activity, intelligence. The word *spirit* is often used to signify the same as *soul*. This should be noticed briefly, at the least.

"And Moses spake unto the Lord, saying, Let the Lord, the God of the spirits of all flesh, set a man over the congregation."—Num. 27: 15, 16.

Here the dual, or compound nature of man—flesh, and spirit—is clearly seen. The term *spirit*, or its equivalent, in ancient times signified primarily, and generally, a real *substance*, though highly refined or sublimated, and not merely disposition, energy, breath, or ardor. Locke, the author of a treatise *On the Human Understanding*, explains it thus:

"*Spirit* is a substance in which thinking, knowing, doubting and a power of moving, do subsist."

And it is clearly of individual, substantive spirits, that Moses speaks in the foregoing text. And the same may be said of the following.

"But there is *a spirit* in man, and the inspiration of the Almighty giveth them understanding."—Job. 32: 8.

So of this:

"The Spirit itself beareth witness with our spirit, that we are the children of God."—Rom. 8: 16.

While the first "Spirit" is undoubtedly the Holy Ghost, the second—"our spirit"—is as evidently the intelligent part of man—the soul. Again:

"For what man *knoweth* the things of a man, save the *spirit* of man which is in him ?"—1 Cor. 2: 11.

Here "the spirit of man," is his intelligent part. And what is true of these texts is true of hundreds more. We have now learned from the Scriptures what part of man is conscious, and therefore responsible. And we shall pursue our further investigation from this standpoint.

We are now prepared to understand the inspired writer when he describes the death of man:

"Then shall the dust return to the earth as it was; and the spirit shall return unto God who gave it."—Eccl. 12: 7.

So also of the following texts:

"Verily, verily, I say unto you, Except a corn of wheat fall into the ground and *die*, it abideth alone; but if it *die*, it bringeth forth much fruit."—John 12: 24.

As in the death of the seed, the living, active part is separated from the mere body that contained it, and then passes with special activity into other living, intermediate conditions before reaching the same kind of a *body* that it leaves; so also it is with the conscious, spiritual part of man. Death is the separating of the vital, active part from the inert. In this view of the matter the words of the proto-martyr Stephen are full of solemn, cheering significance, and are easily understood.

"And they stoned Stephen, [he] calling upon God, and saying, Lord Jeses, receive my spirit."—Acts 7: 59.

Now Stephen knew *where* Jesus was, that he was at the right hand of God in heaven, and he evidently knew his spirit would survive his death, and be separated from his body, and that by God's grace it would go into the presence of Jesus. Hence he prayed in the manner quoted.

While Jesus told the wicked Jews, "ye shall die in your sins; whither I go, ye can not come," (John 8:21); yet he promised his disciples, "Where I am, there shall also my servant be," (John 12: 26. And to Peter,—

"Whither I go thou canst not follow me *now;* but thou shalt follow me afterward."—John 13:36.

And for all his disciples he prayed,—

"Father, I will that they also, whom thou hast given me, be with me where I am; that they may behold my glory, which thou hast given me."—John 17:24.

This hope of being with Jesus, in the presence of God, at death, is sublime, and very, very comforting. Such it was to Paul the Apostle; and such it was to all the intelligent early Christians. A few passages in Paul's writings may suffice for the present:

"For me to live is [to serve] Christ, and to die is gain. But *if I live in the flesh* this [service of Christ] is the fruit of my labor; yet what I shall choose I wot [know] not. For I am in a strait betwixt two, [desires], having a desire to depart, [from the flesh], and to be with Christ; which is far better. Nevertheless to *abide in the flesh* is more needful for you."—Phil. 1:21-24.

The sense of this passage is so manifest that no lengthy explication is needed. The question with Paul was, as to whether it were better, all things considered, for him to "abide *in* the flesh" for the good of the church, or to die, depart from the flesh, and to be with Christ, which, for him, personally, would be "gain"—and, "far better." This sense of the text harmonizes beautifully with what he afterwards, on the eve of his martyrdom, wrote to Timothy:

"For I am now ready to be offered, and the time of my *departure* is at hand."—2 Tim. 4:6.

So also does it with 2 Cor. 5:6, 8.—

"Therefore we are always confident, knowing that, whilst we are *at home in the body,* we are *absent from the Lord;* * * * We are confident, I say, and willing rather to be *absent from the body,* and to be *present* with the Lord."

No amount of skillful perversion can make these texts sustain the mortality, or the sleep of the soul at death, when that term is applied to the spirit or sentient part of man. A *living* man is often called a soul, but a dead man, never. Hence the term always relates to a *living being.* Peter, too, taught the entity, and consciousness of man's spirit after death. He says:

"Yea, I think it meet, as long as *I am in this tabernacle*, [fleshly body], to stir you up by putting you in remembrance; knowing that shortly I must *put off this my tabernacle*, [body], even as our Lord Jesus Christ hath shewed me."—2 Pet. 1: 13, 14.

The evident sense of this is, that Peter, in his intellectual, spiritual nature—the soul—lived in his fleshly body as in a "tabernacle," or house; and that his intelligent soul would "put off" the fleshly "tabernacle" in death, as Jesus had shewed him. (John 21: 18, 19). To say that he would put it "off" from *his breath*, or from his natural life—the blood—is absurd; and to say that his soul or spirit would remain *in him*, *asleep*, at death, is to flatly contradict the text. When persons put "off" their clothing, they are the same *persons* they were when they had their clothing on. So with Peter, his "tabernacle" was his *mortal clothing;* this he could "put off" from his soul, and did put off at his death.

In another place Peter teaches the entity of the spirits of the dead, and their consciousness, when he says:

"For Christ also hath once suffered for sins, the just for the unjust, that he might bring us to God, being put to death in the flesh, [his flesh], but quickened [resurrected] by the Spirit, [Holy Spirit]: by which [Spirit], also, *he* went and preached unto the *spirits in prison:* which [spirits] sometime were disobedient, when once the long suffering of God waited in the days of Noah, while the Ark was a preparing."—1 Pet. 3: 18, 20.

That these were the spirits of the dead, and that Christ preached to them in their disembodied state, is made clear from what follows:

"Who shall give account to him that is ready to *judge* the *quick* [living] and *dead*. For, for *this cause* [the coming judgment] was the gospel preached *also to them that are dead*, that they might be judged according to [the same as] *men in the flesh*, but live according to God [according to God's laws] *in the spirit*."—Pet. 4: 5, 6.

Prof. Taylor Lewis says:

"We are taught that there was a work of Christ in Hades. He descended into Hades; he makes proclamation 'ekeruxen' in Hades to those who are there 'in ward.'"—*Hailey, Discrepancies of the Bible*, p. 192.

Alford says:

"I understand these words to say that our Lord, in his disembodied state, did go to the place of detention of departed spirits, and did there announce his work of redemption, preach salvation in fact, to the disembodied spirits of those who refused to obey the voice of God when the judgment of the flood was hanging over them."—*Ibid*.

Prof. Hindekoper:

"In the second and third centuries, *every branch and division of the Christian*

Church, so far as their records enable us to judge, believed that Christ preached to the departed."—*Ibid.*

For further information in respect to the spirits of the wicked dead being "in prison," we refer the reader to Isaiah 24: 21–23, Zach. 9: 11, Ezek. 32: 18, 21, 23, 27, 31, 32. In harmony with these texts is the saying of the Psalmist,—"The wicked shall be turned into *hell*, and all the nations that forget God."—9: 17. It will not do to say that hell is simply the grave, as some do; for that would rob the passage of its significance. Being "turned into hell," is threatened as a terrible *punishment*, but decent burial in the grave is, by the righteous, esteemed a blessing. That the souls of the wicked, at death, go to "hell," or the "prison," is clearly taught by the Savior:

"But I will forewarn you whom ye shall fear: Fear him, which, after he hath killed, hath power to cast into hell; yea, I say unto you, fear him."—Luke 12:5.

Again:

"And it came to pass, that the beggar died, and was carried by the angels into Abraham's bosom: [presence, society]: the rich man also died, and was buried; and *in hell* he lifted up his eyes, being in torments, and seeth Abraham *afar off*, and Lazarus in his bosom."—Luke 16: 22, 23.

In this the entity of the spirit, and its active, and intense consciousness after its separation from the body, is made as plain as language can make it. To illustrate, and further confirm the grounds we have taken, we appeal to history. Josephus relates of Moses, that in his last address to his people he said:

"When souls are about to *leave the body*, they speak with the sincerest freedom."—*Ant.* B. 4, ch. 8.

It may be well to here remark that Josephus often quotes, from Moses and the prophets, such passages as we have not in the Bible. In his discourse concerning Hades—the state of the dead—he says that the souls of the just dwell in a peaceful, delightful region, where "the countenance of the fathers, and of the just, which they see, always smiles upon them, while they wait for that rest and eternal new life in heaven which is to succeed this region. This place we call *The Bosom of Abraham.*" This makes it plain that the Jews believed in the conscious condition of the spirit after death; and it enables us to see why Jesus used the term "Abraham's bosom." The people to whom he was speaking were familiar with that term, they knew its meaning, hence it was suitable in describing the condition of righteous Lazarus, with the righteous dead.

The Christians of the first three centuries believed the doctrine we advocate. St. Clement in his first epistle to the Corinthians, says:

"Peter, by unjust envy, underwent, not one or two, but many sufferings; till at last, being martyred, he went to *the place of glory* that was due to him. For the same cause did Paul in like manner receive the reward of his patience. Seven times he was in bonds; he was whipped, was stoned; he preached both in the east and in the west, leaving behind him the glorious report of his faith; and so having taught the whole world righteousness, and for that end traveled even to the utmost bounds of the west, he at last suffered martyrdom, by the command of the governors, and *departed out of the world, and went unto his holy place.*"—*Apostolic Fathers; Wake's Trans.* p. 60.

Comment here is needless. Of the martyrdom of St. Ignatius, who, it is claimed succeeded the Apostle Peter at Antioch, it is said in an epistle from the Church at Smyrna, where he suffered:

"Wherefore, with much readiness and joy, he left Antioch and came to Selucia; from thence he was to sail. And after a great deal of toil, being come to Smyrna, he left the ship with great gladness and hastened to see the holy Polycarp, his fellow-scholar, who was bishop there; for they had both of them been formerly the disciples of St. John. Being brought to him, and communicating to him some spiritual gifts, and glorying in his bonds, he entreated, first of all the whole Church, (for the churches and cities of Asia attended this holy man by their bishops, and priests, and deacons, all hastening to him, if by any means they might receive some part of his spiritual gift), but more particularly Polycarp, to contend with God in his behalf, that being suddenly taken by the beasts *from the world, he might appear before the face of Christ.*"—*Apostolic Fathers*, p. 179.

And now in regard to the martyrdom of Polycarp (the one alluded to, historians assert, in Rev. 2:10), and others with him:

"Wherefore being supported by the grace of Christ, they despised all the torments of the world; by the suffering of an hour redeeming themselves from everlasting punishment. For this cause, even the fire of their cruel and barbarous executioners seemed cold to them; whilst they hoped thereby to escape that fire which is eternal, and shall never be extinguished; and beheld, with the eyes of faith, those good things which are reserved for them that endure to the end; 'which neither ear has heard, nor eye seen, nor have they entered into the heart of man.' But to them they were *now* revealed by the Lord; as *being no longer men, but already become* ANGELS."—p. 193.

Eusebius, in giving an account of the martyrdom of Lucius, represents him as saying to his judge:

"I thank thee, for now I am liberated from wicked masters, and am going to the good Father and King, even God."—*Eusebius' Eccl. Hist.*, ch. 17.

Dionysius, Bishop of Alexandria, in the third century, says of the Christian martyrs:

"But these same martyrs, *who are now sitting with Christ*, and are the sharers in his kingdom," &c, &c.—*Vide* ch. 42.

Space would quite fail us to give all the testimonies of the early fathers which sustain the Bible doctrine of the conscious condition of the spirits of the dead. But we must not dismiss Eusebius until we present his testimony concerning the "soul-sleeping" professors of those early days. He says, chapter 37:

"But about this time, (A. D. 244), also, other men sprung up in Arabia as the propagators of false opinions. They asserted that the human soul, as long as the present state of the world existed, perished at death and *died with the body*, but that it would be raised again with the body at the time of the resurrection."

This is, identically, the theory of Mr. S. and his fellows. Through the means of a large council, headed by Origen, these heretics were prevailed upon to abandon their "false opinions."

We must not omit to quote the testimony of another one from among the "cloud of witnesses" furnished us by the primitive Christians. Tertullian, that learned advocate and unflinching defender of the faith of the early Christians, in his book, *De Anima*, says:

"We had a right, after what was said by St. John, to expect prophecyings; and we not only acknowledge these spiritual gifts, but we are permitted to enjoy the gifts of a prophetess. There is a sister amongst us who possesses the faculty of revelation. She commonly, during our religious services on the Sabbath, falls into a crisis or trance. She has then intercourse with the angels, sees sometimes the Lord himself; sees and hears divine mysteries, and discovers the hearts of some persons; and administers medicine to such as desire it; and when the Scriptures are read, or psalms are being sung, or prayers are being offered up, subjects from thence are ministered to her vision. We were speaking of *the soul* once when our sister was in the spirit—I do not recollect exactly what. After the service she allowed the rest of the people to go away, as she always did on such occasions, and then communicated to us what she had seen in her ecstasy, which was then more closely enquired into and tested. She informed us that she had seen a *soul in a bodily shape;* that it appeared to be a spirit; but not empty and formless and wanting a living constitution; but that its form appeared so substantial that you might touch or hold it. It was tender, [delicate], shining, of the color of the air, but in everything resembling the *human form.*"—*Hist. Supernatural*, vol. 1, p. 443.

Tertullian, and also Ireneus, flourished in the second century; the latter being "a disciple of Polycarp." Their testimony is conclusive that the early Christians believed that man's spirit was actively conscious after death; also that the spirit had real substance, and was in the general *form* of the body of man. When we consider that air, light, electricity, magnetism, etc., are real substances, and yet some of them impalpable, and others imperceptible to the natural sight, we may not doubt that spirits have substantial existence, though they be not apparent always to our natural vision.

Doubtless all the enlightened primitive Christians believed as did Tertullian, Ireneus, Polycarp, Lucius, St. Ignatius, and those of their times, that the soul of man possessed consciousness after departing from the body, and that it was in *the form* of the human body; for we find that the disciples mistook Jesus in the obscurity of night for a spirit:

"And about the fourth watch of the night he cometh unto them, walking upon the sea, and would have passed them. But when they saw him walking upon the sea, they supposed it had been a spirit, [spectre] and cried out."—Mark 6:48, 49.

Again, when Jesus was resurrected from the dead he appeared, unannounced, to his disciples who were assembled in an upper room, that was evidently but very dimly lighted, and—

"They were terrified and affrighted, and supposed that they had seen a spirit. [spectre]."—Luke 24:37.

This took place after they had been under the teaching of Jesus for at least three years and a half; and it cannot be claimed that the disciples were ignorant and superstitious in respect to the *existence* and *form* of spirits, for those were topics about which the Pharisees and Saducees were at direct issue, and were likely often discussed, and about which the disciples could but feel deep interest, as they were so intimately related to their mission—preaching the gospel of salvation to all men. They believed in the fact of spirits, and that they existed in the form of man, otherwise they would not have taken the living Jesus to be a spirit. Jesus now instructs them somewhat in regard to spirits when he said:

"A spirit hath not flesh and bones, as ye see me have."—v. 39.

The fact of spirits existing, and in the human form, is here admitted by Jesus; but they did not possess, he said, a body, or "tabernacle," of *flesh and bones.*

We can not better close this part of our subject than by considering a portion of the Revelation of St. John. When on the Isle of Patmos, he was shown a series of remarkable events touching the interests of the church, and among them the overthrow of "Babylon the Great, the Mother of Harlots and Abominations of the Earth." Prior to her complete destruction, and *before the resurrection of the righteous dead*, the following occurs:

"Rejoice over her, thou heaven, and ye holy apostles and prophets; for God hath avenged you on her. And a mighty angel took up a stone like a great mill-stone, and cast it into the sea, saying, Thus with violence shall that great city Babylon be thrown down, and shall be found no more at all."—Rev. 18: 21, 22.

Here we see that "heaven," and "holy apostles and prophets" were called upon to "rejoice over her;" and in the opening verses of the next chapter we get their response:

"And after these things I heard a *great voice of much people in heaven*, saying, Alleluia: Salvation, and glory and honor, and power, unto the Lord our God: for true and righteous are his judgments; for he hath judged the great whore, which did corrupt the earth with her fornication, and hath avenged the blood of his servants at her hand."—19:1, 2.

Now, from what we have seen in the instinctive sentiment of the race, in the experiences of life, in the teachings of philosophy, in the revelations of the Old Testament and the New, as also in the testimonies of the Jewish historian, the early Christians and martyrs, we are by these evidences, great in amount and unimpeachable in character, fully warranted in concluding that the soul of man, after it leaves the body, is intensely and actively conscious and capable; and that the doctrine of the death of the soul with the body, or the sleep of the soul with the body at death, is a base and contemptible heresy.

Mr. S., to establish his soul-sleeping theory, distorts and perverts the Scriptures in a manner that clearly evinces the badness of his case. We will give a few instances:

"The living know that they must die; but the dead know not any thing."

This, clearly, has no reference to the spirit only, or the soul of man, but to *the man*, composed of body and soul. The man proper being dead—his body gone to the grave, and his spirit to God—being disorganized, could not *know* any thing. We might as well expect life and activity in a grain of wheat that has fallen in the ground and died. The life that was once in such a grain is now separated from it, and passed into other conditions; therefore that particular grain is dead, and lifeless, but the *life* that was once in it is still in existence, and active.

"David [says Mr. S.] affirms of the dying man: 'In that very day his *thoughts* perish.'"

Very good; a man's thoughts may perish in many ways, and yet he retains his power to think. But this quotation should be understood, as relating to a living man who dies; that man as a compound being, body and spirit, no longer thinks, or acts, and for the best of reasons, because death has separated his spirit from his body. But the text does not intimate but that *the soul* of that man may think and act. Again he quotes:

"The dead praise not the Lord, neither any that go down into silence."—Ps. 115:17.

This clearly relates to the dead body, that which goes *down* to the dust, and not to "the *spirit* of man that goeth upward."—Eccl. 3:21. Again:

"In death there is no remembrance of thee."—Ps. 6:5.

If Mr. S. had given the context, it would have explained at once the *meaning* of what he did quote. I will give it:—"In *the grave* who shall give thee thanks." This completes the verse, and the sentence, and enables us to better understand the text. This text relates to the body, and *not* to the soul, evidently. Mr. S. next quotes the words of Job 14:21:

"His [the dead man's] sons come to honor, and he knoweth it not; and they are brought low, and he perceiveth it not of them."

This, like the first texts considered, cannot be made to relate to the *spirit* of man, which goes to God at death, but was doubtless intended to apply to that part of man which goes to the grave. And as for Job, his teachings between the beginning of his afflictions and their close, as also those of the "three miserable comforters," whose words are so often quoted by Mr. S. and his co-religionists, we do not accept them in the discussion of doctrine. Elihu, who was sent of God, to Job, says of Job, (34:35), "Job hath spoken without knowledge and his words are without wisdom," and, "he [Job] multiplieth words without knowledge," (35:16). And the Lord says of Job, "Who is this that darkeneth counsel by words without knowledge," (38:2). Please excuse us, Mr. S., if we take no further notice of the teachings referred to in Job.

Mr. S. next quotes:

"And the sea gave up the dead which were in it; and hell [*hades*—the state of the *dead*] delivered up the dead which were in them; and they were judged every man according to their works."—Rev. 20:13.

But where is "death," Mr. S.? You have left that out; but we do not say you did it intentionally; oh no! but the passage as you quote it is much better suited to your theory, if possible, and looks suspicious. John says, "*death* and *hell* delivered up the dead which were in *them*." Here is a delivery of the dead from *two* places.

Plato, the learned Greek, tells us that *hell—hades—*is "the world of spirits," (*Plato, by Pond*, p. 125). As *Hades* is a Greek word, the profound Plato has no doubt given us its true signification. Wm. Smith in his *Dict. Bible*, says:

"The word *sheol* [Hebrew] is *never* used of the grave proper, or place of burial of the body. It is *always the abode of spirits*, LIKE THE GREEK HADES." —*Note on Hell.*

This being true, when "hell delivers up the dead which were in" it, of course it delivers up its spirits. And this makes it conclusive that "death" here means the grave, or other repositories of the bodies of the dead. This renders the text plain to the comprehension.

This second, and last resurrection, is clearly that of "the unjust;" for this is after the "thousand years," (vs. 3, 5, 7), while that of the righteous takes place at the *beginning* of "the thousand years." (vs. 4, 5). So that the spirits that hell now delivers up, are the spirits of the wicked dead, "and they were judged every man according to *their works*.

Mr. S. asserts that—

"Peter, an eye witness of the scene, did not think that Moses' spirit was there, [on the mount with Christ], but *Moses himself*, else he would not have proposed to build a tabernacle for Moses, for he was not foolish enough to talk of building a tabernacle for a spectre."

The disciples, we have seen, thought the resurrected Jesus was "a spirit," and its not *impossible* for Peter to have mistaken the spirit of Moses for Moses *in the flesh*. Yet we do not believe he was deceived at all, but knew that *the spirit* of Moses was present. Peter had more experience in spiritual things than Mr. S., and held entirely different views in respect to the existence, form, power, and ministrations of spirits. The dead body of Lazarus was called *Lazarus*, and such usage was and is common, and why not the spirit of Moses be recognized as Moses, and called Moses. Surely the intellectual man is more worthy to retain the name than the dead body; yet either may do so.

Now Moses' spirit did, evidently, appear with Elias' (or John the Baptist's) spirit, on the mount, and minister to Jesus. That this "Elias" was John the Baptist is seen by reading the 10th to 13th verses, inclusive, of Matthew 17th chapter. After they had seen the vision,

."His disciples asked him, saying, Why then say the scribes that Elias must first come? And Jesus answered and said unto them, Elias truly shall first come, and restore all things. But I say unto you, That *Elias is come already, and they knew him not, but have done unto him whatsoever they listed,* [had beheaded him]. Likewise shall also *the Son of Man suffer of them.* Then the disciples understood that he spake unto them of *John the Baptist.*"

This forever settles the matter, that the Elias who appeared with Moses on the mount to Christ and his three disciples, was none other than John the Baptist, who had been beheaded but a few months before. It was fitting, upon this august occasion, that the two priesthoods, Melchizedek and Aaronic, should be represented by Moses and John the Baptist. Moses had been dead for near 1500 years, and John the Baptist for but a few months; the resurrection had not yet occurred, therefore it was the *spirits* of these servants of God who now appear and minister. Here were "spirits of just men made perfect."

But Mr. S. says this was "a vision." If he intends by this to say that it was not *real*, but merely a trance, then he clearly perverts the sense of the text. Peter declares of this occurrence:

"We have not followed cunningly devised fables when we made known unto you the power and coming of our Lord Jesus Christ, but were *eye-witnesses* of his majesty. For he received from God the Father honor and glory; when there came such a voice to him from the excellent glory, This is my beloved Son, in whom I am well pleased. And this voice which came from heaven we heard, when we were with him in the holy mount."—2 Peter 1:16-18.

It was a *vision*, it is true; and the first and most obvious meaning of that word is actual, literal sight. In this vision the disciples saw *three persons*:

"And, behold, there *talked* with him *two men,* which were Moses and Elias [John Baptist]; who appeared in glory, and spake of his decease which he should accomplish at Jerusalem."—Luke 9:30, 31.

They saw Jesus literally, for Jesus was there *personally*, but not more so, evidently, than Moses and Elias. Now, if John the Baptist and Moses, in their spirit state, could minister on the mount 1800 years ago, why not other servants of God, in their spirit state, minister to and for Joseph and Oliver in this age? Clearly they could; but like Moses and Elias they could only appear "in glory," which they did do. It is not at all strange that the spirits of the just should, on very extraordinary occasions, appear "in glory" and minister to men in the flesh; especially when we remember that they are members of "the family" of God "in heaven and earth," (Eph. 3:15). Paul teaches that the saints, by virtue of being children of God, (of "the family in heaven and earth"), are brought into fellowship with all that pertains to that "family." For he says:

"Ye are come unto Mount Sion, and unto the city of the living God, the heavenly Jerusalem, and unto an innumerable company of angels, to the general assembly and church of the first-born, which are written in heaven, and to God the Judge of all, *and to the* SPIRITS *of just men made perfect*."—Heb. 12: 22, 23.

John Baptist "was a *just man* and a *holy*," (Mark 6:20). Jesus commanded his saints to be *perfect*, (Matt. 5:48); and the *means* for making *just* men *perfect* is made clear in 2 Tim. 3:17, Eph. 4: 13, Matt. 19:21, Col. 1:27, 28, etc., etc. Just men are made *perfect* by gospel means.

The physical *body* is the mortal part of man; the spirit—soul— is the intellectual life, the active "inner man." The latter never dies, in the sense of ceasing to exist, but the body does. Salvation through Christ, by the resurrection, secures immortality to the *body;* hence Paul says:

"This corruptible [body] must put on incorruption, and this mortal [body] must put on immortality."—1 Cor. 15:53.

Thus making man, the compound being, as a whole immortal. The natural man and the physical body, is in a mortal and corruptible condition; but in the resurrection, the body, the man as a whole, will put on the eternal *condition*, becoming immorcal and incorruptible.

Mr. S. contemns the claim of Joseph where he says (D. C. 110: 18) that he could give "a plainer translation" of Mal. 4:5, 6, than that found in the common version, and Inspired Translation. He says Joseph in this repudiates his own translation. We have to remind Mr. S. again, that Joseph did not profess to translate, revise, or correct every part of the Bible; and this is one among many passages that he did not translate. Might not a translator give "a plainer translation" of a passage—giving it in simpler terms, terms easier of comprehension for inexperienced and uncultured minds, and yet give an equally true translation? We think so; and we think this was substantially what Joseph intended.

CHAPTER VI.

Mr. S. quarrels with Joseph and the Book of Mormon, because the latter says that the Nephites, within *thirty years* after they left Jerusalem, appointed Nephi their king, and also built "a temple like unto Solomon's;" and this, too, when Laman and some others were separated from them. Among the first needs of society is that of government—ruling authority—and what is more natural than that these Israelites, few in number though they were, should seek to establish the form of government peculiar to their nation, and the then existing nations of earth? Nothing could be more reasonable. The fewness of their numbers argues nothing. Many governments, ancient and modern, have been founded with but a few persons. Rome, that great nation which conquered the whole known world, was founded by Romulus, B. C. 753, and the few who were with him in his "small castle on the summit of Mount Palatine."

In respect to the "temple," nothing could be more natural, and likely, than for these zealous religionists to desire, and to build at the earliest practicable moment possible, a suitable house for public worship. And nothing could be more likely than for them to build such a house "after the *manner* of the temple of Solomon." They knew of the temple of Solomon—its grand, historic associations—they remembered it with reverent pride as the place where they had worshipped the God of their fathers, and what is more natural, and likely, than for them to build their first house of worship, though it might be very small, and very rude in comparison, after the *form, pattern*, or "manner," of the venerated temple of Solomon? Onias, and the captive Jews in Egypt, "built [in the city of Heliopolis] a temple and an altar to God, *like indeed to that in Jerusalem*, but smaller and poorer. * * * Onias found other Jews like to himself, together with priests and Levites, that there performed divine service."—*Jos. Antiq.*, B. 13, ch. 3. And they claimed to do this in fulfillment of a prophecy of Isaiah:—

"In that day there shall be an altar to the Lord in the midst of the land of Egypt, and a pillar at the border thereof to the Lord. And it shall be for a sign and for a witness unto the Lord of Hosts in the land of Egypt."—Isa. 19: 19, 20.

These captive Jews, and the Nephites, were doubtless actuated by similar impulses, and prompted by similar motives. But Mr. S. says it was an "enormous temple," a "mighty temple," a temple of "huge dimensions,"—and his statements here are just as false as we have found them in scores of other places. Nothing is said, or intimated as to the *size* of the temple, but only as to the "manner," fashion, or model of its construction. "The *manner* of the construction" of it "was like unto the temple of Solomon; and the workmanship thereof was exceeding fine."—2 Nephi 4 : 3. Again:

"And I did construct it after the *manner* of the temple of Solomon, save it were not built of so many precious things; for they were not to be found upon the land."—*Idem*

Mr. S. avers that there could have been "a working force of only eighteen men and boys to build that mighty temple." Let us see. There were four families that went out in the exodus of Lehi, viz:

Lehi, wife, and four sons—total, ... 6.
Ishmael, wife, and five daughters—total, ... 7.
Ishmael's two sons "and their families,"—probable total 12.
Zoram, Laban's servant, ... 1.
Making in all, ... 26.

Zoram and the four sons of Lehi marry the five daughters of Ishmael, giving us *nine* families in all, seven of whom are young families. Lehi, soon after leaving Jerusalem, has two sons born to him (1 Nephi 5 : 36), and after this some daughters (2 Nephi 4 : 2). It is not improbable that Ishmael had children born to him after leaving Jerusalem, but of this we shall not conjecture further.

The increase of this company would naturally be very rapid; (1) because seven of the families were young, five of them very young; (2) because their plain, rural living, would conduce to fecundity; (3) because the people of those eastern countries and warm climates, married young and reproduced abundantly; and, (4) because the Israelites took pride, and religious care in being fruitful in family increase. Marriage in those warm climates took place at as early even as *ten years* with females, and *fourteen* with males. A fair average would not likely be above *sixteen* with females, and *twenty* with males. It would probably be less, especially with this company of Israelites, as all their surrounding conditions would invite early marriages. Malthus claims that one hundred per cent. is the natural average increase of the race (except in times of war, famine, or pestilence) for every twenty-five years. But that is where communities are made up of all ages from the infant to the aged. The increase of these Nephites should not be judged by such a standard, for their situation in respect to age, and manner of life, favored their rapid and large increase.

The four sons of Lehi would easily number, themselves and their children, in thirty years, exclusive of deaths, 48 persons; the two sons of Ishmael, themselves included, 24 persons; Zoram and family, 12 persons; Lehi's two sons, Joseph and Jacob, and wives, (marrying at eighteen years of age), for twelve and ten years, 15; total, 99. The 70 children of the first sons of Lehi, Ishmael's sons, and Zoram, would give us in 18 years after the exodus 7 new families; in 20 years, 3; in 22, 4; in 24, 3; in 26, 4; in 28, 3; in 30, 4; or 28 families in all in that time; and the children of these families—for the first 7, 35; the 3, 12; the 4, 12; the 3, 9; the 4, 8; the 3, 6. Total, 82. To this add like increase for the probable families of the "sisters" of Nephi, and we have at least twenty more, making the total 102. And to this add the number not counted of the children and heads of the first two, and the first seven families 103, and we have a total of 205 persons in thirty years from Lehi's exodus, less Lehi and Ishmael, who died, leaving 203. Now if one fourth of this number were separated from Nephi and his company it would still leave 150. And if one third of them were children under ten years of age it would leave us 100 persons, or more, ten years of age and upwards. Now for a body of people like this to organize a government, in a simple way, isolated as they were, is perfectly reasonable. And for them, being Israelites, to call their ruler a *king*, would be perfectly natural. And for them to build a house of worship after "the manner" of Solomon's temple, is just what we might expect of them. And as to their wars and contentions with the Lamanites, history here repeats itself, for perhaps the thousandth time. And that this company practiced many of the trades of civilization, their tastes and early experiences would lead, and their necessities *compel* them to do so. There is nothing more natural, and reasonable, than all these things, except to the ignorant or wilfully perverse.

In controverting his next subject, that of the reign of the Jaredite kings (Ether 1:1), Mr. S. makes no less than four false assertions. He states, (1) that there were but "twenty-five successive kings," yet the record shows there were *twenty-nine;* the first king of the twenty-nine, Orihah, beginning his reign after the long and eventful rule of the brother of Jared. This last with the "twenty-nine," makes the number *thirty;* though the brother of Jared was not called a *king.* See Ether 1:1; 4:12; and 5:1. He states, (2) that "this last king [Coriantumr] was still alive under the reign of Mosiah the first, about 400 years after Lehi left Jerusalem;—the first Mosiah, who was *visited by Coriantumr,* about B. C. 200." Nothing is said in the Book of Mormon, or intimated even that Coriantumr *visited* Mosiah, or that Mosiah saw him. What information Mosiah obtained in respect to Coriantumr, he interpreted from "a large stone" tablet, containing hieroglyphics.—Omni 1:9, 10. He states, (3) that there was "a space of 2,000 years occupied by the reign of twenty-six [Jaredite] kings;" yet the record claims it was a space dating from some time after the confusion of languages, to about the time the Nephites and Zarahemlaites came from Palestine to America—B. C. 600—a period of probably *not more* than 1600 years, making an average of 53⅓ years for each of the thirty who bore rule. A slight error, Mr. S., of 400 years! But that is nothing for a man with such an unbounded stomach for crooked things as our critic. And this average, 53 years, was not very long, considering the great age to which people lived between the times of the flood and the time of Christ. The longevity of this people is constantly affirmed in the book of Ether, as also the protracted reign of many of their kings.

It is affirmed on good authority (Dr. Mussey, in *"Health, Its Friends and Its Foes,"*) that the Arabians of these modern times even, by virtue of their abstemious habits, and simple vegetable diet, live to a great age—even to that of two hundred years, in some instances. Goodrich, in his *"Universal Traveller,"* informs us that the Peruvians of the present age are very long lived—attaining, in many instances, one hundred years, and more, and that they retain their teeth, their good sight, and very seldom turn grey. The longevity of the Jaredites, a people living under the most favorable circumstances, could not be other than very great.

The Book of Mormon claims that those who should occupy the land after the Jaredites, would not do so till *after* the Jaredites were destroyed (Ether 4:12); and that only their last king should live to see the people who should succeed them (Ether 6:2), and this was fulfilled when the first Zarahemlaites, as they were called, first came from Palestine to America (Omni 1:7, 9, 10) about B. C. 590 to 600. Mr. S. asserts, in effect, (4) that *Ether,* the last Jaredite prophet, writes his "record" of the reign of the kings on the same plates used by the brother of Jared; and to *clinch* his statement quotes, "He [Ether] made the remainder of this record." Now "this record" was simply the "record" of Ether—"the book of Ether" (Ether 1:1). And "the remainder of this record" was simply the remainder of "the book of Ether" which followed from chapter 6, par. 2.

Because Ether, the last Jaredite prophet, possessed the "record" and "interpreters" of "the brother of Jared," which record contained the marvelous things shown to the brother of Jared in the mount, "which were forbidden to come unto *the children of men* until after he [Christ] was lifted up upon the cross" (Ether 1:11); because of this, Mr. S. pretends that the Book of Mormon is false! He says, "How came Ether by the records several hundred years before the cross?" For the very good reason that he was the last of the Jaredite prophets—a prophet of God—and because he was not "the children of men." The term "children of men" means the world—those who are not "the children of God." A very wide distinction, though our hypercritic *seems* to not see it.

We shall, from this on, pass, without notice, some of the lesser and more contemptible objections and quibbles of Mr. S., lest we weary the reader by introducing them.

Mr. S. finds fault because the book of Malachi, as found both in the common version and in the Inspired Translation agree, while the words of Malachi, as delivered by Jesus to the Nephites, are somewhat different. Joseph did not pretend to either translate or correct the book of Malachi, except, possibly, in a *few words*. The words of Malachi, as found in the Book of Mormon (book of Nephi, ch. 11), do differ from the common version, and this fact proves a former assertion of Mr. S. false, where he says: "The fact is, when preparing the Book of Mormon, our version was freely used, with all its defects."

These differing texts are *prima facie* evidence that Joseph did not copy from the common version; and they furnish a strong argument in favor of the divinity of the Book of Mormon. The superior sense of these differing texts is always found in the Book of Mormon.

Mr. S. next complains that Moroni *saw* the "three Nephites," whereas "Mormon [his father] testified that they were taken away out of the land when he was fifteen years old." "How," says Mr. S., "could Moroni have seen them if they were not in the land?" To this acute, and *profound* question we reply; (1) Moroni could scarcely see them unless they were *in the land;* and (2) Moroni likely saw them when they came back *into the land;* for, in going away, we have no reason to suppose that they were prohibited from returning. We hope this matter will no longer perplex our burdened critic.

Another difficulty in the way of Mr. S. is the gathering up of the Nephites prior to their national destruction. He says they "were gathered from remote regions in the short space of *four years,* * * * men, women, and children, without the aid of railroads, from Minnesota, Maine, California, Florida, and every other locality, from the Atlantic to the Pacific, to the land of Cumorah, in New York, all this, too, within *four years.*" Wonderful, if true! But the record informs us that this Nephi—Lamanite war *began* in about A. D. 320, (book of Nephi 1:11, with book of Mormon 1:1, 2), and continued until *after* A. D. 384, (book of Mormon 3:1, 2); a period of *sixty-four years.* Mormon says:

"And when three hundred and eighty and four years had passed away, we had gathered in *all the remainder* of our people unto the land Cumorah."—3:1.

But for *sixty-four* years the wars had been in progress, the Nephites fleeing many times before the Lamanites, generally, if not always, toward the north and east, till they finally reached Cumorah.

Similar objections are raised by Mr. S. in regard to the Jaredite wars. He *intimates* that they were of but *four years'* duration, whereas, they continued through a long series of years, as any one may learn by reading Ether, chapters 5, 6, and the latter part of ch. 4.

Mr. S. asserts that the Jaredites and Zarahemlaites lived near each other "about 400 years; and once the Jaredite flocks made a stampede into the land of Zarahemla." Yes, Mr. S., into the land that was afterwards "called by the Nephites, Zarahemla" (Ether 4:4) just as you have called their lands Minnesota, California, &c, &c. This account is in *Moroni's abridged record* of the book of Ether. Ether 1:1; 4:1; 6:1, etc. Hence it is Moroni and not Ether, as you insinuate, who says the land afterwards, after the times of the Jaredites, "was called by the Nephites, Zarahemla."

We have shown on p. 32, that the Jaredites, with the exception of their last king, were destroyed before the Zarahemlaites came to America.

Another difficulty is sought to be conjured up as follows:

"And in the days of Coriantor there came many prophets, and prophesied of great and marvelous things, and cried repentance unto the people, and except

they should repent, the Lord God would execute judgment against them to their utter destruction; and *that the Lord God would send forth another people to possess this land*, by his power, after the manner which he brought their fathers."
—Ether 4:9.

Of this prophecy Mr. S. says:

"Here Joseph makes a serious blunder, for the Nephites had been brought over the water about 350 years *previously*."

This is not true. We have already proven on pages 34 and 127 that the Zarahemlaites (and the Nephites came about the time they did) did not come to America till *after* the destruction of all the Jaredites except their last king.

Mr. S. claims that the Book of Mormon conflicts with the Bible when it says, "He did not confound the language of Jared," (Ether 1:1), while the Bible states, "The Lord did there confound the languages of all the earth." It is said in the Bible, too, "*All* countries came into Egypt to Joseph for to buy corn," (Gen. 41:57); "And there went out unto him *all* the land of Judea, and they of Jerusalem, and were baptized of him in the river Jordan, confessing their sins" (Mark 1:5). No sensible person by these latter texts understands that "all," as used in them, means exactly, and absolutely, the *whole*, and *every one*, but, rather, the larger part; or, a large part. The (one) language of all the earth was confused, but that is not to say but that certain favored persons might have retained their original language.

CHAPTER VII.

"Joseph says," continues Mr. S., "'He that kills shall not have forgiveness in this world nor in the world to come.'—Doc. & Cov., p. 142. Yet," says Mr. S., "we are told that Nephi, the hero of the Book of Mormon, 'took Laban by the hair of the head and smote off his head with his own sword.'—1 Nephi 1:35."

Yes, Mr. S., this is all true; and to be consistent you should have quoted Moses, who said, "Thou shalt not kill" (Ex. 20:13), and then told us about Samuel, the great prophet, who "hewed Agag in pieces before the Lord in Gilgal" (1 Sam. 15:33). Laban had records that possibly might have belonged in part, or in whole, to the house of Lehi; at least they were essential for them to have in future time and which they were authorized of God to obtain, (ch. 1:20, 23, 25). The killing of the prisoner Agag, was immeasurably more condemnable than the killing of Laban. Laban had *robbed* Nephi and his brethren, and also sought to kill him (1 Nephi 1:28). There were no such justifying causes recorded in the case of Samuel as in the case of Nephi, for the record shows that Nephi slew Laban by direct commandment of God. And in respect to the quotation from Joseph, "thou shalt not kill," etc., it is a part of a series of commandments given to the church in these latter days.

What might have been justifiable in Nephi's time, and in the times of Samuel, may now be very condemnable. Men were justified under Moses' law in putting away their wives for trivial causes; but under the gospel they are not. The character of an act is, of right, determined by the condition and surroundings of the one who performs it.

Mr. S. avers that a revelation given by Joseph is false, because it says:

"So shall the knowledge of a Savior come unto my people, and to the Nephites, and the Jacobites, and the Josephites, and the Zoramites through the testimony of their fathers."—D. C. 2:6.

Mr. S. says "there are no Nephites now in existence, according to the Book of Mormon." They lost their *national* existence, it is true; but a remnant of them were to be preserved *forever*, (1 Nephi

4:2; 7:1, 2; 2 Nephi 2:1, 2, 3, 4; 7:1, 2; 11:6; 12:9, 12). There were large bodies of the Nephites, Jacobites, Josephites, and Zoramites—all called Nephites—who dissented from the Nephite people, and united with the Lamanites (Alma 21:29; 22:3). And this continued from time to time till the *nation* of the Nephites was blotted out in their last battle (book of Mormon 3:3). Large bodies and small ones, went off by themselves, both by land and sea (Alma 30:3, 4, 5; book of Mormon 3:3, etc., etc.). In these various ways the seed of the Nephites, Jacobites, &c, were to be, and were, preserved; and all this "according to the Book of Mormon."

Mr. S. says the Zion mentioned in a revelation through Joseph in March, 1833, D. C. 87:8, has been "moved out of her place;" and that therefore the revelation is false; for it states that "she shall not be." To this we answer, that the thing intended, was, evidently, the locality, site, or place for the building up the city of Zion The same thing is said in another revelation, D. C. 98:4—

"Zion shall not be moved out of her *place*, notwithstanding her children are scattered, they that remain and are pure in heart shall return and come to their inheritances; they and their children, with songs of everlasting joy; to build up the waste places of Zion."

The meaning in both revelations is obvious,—the *site* or place for building up the city, Zion, should not be changed. Mr. S. quotes:

"And behold there is *none other place appointed* than that which I have appointed, neither shall there be any other place appointed than that which I have appointed for the work of the gathering of my saints, until the day cometh *when there shall be found no more room for them;* and then I have other places which I will appoint unto them, and they shall be called stakes."—*Ibid.*

He avers this is false, because other places for gathering were subsequently appointed. Other places were appointed, but not until it was found that there was "no more room" *for the saints in or about Zion*, or in Jackson county, or, finally, in the *state* of Missouri. For the saints were driven by force, and great violence, first from Independence, the place for Zion, and then from Jackson county, and then, in December, 1838, from the state of Missouri. This was not done by "lewd fellows of the baser sort" alone; but by lawyers, doctors, judges, editors, county officials, the clergy (to their eternal shame), and, finally, by the state authorities, sanctioned by state law!

Bigotry, political ambition, love of plunder, fear of the abolition sentiments of the saints, stimulated and urged on by falsehood through the pulpit and the press—these things, with the wicked conduct, and the heretical and foolish teachings of a few saints were *the causes* in bringing about the condition provided for, viz: "when there is found no more room [in Zion] for *them* [saints], * * * then I have other places which I will appoint unto them, and they shall be called stakes." The saints were commanded to not resist evil; and to "be subject to the powers that be," and to let "let no man break the laws of the land, for he that keepeth the laws of God hath *no need* to break the laws of the land."—D. C. 53:5. Therefore, when driven by mobs, some of whom were organized and officered by men holding civil authority, and by ministers of religion, and finally, when driven by the sanction and order of state authority, certainly there was "no more room" in Zion for the Saints. The evils of Brighamism, and other isms that have sprung off in the apostasy from the original faith and doctrine of the church, are but the legitimate fruit of the *desperation* to which many were forced in the numerous persecutions and drivings of the saints either sanctioned or winked at by the civil authorities—town, county, state, and national—in Missouri, and in Illinois. These authorities, when they in any manner encouraged these persecutions, and when they did not faithfully seek to prevent such things, and to punish, adequately, those connected with them, "they sowed the mind!" and they may blame themselves when they "reap the whirlwind!!" Their treatment of the saints drove thousands of the honest, confiding ones, into the blinding, bitter bondage of priestcraft, and thrust them under the influence, and into the very jaws of "devouring wolves," so that but "few" of that old stock will stand, or remain to receive an inheritance in the original Zion.

In order to make the revelations quoted conflict with the revelation of 1841, in respect to building up Zion in Missouri, Mr. S. quotes but part of a clause of the latter revelation, thereby perverting its sense. The entire clause reads:

It behooveth me to require that work [of building the city and temple in Zion, Missouri,] no more at the hands of *those sons of men.*"—D. C. 107:15.

But this garbler quotes it, "will require that work no more;" leaving out, we see, the concluding and qualifying part of the clause. Such is the pious (?) method of this man who boastfully promises to dig Mormonism up by the roots!

He finds fault because the formula of words used in baptism, as found in the Doctrine and Covenants,—"Having *been commissioned* of Jesus Christ, I baptize you," &c., is different, *in letter*, from that found in the Book of Mormon—book of Nephi 5:8,—"Having *au-*

thority given me of Jesus Christ, I baptize you," &c. The sense of the two passages is identical. The latter form was given eighteen hundred years ago, to the Nephites; while the other is given in this century to the church of the Saints. What a prodigious evidence that Joseph is a false prophet!

Mr. S. says "it is a well authenticated fact that Christ was born several years before the vulgar Christian era began." And he argues therefrom that the commandment is false which says:

"The rise of the Church of Christ in these last days, being one thousand eight hundred and thirty years since the coming of our Lord and Savior Jesus Christ in the flesh."—D. C. 17:1.

If the reckoning of Mr. S. should by any means prove true, still the revelation would not be false; for it would be 1830 years, *and more;* but 1830 years at any rate. It is *not* a well authenticated fact, chronologically, that Christ was born four years before A. D. 1. The time of his birth is still a disputed point. Scaliger says, "to determine the day of Christ's birth belonged to God alone, not man. (Types of Mankind, p. 666). Says Dr. Moshiem:

"The year in which it happened has not hitherto been ascertained, notwithstanding the deep and laborious researches of the learned. There is nothing surprising in this, when we consider that the first Christians labored under the same difficulties, and were divided in their opinions concerning the time of Christ's birth."—*Church Hist*, part 1, ch. 3, 1.

In D. C. 45:3–10, is a revelation as to what Jesus said to his disciples on the Mount of Olives in respect to the calamities coming upon the Jews, the second coming of Christ, the end of the world, etc.; and in the 11th paragraph it is said to Joseph and others, "behold I say unto you, it shall not be given unto you to know any further concerning *this chapter,* (Matt. 24), until the New Testament be translated." Mr. S. thinks this promise has failed. Let any one read the Inspired Translation, and they will find a vast amount of added information concerning the subject matter of that chapter, especiall yin Luke 17th and 21st chapters; also in Mark 13th and Matthew 24th chapters.

Of the revelations given by Hiram Page concerning the order of the Church, the building up of Zion and other matters, Mr. S. enquires:

"Why had not Hiram just as good a right to write from a stone as Joseph had? And if Satan could deceive Hiram through a stone, why could he not deceive Joseph in the same way?"

We reply, (1) that it was utterly contrary to the established order of the Church for any but those who were called of God to that special work, to receive revelations and commandments touching the law and general order of the Church. This may seen by consulting D. C., sec. 19, a revelation given to the Church at the very time the Church was organized. Joseph, alone, was called to that work. The case of Aaron and Miriam, where they usurped the prerogatives of Moses, is right in point. See Num. 12:1-8. They erred greatly in seeking to get into Mosses' place. Hananiah usurped the special calling of Jeremiah—Jer. 1:5-10, with ch. 28. Satan deceived Hananiah, moving him to supplant Jeremiah. There is specific order in the government of God's church, as is seen in the cases cited, and as may be further seen by consulting Gal. 2:12, with acts 15:19, 28, etc., etc. Hiram violated the provided order of the Church; and seeking the office of another, he was in a condition to be deceived by Satan. When persons attempt to officiate in the things of God, when not properly called and set apart to that work, they are serving the wicked one, and are in a condition to be easily deceived. We reply, (2) that Satan could not deceive Joseph in the same way he did Hiram, first, because Joseph had great experience in the spiritual things of God, and had witnessed much of the cunning wiles of Satan during the seven or eight preceding years; and in the next place, the Lord will not call a person to the specific work of receiving revelations and commandments for his church, and then permit him, if he is faithful, to be deceived by Satan so as to receive and give to the church false revelations. God has promised to be with, and protect, and preserve, his ministry, on the grounds, of course, of their faithfulness in *their own calling and office.* A counterfeiter can not impose his spurious notes on the skillful, experienced, and faithful cashier on whose bank the notes are drawn, but he may upon the inexperienced, the unwary, the officious and conceited.

Mr. S. says, "Joseph and Oliver differ in their testimony concerning the statement of the angel at their ordination." That is true; but it consists in omissions. Joseph omits in his statements some things mentioned by Oliver, and Oliver omits some things mentioned by Joseph, yet their testimony is essentially the same. They can not be charged with collusion. Furthermore, they do not differ near so widely as do the evangelists in respect to the teachings of

Jesus, or as does Paul in respect to his own conversion. Acts 22: 6–16; 26:13–18.

He inquires: "And if the priesthood had been lost so long, why was it not restored before?" For the very good reason (1) that the world was not prepared for it before. The religious intolerance, and the priestly despotism that, by the sanction and aid of civil rulers, had so long held the world under their blinding and tyrannical sway, had to be subdued in part, or be removed, ere such a work could be accomplished. Civil and religious liberty must be firmly established before it was practicable, if indeed possible. The Reformers did good work in *preparing the way*, but it remained for "free America," which is pledged to protect and defend the religionist of every creed and belief, to be raised up to an honored and commanding position among the nations before "the dispensation of the fulness of times" could be successfully ushered in. It required peculiar conditions in national and religious matters, under which to begin the sojourn in Egypt, the exodus of Israel, the return from the "seventy years' captivity," and especially the order of the "new covenant," under Jesus and his Apostles. And in the latter days proper conditions must be had in civil and religious affairs ere the priesthood could be restored, and God's "marvellous work and a wonder" be begun. We reply, (2) that it was not restored before, because *it was not so appointed of God.*

Mr. S. next inquires: "Would the world have gone to ruin if Joseph had died in his infancy?" And to this we reply, "would the world have gone to ruin if John the Baptist had died in his infancy? God will judge all men according their light and their works. The Lord, "whilst he is no respecter of persons," does respect the *works* of men, "to give unto every man according to his ways, and according to the fruit of his doings," (Jer. 17:10), whether he has heard the gospel or not. The almsdeeds, the justness, the piety and godly reverence of Cornelius, the heathen man, pleased the Lord, and called forth the angel from the heavens in order that this man and his house might be brought nigh to God, and made partakers of gospel salvation in its fulness and perfection.

The Lord will finally judge all men, and "give every man according as *his work* shall be," (Rev. 22:12), whether John the Baptist, Joseph Smith, or even Mr. S. had died in their infancy.

Mr. S. seeks to make capital out of a revelation to O. Cowdery in April, 1829, relative to his translating. The Lord had said to him in the preceding revelation that if he sincerely desired it, and was very faithful, he should "receive a knowledge concerning the engravings of the old records * * * by the manifestation of my [God's] Spirit; yea, behold I will tell you in your *mind* and in your *heart* by the Holy Ghost, which shall come upon you, and which shall dwell in your heart. Now, behold this is the Spirit of revelation."—D. C. 7:1, 2.

The promise to him was, not that he should have the Urim, but that he should, if he complied with the specified conditions, receive knowledge "of the old records" by "the Spirit of revelation" in his "mind" and in his "heart."

"His word was in my heart as a burning fire shut up in my bones."—Jer. 20:9.

The next revelation informs us that he failed to comply with the said conditions, and therefore failed to translate. Peter failed in his faith and therefore sank. (Matt. 14:30, 31).

Mr. S. thinks that if Joseph did not have the plates immediately before him when he was translating them, (as stated by D. Whitmer to a *Chicago Times* reporter, in August, 1875), he had no need to have dug them up. We do not question but what God might have *revealed* the contents of the plates, through his Spirit, as easily as to reveal any other secret thing; but this *was not done*. Undoubtedly God, in his wise Providence considered it far better that the plates should be obtained, and kept at hand, and *seen* and *handled* by many chosen and reliable witnesses, and then exhibited—*the same plates*—by the angel of God to David Whitmer, Oliver Cowdery, Martin Harris, with Joseph, while the voice of the Lord out of heaven testified to the fact and truthfulness of their translation by Joseph. This course multiplies and strengthens the evidences relating to the truly wonderful matter.

Mr. S. tells us that "there are a *few* Mormons who repudiated the revelations of Joseph, and yet cling to the Book of Mormon, thinking that Joseph was all right when he translated, and apostatized before giving the conflicting revelations." We are not aware of any Saints who *profess* to repudiate *all* Joseph's revelations. There are a *very few* who repudiate his revelations after about 1833, when they claim he fell and lost his gift. And there are a great many who *in practice* repudiate his revelations to the Church, the most prominent and numerous of whom are the Utah Mormons.

We do not believe, with Mr. S., that "he was used alternately by the Lord, and by the Devil,—by the Lord to translate, and at this same time by the Devil to give revelations."

"The story of engraving such a large book as the Book of Mormon on such a small number of plates as Joseph pretended to find, is preposterous," avers Mr. S. He says that the language in which the plates were written is "claimed to be *a little less* than the Hebrew," "the *elaborate* Hebrew." These statements are not true. What the Book of Mormon states is this:

"If our plates had been sufficiently large, we should have written in Hebrew." —Mormon 4:8.

The plates were written in characters called among the Nephites "the reformed Egyptian." *Ibid*. The Egyptian, proper, combines in style the ideographic, and the phonetic; and is very comprehensive. Mr. S. thinks that one page of their language could not make more than three pages of English. He thinks this a very great difference in the languages, and seeks to invalidate Mr. Smith's prophetic mission, and the Book of Mormon on this hypothesis. Now, if he proposes to prove Joseph a false prophet because so large an amount of information is contained in so small a space as would be afforded by the plates, why not be consistent and convict another translator on similar grounds?—"*Mene, Mene, Peres*"—three small words were translated by the prophet Daniel (5:26-28) "God hath numbered thy kingdom and finished it. Thou art weighed in the balances, and art found wanting. Thy kingdom is divided, and given to the Medes and Persians." The first words have thirteen letters, and the latter one hundred and thirty-one. Here is more than ten-fold difference! There may have been even a wider difference than this between the "reformed Egyptian" and the English.

In the book of Omni 1:7, it is said:

"The people of Zarahemla came out from Jerusalem at the time that Zedekiah, King of Judah, was carried away captive into Babylon."

They are mentioned also in Mosiah 11:8, Helaman 2:27, and 3:6. In the two last cited places we are informed that with this people came "Mulek," a son of King Zedekiah, not "a leader" of the colony, as Mr. S. asserts, but simply a member of that colony.— Nephi, reasoning with the people, said,

"Will ye say that the sons of Zedekiah were not slain, all except it were Mulek? Yea, and do ye not behold that the seed of of Zedekiah are with us, and they were driven out of Jerusalem?"

Mr. S. tells us this account can not be true, for the reason, he claims, that *all* the sons of Zedekiah were killed by the King of Babylon. It is true that it is stated, 2 Kings 25 : 7, and Jer. 39 : 6, that "they slew the sons of Zedekiah before his eyes;" yet this does not render it impossible for *one*, or even more of his sons to have been spared. Josephus informs us that he had many wives. He likely had many sons. Pharaoh commanded the Hebrew midwives to slay *all* the sons born to the Israelites, yet in the providence of God Moses was secretly saved. An Egyptian historian, recording that slaughter, and not knowing of the escape of Moses, would, unquestionably, have stated that *all* the doomed innocents were slain. Jewish historians are distinguished for their florid, poetic, and exaggerative style—a style lacking the nice precision, and fulness of detail, that distinguishes the historian of Greece, and Rome, and the enlightened nations of these later centuries. For instance, Josephus tells us that "when Cestius had marched from Antipatris to Lydda, he found the city empty of its men, for *the whole multitude were gone* up to Jerusalem to keep the feast of tabernacles; yet did he *destroy fifty of those that showed themselves*, and burnt the city."—*Wars*, B. 2:19. "The *whole multitude were gone*," "*yet did he destroy fifty of those that showed themselves*. Paul, in Colossians 1 : 23, says the gospel "was preached to *every creature which is under heaven*." Yet this could have been strictly true of only a part. Daniel prophecies that the third kingdom in the succession from Babylon, the Macedonian, "shall bear rule over *all* the earth" (Dan. 2 : 39), yet there were large portions of Europe, Asia, and Africa, to say nothing of America, over which the Macedonian kingdom did not bear rule. Mr. Newton, in his works, p. 192, makes these judicious remarks, which we submit for the information of Mr. S. and his admirers:

"General prophecies, like general rules, are not to be understood so *strictly* and *absolutely*, as if they could not possibly admit of any kind of limitation or exception whatever. * * * The prophets exhibit a general view of things, without entering into the particular *exceptions*. It was predicted that 'Canaan should be a servant of servants unto his brethren,' and *generally* his posterity were subjected to the descendants of his brethren; but yet they were not always so; upon some occasions they were superior."

And this rule applies with greater force to history, as our quotations prove. These thoughts are presented, and these quotations made, that we may be guarded against putting too great exactitude and *precision*, upon passages where the writer thereof did not intend it. That the King of Babylon killed the sons of Zedekiah before his eyes, we do not doubt; yet to believe the Bible we *must* believe that at least *one* (Mulek) was saved from that fate. We turn to the "more sure word of prophecy," and by that we learn that the Lord, very shortly before Zedekiah and his family were taken captive, made promise through his prophet Ezekiel, in respect to the seed of Zedekiah:

"Thus saith the Lord God; I will also take *of* the highest branch of the high cedar, and will set *it;* I will crop off from the top of his *young twigs a tender one,* and will plant *it* upon a high mountain and eminent: In the mountain of the height of Israel will I plant *it*."—Ezek. 17:22, 23.

"The *highest branch* of the *high cedar*" clearly relates to the *then* reigning king of Judah, which was Zedekiah (as "the highest branch of the cedar," of verse 3, related to king Jehoiachin). And "his young twigs," as clearly relates to the king's seed. And, "a tender one" "*from the top* of his young twigs," can only mean the *most eminent one* of his seed. And when the Lord says, "*I will* also take *of* the highest branch of the high cedar, and *will set it; I will* crop off from the top of his young twigs a *tender one,* and will *plant it,*" etc., etc., it can only mean that the Lord, in some *special* and *extraordinary way,* will take "a tender one" of King Zedekiah's seed, and will establish it, and nurture it, in a superior place—"a high mountain and eminent"—in some land that belongs to Israel (not Judah). This prophecy must have its fulfillment; but it could not if the claim of Mr. S., that *all* Zedekiah's sons were slain, was true. The Book of Mormon affords to this an easy and rational solution; otherwise it would be an insuperable difficulty. It must be fulfilled in *a manner* like that claimed by the Book of Mormon; and America being *the land of Israel,* as claimed by the Book of Mormon, and as is shown by prophetic blessings (Gen. 49: 22–26; 48:15–21; Deut. 33:13–17), it was fitting to describe this choice land as being "a high mountain and eminent * * * the mountain of the *height* of Israel." Mr. S. says that Joseph got himself "in a trap," when stating that one of Zedekiah's sons came to America. If Joseph had "copied from the common version, with all its defects," as averred so often by Mr. S., he certainly would not have said that one of Zedekiah's sons came to America. Neither would Mr. Spaulding have said so, had he written the book. The book he claimed to translate does make such claim, and Ezekiel's prophecy sustains it; thus confirming the truth of the book, the divinity of Joseph's mission, and catching Mr. S. in the trap he laid for others.

Mr. S. is horrified at the idea that God should prepare a "compass," or "directors," to guide Lehi and his family, yet he professes to believe that God provided a beautiful *star* to guide the wise men to him that was "born King of the Jews" (Matt. 2:1, 2, 9, 10). He says "the story about the interpreters, or stone spectacles, is too marvelous for credence;" yet he can *easily* believe that Joseph had a silver cup through which he obtained revelations (Gen. 44:5), and that the Urim was a means of revelation also (Num. 27:21; 1 Sam. 28:2). He says "the story of Ether's stone candles overtaxes marvelousness;" yet he readily believes that the "pillar of cloud by day, and the pillar of *fire* by night" attended Israel in their exodus; and that "cloven tongues like that of *fire*" sat upon the disciples (Acts 2:3); and that unconverted Saul "saw in the way a light from heaven, above the brightness of the sun," shining about himself and those that journeyed with him (Acts 26:13). He shudders at the thought that Nephi and Lehi, missionaries whose lives were endangered by enemies, "were encircled about with a pillar of fire" (Helaman 2:18); yet he can take in at one gulp the three Hebrew children and the fiery furnace (Dan. 3:19–27); and with credulous gaze can see Elijah go up into heaven "by a whirlwind," attended by "a chariot of fire, and horses of fire" (2 Kings 2:11).

Bible miracles he rather likes, but those from any other direction he cannot and will not believe, because they are not *fashionable*, probably; and because they have not the sanction of his modern creed of unbelief in the word of God. Such clear sighted people as our critic can see that miracles are easy to be believed if they are only the ones done two thousand years ago and ten thousand miles away, and related in their Bible; but any thing outside of that should be belittled, belied, and branded as an imposture. We are forcibly reminded of the ancient Pagans; they could easily believe all the miracles imputed to *their* deities, but the miracles of the early Christians were *spurious!* The Jews could believe in the miracles wrought among their forefathers, but the miracles of Jesus and his disciples were either impositions, or were done by Belzebub. Mr. S. would not for the world question but what Elisha made the axe-head to swim (2 Kings 6:6); and that Jesus wrought a miracle in order to pay poll-tax for himself and Peter; but no miracles must be wrought in bringing out to America a righteous colony, nor in sustaining them when here! The sun standing still at the behest of Joshua is all right with Mr. S., but Israelites on this continent must make no claim to miracles.

"Hush, hush, my son," said the pious old lady to her idolized sailor-boy, as he related to her that among the wonders there were flying-fish in the sea, "don't impose on your old mother, and try to fool her with any of your big sailor yarns;" but when he told her, in solemn tones, that their vessel's anchor dragged up one of the veritable chariot wheels of old Pharoh, lost in the Red Sea, she exclaimed with reverential awe, "La's a me! and did you bring the precious relic home?" Some people will spurn any truth, if it conflicts with their creeds and traditions.

Orson Pratt describes the body of the plates from which the Book of Mormon was translated as being about eight inches long, seven inches wide, and six inches thick; which would contain 336 cubic inches. Mr. S. thinks gold plates to this amount would weigh "near 200 pounds." Here, as usual, he goes wide of the truth. A body of *solid* gold of such dimensions and of such quality as needed would not weigh near so much; and a body of finely and elaborately engraved plates of such dimension would weigh far less; probably much less than 100 pounds.

Mr. S. now has another fearful *spell* about the "interpreters." He seems as rabid at the thought of them as a mad dog at the sight of pure, cool water. For information we refer him to pages 28–34 and 71, 84, where we have already disposed of that matter.

He thinks the story of the utter extermination of the Jaredite nation on this continent is too marvelous for credence; and so of the Nephites. He admits that an intelligent class of people dwelt on this continent at one time, but claims that it was "prior to the great deluge!" He says further: "The many traces of an early settlement date back to that dispensation!" Humboldt, Josiah Priest, Stephens, Baldwin, Delafield, and many others who have studied the antiquities of America never dreamed of the sweeping method of this genius from Broadhead! What a pity they had not met and consulted this prodigy of invention! and that, too, before they had spent so much time and money in elaborating their theories. The idea that Mr. S., who never *saw* any of these antiquities, and whose ignorance on these matters, he now so plainly exhibits, the idea, I say, that he should oppose his opinions to those of the most renowned antiquarians and scientists of the age, makes him slightly ridiculous. Mr. Delafield has furnished the world with an Aztec

Map which outlines the route of those who came and settled in Mexico and Central America, and this puts the settling of America this side the Deluge. The Mexicans, and Peruvians, with many of the Indian tribes, and many of the islanders of the Pacific, have a well defined tradition of the Flood, but these all locate the flood *before* the building up of these great cities and roadways that so abound in America. Mr. Delafield assures us that the style of architecture seen in these ancient ruins is clearly Egyptian. He also assures us that there are striking analogies between the ancient languages of America, and those of Asia—the Egyptian and Hindoo, especially. And further, that there are strong analogies in the religious notions of the ancient Americans, and the Asiatics, as seen in their traditions, their sculpturing, their religious symbols, etc. He likewise tells us that their style of hieroglyphics bears a striking resemblance to the Egyptian. How exactly this accords with the claims of the Book of Mormon, where it says, in no less than three different places, that the Nephites wrote in Egyptian, the reformed Egyptian.—1 Nephi 1:1; Mosiah 1:1; book of Mormon 4:8. Delafield further remarks, that Mexican astronomy, with its divisions of time based thereon, are, in many leading respects identical with that of Egypt. At this, Latter Day Saints are not surprised, for they know by the Book of Mormon that two colonies of intelligent Israelites, who could not be otherwise than well acquainted with the then prevailing system of astronomy of Egypt, came to this land 600 years B. C. and grew into mighty nations. Mr. Delafield claims that in all the analogies discovered, as also in tradition that they have "positive evidence of an early identity between the aboriginal race of America and the southern Asiatic and Egyptian family."—*Antiquities of America*, p. 51.

The Book of Mormon asserts that America was settled by *two distinct peoples, at two very remote periods of time;* the Jaredites commencing their settlement some 2150 or 2200 years before Christ, and continuing over a period of from 1500 or 1600 years to the exodus of Lehi, and Mulek and his company, B. C. 600, when the Nephites and Zarahemlaites succeeded them and continued for 1000 years, and were themselves succeeded by the Lamanite nation. It represents the Jaredites, and the Nephites, as being highly skilled in the arts and sciences of civilized life. Now, Baldwin, in his "*Ancient America,*" pp. 155, 156, 264, 271, etc., confirms this view. He says "these old constructions [ruins] belong to different periods in the past, and represent somewhat different phases of civilization." So say other authors.

This theory of Mr. S., like many other of his positions, lacks the essential elements of truth, and common sense; and when these bubbles are pricked they collapse, and leave a blot on the record of him that created them.

Mr. S. thinks that Amos, the son of Amos, could not have kept the records for so long a time as is claimed; neither Ammaron, his brother. Holy men of old lived to great ages. Abraham begat a son when he was one hundred years old. Moses, when he died, aged one hundred and twenty years, was in the full vigor of life. Ezra, and Daniel, and many others of God's worthies lived to be very old, and their habits of business followed them to their latest years. Mr. S. labors hard to make the record claim that Amos and Ammaron were aged respectively 150 and 160 years. This method of perversion is a favorite trick with him. Amos 2d might have been less than 130 years old at his death, and Ammaron no older as will appear on examining the record.

Golour M'Crain, of the Isle of Jura, who died in the reign of Charles I., of England, was over 180 years old. Thomas Parr died in A. D. 1635, aged 153 years; and James Bowles, of Killingworth, in 1656, aged 152 years; and Lady Eccleston, Ireland, in 1691, aged 143 years. In A. D. 1588, Jane Britten died, in Somerset, England, aged 200 years; and J. Forathe, Glamorganshire, A. D. 1621, aged 180 years. Joseph Crele, of Caledonia, Wisconsin, died in 1866, aged 140 years.—*Haydn, Dict. Dates.* These are a few from the very many cases of longevity since the times of Christ. So the great ages of Amos and Ammaron are not highly improbable, as Mr. S. pretends.

Of the *brass plates* brought out from Jerusalem, (1 Nephi 1:46, 47, 48; Alma 17:5), Mr. S. says:

"If these unfound brass plates are yet to be seen by all nations," etc.

There is no promise that they were to be "seen" by all nations; but only that their contents, in part, or in whole, were to go to all nations. And that is being fulfilled, in part, by the circulation of the Book of Mormon; for it is made up, in a measure, of facts contained on those plates.

Mr. S. thinks it contrary to the belief and teachings of the saints that Alma (Mosiah 11:22) should be born of the Spirit (or have his sins pardoned, as he puts it) before baptism by water. Nothing more strange, Mr. S., than the case of Cornelius, as treated on p. 51. God may pardon peoples' sins before baptism, and give them the Spirit in great power, also; yet it is out of the ordinary course. The Lord increased the widow's oil and meal (1 Kings 17:14), but that is not the common way for him to supply the wants of the needy.

He cavils about the commandment concerning candidates for baptism, where it says:

"All those who humble themselves before God and desire to be baptized and truly manifest by their works *that they have received* [of] the Spirit of Christ unto the remission of their sins, shall be received by baptism into his Church."—D. C. 17:7.

Mr. S. leaves out the word *of*, inclosed in brackets, when quoting; and then says:

"Here the reception of the Spirit and remission of sins is made a prerequisite to baptism."

Not quite so fast, Mr. S.; a man may receive *of* a cup of wine, and still not receive the cup. Receiving "of the Spirit of Christ *unto* the remission of sins," means, simply, receiving that which leads, or moves toward that condition. The words *to* and *unto* are synonymous. A man may start *to* New York, and yet never get there.

Mr. S. says:

"The Mormon doctrine of baptism by proxy—baptizing the living for the dead—establishes the doctrine of salvation *without repentance* on the part of the sinner."

This is not true, and Mr. S. *knows* it is not the doctrine of the Saints. The doctrine and belief of some of the Saints is that, as the spirit of man, after death, is active and capable, and that, as the judgment of the wicked dead does not take place till after their resurrection, there is in this fact strong presumptive evidence in favor of the idea that the spirits of the wicked dead are, in the intermediate state, placed under reformatory influences. The statement in Isaiah 24:21, 22, that the "prisoners" shall "be visited," "after many days;" and the statements (1 Peter 3:18–20; 4:5, 6) that disobedient spirits shall be preached to in the prison, treated on p. 114; with other texts, among them Jonah (2:1–4) give ample grounds for believing that sinners, except those of the highest degree, may hear the gospel in the world of spirits, and *repent*. And it is for this class that baptism is to be administered by proxy. And, as for *baptism for the dead*, why did Paul speak of it as though practiced in the Church, if it was not so practiced?—

"Else what shall they do which are baptized for the dead, if the dead rise not at all."—1 Cor. 15:29.

Now it will not do to say that "the dead" here spoken of is the dead Christ, as some do; for here "the dead" is from the Greek, *nekron* and is a *plural* noun. Besides, it is historically true that such a practice was had in the days of the first Christians. And yet this is not a fundamental doctrine—a formally authorized doctrine—of the Church of the Saints.

ENDLESS PUNISHMENT.

Mr. S. strives to make a conflict in the teachings of our standard works in respect to *endless punishment*. He argues that when a person suffers "endless punishment," "eternal punishment," "everlasting punishment," "eternal torment," etc., he necessarily suffers that punishment—torment—*eternally*, in the most absolute and extended sense of that term. Now the Book of Mormon, like the Bible, uses the words *eternal, forever, everlasting, endless*, etc., to signify lengthy periods, but not always absolute, unending duration. And this is especially true when describing punishment. See 2 Nephi 1:4; Mosiah 11:22; Alma 17:2; book of Mormon 4:6, etc. Exodus 12:14, 17, 24; Lev. 25:46; Num. 18:8; 1 Sam. 3:13; Isa. 34:10; Amos 1:11; Jonah 2:6; Gen 17:8; 48:4; 49:26; Lev. 16:34; Hab. 3:6; 1 Tim. 1:14. The "everlasting punishment" mentioned in Matt. 25:46, it is held by the most eminent scholars of the primitive church, and also of the present times, to mean punishment during a period, the *age* to which it relates. They inform us that *olam*, Hebrew, is the same in sense and meaning as *aionias*, Greek, and that both ordinarily signify *age* or *life;* and sometimes an indefinite period. Now the sentiments advocated in D. C. 18:1, 2, about which Mr. S. makes such an ado, are similar to those just noticed. "Endless punishment," is treated of in the revelation cited as *a condition* into which persons may be placed, and from which they may be delivered. This is the sum of the matter. The meaning of a word, and the signification of a sentence, can only be determined by what is directly connected with it. Of this Mr. S. seems quite oblivious.

THREE HEAVENS.

He says Mahomet had seven heavens while Joseph teaches three kingdoms in the future world. Well, Paul (2 Cor. 12:2) tells of "the third heaven;" and inasmuch as there is "the third heaven," there must be the first, and the second. He also tells us, in describing the resurrection of the dead (1 Cor. 15:41, 42), that

"There is one glory of the sun, another glory of the moon, and another glory of the stars: for one star differeth from another star in glory. So also is the resurrection of the dead."

Joseph and Paul agree, only Joseph calls those conditions *kingdoms*, while Paul calls them *glories*. The *departments*, or conditions, are the same, yet described under different forms of speech. God has promised to judge all men according to their works (Rev. 22:12; Rom. 2:6; 14:12; Rev. 20:12, 13; Matt. 16:27, etc., etc.), and has promised that the faithful Saints shall be *with Christ* (John 17:24; 14:3; 1 Thess. 4:16, 17) and that they shall be *like Christ* (1 John 3:3; 1 Cor. 15:49; Phil. 3:21; Col. 3:4; Rom. 8:16, 17); they, then, possessing the same glory, or heavenly condition with Christ, who will occupy the two lesser glories? Evidently those whose "works" under the equitable and gracious judgment of God, render them meet for them.

Joseph the seer teaches that men's *rewards* or future condition, will vary as their "works" shall vary; and that, too, even among sinners. John teaches (Rev. 22:14, 15) that while "they that do his [Christ's] commandments" "have right to the tree of life, and may enter in through the gates into the city," yet that "without [*i. e.*, on the outside of the city] are dogs, and sorcerers, and whoremongers, and murderers, and idolators, and whosoever loveth and maketh a lie." We should be glad that after suitable, though terrible punishment, there is something better than eternal sleep, or annihilation, for even them who love and make lies! In these teachings Joseph and John are identical. Jesus says:

"All manner of sin and blasphemy shall be forgiven unto men: [on their repentance, evidently]: but the blasphemy against the Holy Ghost shall not be forgiven unto men. And whosoever speaketh a word against the Son of Man, it shall be forgiven him; but whosoever speaketh against the Holy Ghost, it shall not be forgiven him, neither in *this* world, neither *in the world to come*."—Matt. 12:31, 32.

The plain inference from this passage is, that "in the world to come," all sins except the one may be forgiven. Here, then, are three testimonies agreeing, essentially, in the same ideas. The doctrine held by Mr. S. and others, that all who do not profess christian faith in this present life are doomed to an absolutely endless *sleep*, or endless torture, is as horrid and hateful, as it is irrational and unscriptural. Those who can see nothing better, should not boast of their insight.

CHAPTER VIII.

BOOK OF MORMON.

Mr. S. quarrels with the idea that Psalm 85:11, is applied in proof of the coming forth of the Book of Mormon. He says "the Book of Mormon did not 'spring' out of the earth, but was simply *dug* out." How profound! Webster says *spring* means "to proceed," "to issue," "to issue into sight or notice." And this is precisely true of the coming forth of the Book of Mormon. He also quarrels with the application made of Isaiah 29th chapter in proof of the Book of Mormon. He says the passage: "And the vision of all is become unto you as the words of a book that is sealed, which men deliver to one that is learned, saying, Read this, I pray thee," was not fulfilled in connection with the Book of Mormon, because only Martin Harris delivered them to the learned man. But Mr. S. should bear in mind that Joseph was a party to this delivering "the words of a book that is sealed" to Mr. Anthon, just as much as Solomon was a leading party in building the temple, though doing none of the mechanical work. "Men" did deliver "the words of a book that is sealed" to the "learned;" for Joseph *sent* Martin for this very purpose.

He says Jesus applied verse 13 "to the Jews in his day." Yes, but he did not claim it had its final fulfillment there and then. The 13th verse fitted their case and condition, but only in part. Peter accommodates Joel 2:28–32, to the day of Pentecost, yet it was not finally fulfilled on that occasion. This practice was frequent with the Apostles. "Out of Egypt have I called my son," (Matt. 2:15), was applied to the bringing of Christ out of Egypt; but primarily it related to the calling of *Israel* out of Egypt (Hosea 11:1). This is one specimen out of many that might be cited. Newton remarks, in his work on the fulfillment of prophecy, that "many prophecies of Scripture have a double meaning, literal and mystical, *respect two events*, and have a *two-fold completion.*"—P. 71.

Mr. S. says "the 'vision of all,' verse 11, had then (in the days of Christ) become to the Jews like a sealed book, that could not be read by the learned, or the unlearned—instead of one that could be read by the *unlearned* Joseph." But Mr. S. should remember, what is fatal to his logic, viz., that "the words of the book" would be read; for in verse 18 it is said:

"And in that day shall the deaf *hear the words of the book*, and the eyes of the blind shall see out of obscurity, and out of darkness."

So, we see, "the words of a book that is sealed" would be uttered, and heard—hence "read." And when Isaiah predicts that the "learned" could not read "the words" of the book that was sealed, it was equivalent to predicting that its *language* was such as he could not read. For it was not "the book," that he was requested to read, but "the words of" a sealed book. Isaiah predicts that "the words" of the sealed book should be delivered by "men" to the "learned" and this was done by Joseph and Martin, to Mr. Charles Anthon, Professor of languages in Columbia College, N. Y. So precise is the prophecy, and so exact its fulfillment.

That Isaiah 29th chapter, 4th to 24th verses, did not have their fulfillment in the days of Christ, nor near to that time, but that they were to be fulfilled in these latter days; is made conclusive from the following facts: Firstly, In the the days of Christ there was no "book," neither "the words of a book that is sealed," that was given to the "learned" or the "not learned." The Jewish people had possessed "Moses and the prophets" many centuries before the coming of Christ, the New Testament was not compiled and pronounced canonical till the third Council of Carthage, A. D. 397, and the first book of that compilation (Matthew) was not written till between A. D. 50 and A. D. 60. These books, then, or any part of them, can not be "the book" or "the words of a book that is sealed;" therefore this prophecy did not have its fulfillment in the times of Christ; and, consequently, the immediate context could not have been fulfilled then.

Secondly, It is said in the 17th verse:

"Is it not yet a very little while and Lebanon shall be turned into a fruitful field, and the fruitful field shall be esteemed as a forest?"

Here a highly important truth is declared in an interrogatory form,—"Is it not yet a little while?" meaning, simply, that it would be *but a little while* after the events mentioned in the preceeding verses had transpired, until "Lebanon shall be turned into a fruitful field, and the fruitful field shall be esteemed as a forest." That this term, Lebanon, means the same as in Jer. 22:23, Ezek. 17:3, 2 Chron. 25:18, Zech. 11:1, etc., viz., the land of Judea, is, we think, quite plain. It certainly relates to a *land*, that, prior to the change promised, had been barren and desolate. For it is to be "turned into a fruitful field;" and yet it shall, after this change, for a time at least, be "esteemed as a forest"—an uncultivated and unimproved tract of land. Now the land of Judea, soon after the time of Christ, became desolate and barren, as predicted by the servants of God, Lev. 26:33-43; Deut. 28:24; 29:22, 23; Ezek. 36:3-6, 33, 34; Dan. 10:27, etc., etc., but soon after the coming forth of the "book that is sealed," it is to be restored from its barren and unfruitful condition, a change, the very opposite of that which took place soon after the time of Christ. It is a fact, of which all may inform themselves, that in this nineteenth century, and since A. D. 1827—the time the Book of Mormon was revealed—the land of Judea—Lebanon—has been turned into a state of great fertility and fruitfulness. Its "former and latter rain" have been restored, the latter, for the first time with regularity for many centuries, in the fall of 1852. As a result, this land so long barren and desolate, is bringing forth in its ancient strength and fertility wherever the hand of enterprise and tilth is applied. Here, then, are incontestible proofs that the prophecy indicated did not have its fulfillment in the time of Christ, but that in these days it is having a most wonderful, literal, and glorious accomplishment.

Thirdly, In the twenty-second verse it is predicted:

"Therefore thus saith the Lord, who redeemed Abraham, concerning the house of Jacob: Jacob shall not *now* be ashamed, neither shall his face *now* wax pale."

From this we learn, that at the time Lebanon is turned into a fruitful field—after the coming forth of the "book that is sealed"—the "house of Jacob," including the Jews, of course, would be found in a highly favored condition—"Jacob shall not *now* be ashamed, neither shall his face *now* wax pale." For seventeen centuries and more, *shame*, and *fear* have been the portion of the Jews in their captivity and tribulations amid the nations, and this, too, in fulfillment of prophecy—Lev. 26 : 36–38; Deut. 28 : 65–67; Zeph. 3 : 19, etc., etc.; and *now*, within the last one hundred years, and more particularly within the last fifty years, and more especially within the last thirty years, the Jewish race has become eminent in the nations where they dwell, and are highly favored, and are made partakers of honor and fame in well nigh every department of civilized life. Immediately after the time of Christ they were brought to shame, and their faces "waxed pale," through fear, famine, and despair; but now their shame and fear are removed, and their faces no longer "wax pale;" therefore, these are the days for the accomplishment of the prophecy under consideration, and these are the times for the coming forth of the "book that is sealed." The Almighty has fixed these periods, and marked them in such a manner that the sophistry of "blind guides," nor the "cunning craftiness" of the worldly wise and prudent can disguise their exact location in the world's history, their importance and signification. The nineteenth century being thus definitely marked of God, in prophecy and history, as *the* time, and the *only* time, in which Isaiah 29 : 4–24 finds its fulfillment, we enquire for the "book that is sealed," and for "the words" of that book and can find nothing that fulfills the prophetic description but the Book of Mormon. It comes forth in *the exact time* required; it comes forth "out of the ground," as required; its "speech" whispers out of the dust, as required; it is the "speech," and "vision," of those people who went out from Jerusalem before its destruction by Nebuchadnezzar, (intimated in the first four verses), as required by the prophecy. Its language, in the original, was "sealed," so that the learned could not read it, as required by the prophecy; its words were delivered by "men" (Joseph and Martin) to the "learned," just as required. Though the learned could not read "the words" when first delivered, yet after being given to the unlearned *they are read*, just as required by the prophecy; it comes forth a little while before Lebanon—Judea—is "turned into a fruitful field," as the prophecy requires; and in, and after, the time of its coming forth, the Jews, for a wonder, are found in a highly favored and prosperous condition, as required by the prophecy. It comes richly laden with instruction in spiritual things, and thoroughly freighted with the essential doctrines of the Savior, the Lord Christ, as is intimated in the prophecy; for, "They also that erred in spirit shall come to understanding, and they that murmured shall learn doctrine" (vs. 24). Now, in all these particulars, as well as in others, the Book of Mormon corresponds to, and agrees with the prophecy under consideration, *and no other book or work under heaven does*. For these reasons it is conclusive that the book is of divine origin.

The Book of Mormon having been written by Hebrews who came out from Jerusalem B. C. 600, we might reasonably expect them to be acquainted with, and skilled in the Hebrew language, especially as they carried with them valuable records of their nation; and the book claims that there were. Nephi, in first book of Nephi 1:1, says:

"I make a record in the language of my father, which consists of *the learning of the Jews*, and the language of the Egyptians."

And Moroni says:

"And if our plates had been sufficiently large we would have written in Hebrew; but the Hebrew hath been altered by us also; and if we could have written in Hebrew, behold, ye would have had no imperfection in our record."—Book of Mormon 4:8.

Now this remarkable and important claim, that one portion of the ancient inhabitants of America were skilled in writing a modified form of the Hebrew language, is fully sustained by discoveries of such writing, made by scientists and antiquarians long since the coming forth of the Book of Mormon, these discoveries being in no wise connected with the people who believe in the divine authenticity of the book. We first present an article from *The Israelite Indeed*, a paper edited by G. R. Lederer, a converted Jew. Of course we do not endorse the groundless and absurb conclusions of the writer as to *how* the writer, or writers, of the described *relic* came to America. It will be seen that Mr. Lederer perceives that the Hebrew in which this *relic* is written is "changed" from the ancient form somewhat, and yet it is not in "the modern Hebrew," which would most likely be the case if a forgery were possible. It will be further seen, that Mr. Lederer thinks the writer of the *relic* could not have been a Jew, because the Ten Commandments are there rendered differently than in the Bible. The Hebrews of the Book of Mormon having slightly "changed" the language, which a superstitious Jew would not dare to have done, it is not at all strange that they should modify the form and letter of the commandments, though careful to retain their essential import and meaning. Here is the article referred to:

"HEBREW RELICS.

[These two inscribed stones have been sent to New York by their discoverer and proprietor, Mr. David Wyrick, of Newark, Ohio, to Mr. Dwight, to be submitted by him to the examination of the learned, accompanied with full accounts of the discovery, and maps and drawings illustrating the place and circumstances].

"We suppose that many, if not most of our readers have seen, in religious as well as in secular papers, the accounts of some relics which were found a few months ago in a mound near Newark, Ohio. These relics consist of stones, in strange shapes bearing Hebrew inscriptions, which makes the case particularly interesting to me, as a Hebrew. I have read, therefore, with great interest, all that has been published concerning them, and studied the opinions of different men of science and learning, who have expressed them in public; but I desired to see the objects themselves, to put my finger on these relics, which bear inscriptions of the holy language which once was written with the finger of God upon tables of stone; a language spoken and written by the prophets of Israel, who predicted the main features, not only of the history of Israel but also of the world at large. It is one of the peculiar and national characteristics of the Jews, to feel a sacred awe for that language, and even for "the square characters" in which it is written, so that every written or printed Hebrew page is called "Shemos," by which the people mean to say, a paper on which holy names are printed or written. A pious Jew would never use any Hebrew book or paper for any secular purpose whatever, and carefully picks up every bit and burns it. Being now, by the grace of God, an "Israelite Indeed," believing in Him concerning whom Moses and the prophets did write, that sacred language has increased in its charming influence, upon my mind; this may explain my anxiety to see those relics with the Hebrew inscriptions, without, however, entertaining the least hope of ever having that wish realized. This time, however, I was gladly disappointed; for, in calling a few days ago on my friend, Mr. Theodore Dwight, (the Recording Secretary of the "American Ethnological Society," and my associate in the editorship of this Magazine), my eyes met with the very objects of my desire. That I examined these antiquities carefully, none of our readers will, I think, entertain any doubt. I recognized all the letters except one, (the *ayin*), though *the forms of many* of them *are different* from those *now* in use. This, however, is not the case with the stone found first, (viz., in July 1860), which has the form of an ancient jar, bearing Hebrew inscriptions on its four sides, which are in perfectly such characters as those generally in use now. I can not form any opinion concerning the use or meaning of this, which was found first, as the inscriptions do not lead to any suggestions whatever. They are as follows: 1. "*Debar Jehovah*," (meaning the Word of Jehovah). 2. "*Kodesh Kodeshim*," (The Holy of Holies). 3. "*Thcrath Jehovah*," (The Law of Jehovah), and 4. "*Melek Aretz*," (King of the Earth).

"What was it intended for? Is it, as some suppose, a relic of ancient Freemasonary? We can not concur with that idea, because the first question which would suggest itself to our mind is: How did this relic get into a mound of the ancient Indians, and this, too, at such a considerable depth, and altogether singular? We must leave the solution of this problem to after-days, when men of industry and love for antiquities shall perhaps succeed in discovering more relics, by which the present ones may find an explanation.

"This, however, is not the case with that before mentioned, which was found on the first of November, last, [1860]. It is evident—at least to my mind—that the writer, or carver, intended to perpetuate the essence of the Divine law, which could not have been done in a better way than by engraving it on a stone, of such a nature as should be able to resist all influences of the destroying tooth of time. It is also evident to my mind, that the writer was not a Jew or an Israelite, as some suppose, but a proselyte, one who had been taught by a Ḥebrew, and perhaps converted to abandon his idols, to believe in one living and invisible God, and to keep his commandments. My reasons for believing the writer not to have been a Jew, are briefly these: 1. The veneration which the Hebrews of all classes pay to the Holy Scriptures, and particularly to the five books of Moses, is so great that the *slightest alteration*, even of a point, is considered sinful; and the roll from which they read in the synagogue, in which is found any alteration, transposition of letter, or incorrectness—as, for instance, a *cheth* instead of a *hay*, must be immediately laid by, and not allowed to be used, until corrected. A Hebrew, therefore, who knew how to write the Ten Commandments, would have either written them perfectly, or not at all; and as there are many mistakes in that engraving: some letters entirely wanting, some transposed, and some superfluous, I conclude the writer was not a Hebrew. 2. The order, or rather *disorder*, in which the Ten Commandments are engraved —of which we have nothing of a similar kind elsewhere—proves that the author was not a Hebrew. 3. The presence of a human figure, however, is the strongest objection against the supposition that the writer was a Hebrew. Though, in more recent times, after the invention of printing, the Jews began to imitate the Gentiles, in having the figures of Moses, Aaron, David, and Solomon on the title-pages of their printed Bibles and prayer-books; yet, in ancient days—the age when this stone must have been prepared—no Hebrew would have dared to carve any human figure, even that of Moses, in connection with the Ten Commandments. That this figure led to a fatal mistake, is evident from the fact, that the Reverend and learned John W. McCarty, of Newark, Ohio, who first deciphered and read the inscription, read the word *Moshe*—Moses—over the head of the figure, in connection with the next line on the bas-relief, commencing: "Who brought thee out from the land of Egypt;" thus making Moses instead of Jehovah, the real deliverer of Israel.

"The discovery of that very remarkable antiquity confirmed me in my opinion, not that the aborigines of America are of Hebrew descent, but that, at some *remote age* and in some now *unknown way*, one or more pious and *distinguished Hebrews came over to this continent*, became the teachers of some of the wild tribes of America, and thus introduced not only the knowledge of the true and living Jehovah, but to some extent Jewish, or rather *Mosaic rites* and *ceremonies also*. This, I think, is the real reason why, after the invasion of this continent by the priest-ridden and fanatic Spaniards and Portuguese, *so many things resembling Judaism*, and the belief in *one who came to enlighten them*, departed and *promised to come again*, was found among the southern tribes of Indians, and all *pictures*, *engravings* and *signs* of it were destroyed by superstitious priests and monks.

"One, or a number of those believing Indians, seeing that, in the absence of their teachers, the people were falling gradually back into their old pagan habits, became alarmed, and fearing that, in a short time, all would be forgotten and lost, concluded to *preserve the essence of faith* at least, by *engraving* it on a *table of stone*. They did it with the best of their knowledge of the *Hebrew writing*, as well as of the construction of the passage.

"The *form* of the characters is neither the modern Hebrew, (adopted by the High council in consequence of the fact that the "Cuthiyiun," or Samaritans, adopted the ancient Hebrew), nor is it the Samaritan, which shows again that the writer or writers had already *forgotten much*. Of one thing, however, I am morally convinced: that this stone is a *genuine relic of antiquity*, as it would be a greater difficulty to believe in the invention of such a strange mixture of characters, disorder of combination, and *innocent blunders*, than to believe it the handiwork of a generation long since passed away."—G. R. LEDERER, in "*Israelite Indeed*," May, 1861.

We next present our readers with an article on the same general subject from *The Prophetic Watchman*:

"CURIOUS RELICS—ANCIENT ISRAELITES IN AMERICA.

"We are all more or less acquainted with the so-called 'Indian Mounds,' found in various parts of our country. There are hundreds of them in Ohio alone— several near Newark, Licking Co. Pipes, copper beads strung upon a vegetable fibre, human skeletons, skulls, bones of animals and birds, some charred by fire, as if they had been sacrificed upon a burning pile, have been obtained from them. For centuries it has been a most interesting subject of inquiry as to who built these mounds, and whence came their builders. Within the past few years some relics have been discovered, which are thought to throw light on the subject:

"The first is a little coarse sandstone, not quite an inch and a half high by about two inches long. It was found in the 'Wilson Mound,' and bears the face of a human being. On the forehead are five distinct *Hebrew characters*, which are interpreted to mean: "May the Lord have mercy on him (or me) an untimely birth," evidently an expression of humiliation.

"The second relic from the same mound is stone closely resembling limestone. It is rather triangular than square in its form, and yet it differs widely from both. It represents an animal, and contains four human faces, and three *inscriptions in Hebrew*, signifying devotion, reverence, and natural depravity.

"The third stone was found in 1860, about three miles from Newark. It has a shape like a wedge, and is about six inches long, tapering at the end. On one end is a handle, and at the top are four *Hebrew inscriptions*.

"The last relic is an object of much interest. It was found in 1860, and has engraved upon it a figure of Moses, and the Ten Commandments. One side is depressed, and the reverse protrudes. Over the figure is a *Hebrew word* signifying "Moses." The other inscriptions are *almost literally* the words found in some parts of the Bible, and the Ten Commandments are given in *part* and *entirely*—the longest being *abbreviated*. The alphabet used, it is *thought*, is the *original Hebrew* one, as there are letters known in the Hebrew alphabet [not] now in use, but bearing a resemblance to them. All things on this stone point to the time *before Ezra*,* to the lost tribes of Israel, and the theory is, that some one of these tribes found their way into this continent, and settled where the State of Ohio now exists."—From the *Prophetic Watchman*, Sep. 14, 1866.

Our next is the sum of a lecture delivered in Allegheny City, Pa., in 1866:

"AMERICAN ANTIQUITIES.

"A short time since a notice was published in the city papers that there would be an exhibition and a lecture deliverd by the Rev. R. M. Miller, in the First Presbyterian Church, Allegheny, upon some Indian relics lately discovered in some mounds near Newark, Ohio, containing *Hebrew inscriptions*, and as a matter of course I attended the lecture, as all Latter Day Saints feel considerable interest in all the testimony pertaining to the ancient inhabitants of this land; not because they are any way in the dark upon the history of the past in relation to them, but because additional testimony strengthens the evidence in regard to the divine authenticity of the Book of Mormon, in which they have perfect assurance as being a sacred record, containing the covenant for the gathering of Israel, in conformity with the testimony of prophets.

"The reverend gentleman commenced his lecture by giving a general description of the mounds and ancient fortifications in Ohio and the western country. He said that it was estimated there were in the state of Ohio, alone, ten thousand of them. He gave a very clear and distinct description of the situation and construction of several of them in the neighborhood of Newark, Ohio, from whence the relics he exhibited were obtained. I believe the mounds were from ten to twelve miles apart, where they were found.

"The first piece he exhibited was a stone head, (or rather a photograph of it), which was cut off of the neck, close to the ears. On the forehead was written, in Hebrew, "May the Lord have mercy upon an untimely birth." He gave it as his opinion that the person who had it deposited with his remains, had been executed, perhaps decapitated. There was charcoal and burnt bones of animals and men in the debris. The original is in the possession of Mr. Tennant, of Newark, Ohio. It was found in a mound three miles from Newark. In the same mound was found a three cornered piece, upon which was carved two human faces and an animal. On the forehead of one of the figures of a human face was a phylacter, in the form of a skull, upon which was carved the letter used to denote the name of the Almighty. On the forehead of the other carved human figure was written in Hebrew, "It is good to love the aged." On the side of the animal was written *in Hebrew* something denoting natural depravity. The reverend gentleman said it was *the same as found in Jeremiah:* "the heart is deceitful," &c. Mr. Strock, of Newark, owns this.

---

* It appears that "the alphabet used, *it is thought*, is the original Hebrew," and why do the Hebrew scholars who have examined the inscriptions only *think* so, and why are they not certain about it? Evidently because there is *only in part* a resemblance between the letters in these inscriptions, and the most ancient Hebrew alphabet of which Hebrew scholars have a perfect knowledge. The facts developed by these discoveries, coincide perfectly with a statement of Mormon in Book of Mormon chap. 4, par. 3, who says: "If our plates had been sufficiently large we should have written in Hebrew, but the Hebrew hath been altered by us also." Again, the Nephites and Zarahemlaites came out from Jerusalem just before the time of Ezra, therefore the coincidence is but reasonable.

"The third piece was in the shape of a wedge. On one side was written, in Hebrew:

"First side.—*"The Lord is king of all the earth."*
"Second side.—*"The sword of the Lord is the law."*
"Third side.—*"The Holy of Holies."*
"Fourth side.—*"The Jew of life is the Lord awaking souls."*

"The fourth piece was what he called a Teraphim, a household god, and quoted Judges 17 to prove it.

"This is a stone about eight inches long, three wide, and two thick. There is a depression on one side of about half an inch deep, and in the depression there is cut the figure of a man dressed in priestly robes, and over his head, in the depression, is written the word "*Moses*," and in lines on the back and edges is written in *Hebrew* the *ten commandments to Israel*, written upon the tables of stone by the finger of the Lord, and given to Moses upon the mount. There is *some little difference* between it and the version we have of it in the Bible. It is a little more brief. For instance, it says, "*Who brought thee from the land of bondage,*" and "*six days shalt thou labor.*" In our version we have this addition: "*and do all thy work.*" These are all I can now remember, but I thought the brevity made them more perfect.

"This Teraphim was found about two and a half miles from Newark, near the base of a very large mound. This mound is composed of stones, and it is thought that 20,000 wagon loads have been carried away, to build the canal some years since. It was 400 feet at the base and 50 feet high. Near its base a small mound was noticed, which was composed entirely of fire-clay, and some of the men at work in that neighborhood, thought for curiosity they would dig into it, and see if any particular was in it. The person dug until he came to a piece of wood, upon which he found some copper beads. He took them away and of course exhibited them. This aroused the curiosity of another party, and some two or three persons went and made further search into the fire-clay, and upon lifting up the wood, it proved to be the *lid of a box*, lined inside with some kind of coarse cloth, but so entirely rotten that it crumbled at the touch. The box contained a skeleton and what had been a neck-lace of copper beads, but the string was also rotten. The party removed the wooden box, and began to dig some deeper. They soon struck *a stone box* of an oblong shape, cemented together in the middle. They shook and found it contained something, as it made a rattle when shaken. They forced it open, and found its contents to be the Teraphim, or image, having these *Hebrew inscriptions upon it*. If I remember correctly, this was found in the year 1865, the others some year or two before. This Teraphim is now the property of Mr. David Johnson, of Coshocton, Ohio. The Rev. Miller seems to be a good Hebrew scholar, as he read and criticised the language in the presence of several of the theological professors of the Presbyterian College, Allegheny City. He stated that he had taken them to Cincinnati, and shown them to several learned Rabbies, and they were agreed that the *Hebrew characters* were of a date *beyond the time of Ezra*. He described, on a board, the difference of the formation of the letters before and after that period.

"I will not repeat their *theories and conjectures* respecting the wanderings of the Israelites to reach this land, but this he said was his conclusion:

"First.—That some of the *tribes*, or *parts of tribes* of Israel, had once *inhabited this land*.

"Second.—That they were the mound builders; but whether the modern Indians are their descendants, or whether they had destroyed the Israelites, he could not say; but if the Indians are not the descendants of the Mound Builders, but had extirpated them, then the question remains, where did these Indians come from? Who are they?

"My own conclusion respecting these things is that of every Latter Day Saint. The relics were hid up, in the providence of God, as collateral testimony of the Latter Day Work, and especially of the Book of Mormon.

PITTSBURG, Pa., August 12, 1866.   JOSIAH ELLS."

Now, from these relics we learn, just what was claimed by the Book of Mormon over thirty years before their discovery, (1) that the ancient inhabitants of America possessed a knowledge of, and wrote upon enduring substances, a modified form of the Hebrew language; (2) that they possessed the writings of Moses and the prophets up to the times of Jeremiah, including *the first part of his writings to chap. 17, verse 9,*—"The heart is deceitful," etc. For of these records it is said by Nephi:

"My father, Lehi, took the records which were engraven upon the plates of brass, and he did search them from the beginning. And he beheld that they did contain the five books of Moses, which gave an account of the creation of the world, and also of Adam and Eve, who were our first parents; and also a record of the Jews from the beginning, even down to the commencement of the reign of Zedekiah, king of Judah; and also the prophecies of the holy prophets, from the beginning, even down to the commencement of the reign of Zedekiah; *and also many prophecies which have been spoken by the mouth of Jeremiah.*"—1 Nephi 1:46.

We find (3) that these sacred writings were hidden up in "a stone box," as were the plates of the Book of Mormon. Here, then, is a chain of evidence in support of the claims of the Book of Mormon, that is as strong as it is strange, and one that cannot fail to fasten conviction upon the mind of the unprejudiced inquirer, while it joyfully confirms the faith of the believer. But we have not done with this language question. In our quotation from 1 Nephi 1:1, we see that the ancient Hebrews on this continent were not only skilled in writing Hebrew, but also in "the language of the Egyptians." It is stated in Mosiah 1:1, that Lehi had been "taught in the language of the Egyptians," and that he taught the same to his children; and in Book of Mormon 4:8, Moroni informs us that he wrote the entire record from which the Book of Mormon was translated, "in the characters which are called among us the reformed Egyptian." Now when we find by testimony outside of the Book of Mormon, that the ancient inhabitants of America possessed a knowledge of Egyptian hieroglyphics, and sculpturing, and architecture, we have another strong evidence of the divinity of that book. This evidence we have presented, in part, on pages 153 to 158, and we now give more. Mr. Delafield says, in his *Antiquities of America*, page 41:

"Still further and more important evidence, however, renders the point conclusive that southern Asia was the birth-place of this [ancient American] people, as we detect among them actual traditions of the flood, the building of Babel, and the death of Abel."

Again:

"One of the most interesting sources of comparison between Mexico, Peru, and Egypt, is to be found in an investigation of their *hieroglyphic system*. Each of these countries had a peculiar method of recording events by means of hieroglyphic signs, sculpturing them on monuments and buildings, and portraying them on papyrus and maguey."—p. 42.

Further:

"Baron Humboldt considers the Mexican paintings as rather corresponding with the hieratic than the hieroglyphic writings of *the Egyptians*, as found on the rolls of papyrus in the swathings of the mummies, and which may be considered paintings of a mixed kind, because they unite symbolical and isolated characters with the representation of an action. It is the opinion of the author that further investigations and discoveries in deciphering Mexican hieroglyphic paintings will exhibit a close analogy to *the Egyptian* in the use of two scriptural systems; the one for monumental inscription, the other for the ordinary purposes of record and transmission of information. We find the three species of *hieroglyphics common to Mexico and Egypt*."—p. 46.

On page 65, Mr. Delafield reviews:

"The analogical evidence of an identity of the family of Mexico and Peru with that of Hindostan *or Egypt*, to simplify which we name the several coincidences, which have been specified, in their proper order.

"I. PHILOLOGICAL. The various analogies in language.

"II. ANATOMICAL. The peculiar craniological formation common to those countries, as asserted by Dr. Warren.

"III. MYTHOLOGICAL. The existence of two peculiar modes of worship, [that of Nephites and Lamanites?] addressed to two deities; one sanguinary, the other peaceful. * *.

"IV. HIEROGLYPHIC. The use of three peculiar systems of hieroglyphic writing of *the Egyptians*.

"V. ASTRONOMICAL. 1. Identity in the division of the year, month, and week; and the calculations thereof. 2. Identity in the use of intercalary days. 3. Identity in zodiacal signs.

"VI. ARCHITECTURAL. 1. Identity in sepulchral tumuli [mounds for burial]. 2. Identity in pyramidal temples. 3. In the uses of these temples. 4. In the mechanical power which enabled them to move masses that no other races have ever accomplished. 5. Their use of hieroglyphic sculpture on all their sacred buildings. 6. Similarity in zodiacal and planispheric carvings. 7. Identity in sepulchral ornaments.

"VII. Identity in practice of embalming and preservation of the royal corpses."

The ancient Nephites, and Zarahemlaites, were, no doubt, not only acquainted with the language, but also with much about the habits, customs, arts, and sciences peculiar to Egypt; for the Israelites, in all their history from Abraham to Zedekiah, and after, had direct and intimate intercourse with the Egyptians. Therefore it is not strange that we find in Mexico and Peru, as stated by Mr. Delafield, these evidences of Egyptian art and manners, especially that of hieroglyphic writing. In conclusion upon this point we have only to say, that the claim of the Book of Mormon—that the ancient inhabitants of America were skilled in the Egyptian language, is now fully vindicated. And here we have another unanswerable proof of the truth of the book.

Further proof of the Book of Mormon is seen in its statements that highly civilized and cultivated peoples located anciently in the northern part of South America, Central America, and in the southern part of North America, where they builded very large and splendid cities, especially in Central America, and near "the narrow neck of land," (Isthmus of Panama), making these statements when little or nothing was known to the generality of mankind, in respect to the last named region. Since the coming forth of the book, the discoveries of Stephens and Catherwood, and others, have disclosed the fact that in the very region where the Book of Mormon locates them there were many magnificent cities built up by the ancients. Up to the time of the discoveries by Stephens and Catherwood, in 1839–1843, that region known as *Central America* was not supposed to contain any interesting antiquities, though considerable had been learned in regard to the antiquities of Peru, and of Mexico. It remained for these gentlemen to bring to light rich treasures of information in respect to the ancient civilizations of this region, and to disclose to the world the fact that here had been the theatre of the grandest industries, and the site of the most cultivated, opulent, and enlightened nations of all antiquity. For ten or twelve years the Book of Mormon had been quietly proclaiming these facts, when its statements were fully confirmed by these timely discoveries. Who is there so blind as not to see the overruling hand of God in these things! Such coincidences are not the result of chance. They exhibit too clearly the work of an All-Wise mind, to be so considered. Mr. Stephens, in his "*Central America, Chiapas, and Yucatan,*" vol. 1, p. 98, says:

"Of the great cities beyond the vale of Mexico, buried in forests, ruined, desolate, and without a name, Humboldt never heard, or, at least, he never visited them. It is but lately [Mr. Stephens writes in 1841] that accounts of their existence reached Europe and our own country. These accounts, however vague and unsatisfactory, had roused our curiosity; though I ought perhaps to say that both Mr. C. and I were somewhat skeptical, and when we arrived at Copan, it was with the hope, rather than the expectation, of finding wonders."

But it was not long before their labors were rewarded in discovering the ruins of many ancient cities, which have been visited since by other antiquarians.

Another evidence in favor of the Book of Mormon is seen in the fact that it teaches, in Alma 16:26, and in Ether 1:11, and elsewhere, that the ancient inhabitants of America knew concerning the crucifixion of Christ, both by revelation and by history, and were therefore acquainted with the *cross* as a religious symbol; and in the further fact that the antiquities of America disclose that the cross was so used by the ancients. Baldwin, in "*Ancient America,*" mentions this fact on pages 109, 110, and 293. Stephens does also, in his "*Central America,*" vol. 2, p. 347, and elsewhere. The testimony of the Book of Mormon, and of the antiquities of America, are one upon this point; the latter and the latest confirming the former.

The Book of Mormon states that many of the ancient inhabitants of America became idolators (book of Mormon 2:3), and the discoveries of American antiquarians fully confirm this.

The Book of Mormon states that America abounds with gold, silver, and many other precious metals; and discoveries since 1849 give special confirmation to this claim. And here we may remark that America, the Book of Mormon claims, is the special heritage of Joseph and his posterity, as provided for in the prophetic blessing of Jacob (Gen. 49:22–26, with Gen. 48:16–19), and the prophetic blessing of Moses also (Deut. 33:13–17). Moses says of Joseph:

"Blessed of the Lord be *his land,* for the precious things of heaven [the revealed will of God], and for the *dew* [its universal distribution], and for the deep that coucheth beneath [springs, rivers, lakes, seas, and their products], and for the precious fruits brought forth by the sun [by the action of its light in the vegetable kingdom], and for the precious things put forth by the moon [in the action of its light on the vegetable kingdom and in respect to the tides], and for the chief things of the ancient mountains, and for the precious things of the lasting hills [their various metals, minerals, etc.], and for the precious things of the earth and fulness thereof [embracing the animal, vegetable, and mineral kingdoms of earth, in their 'fulness'], and for the good will of him that dwelt in the bush [the Lord—see Acts 7: 30–34]."

Joseph's portion in Palestine could never fill this description, but the land of America, and that alone, does. The "precious things of the ancient mountains" used in building and beautifying the temple of Solomon did not come from Joseph's portion in Judea, yet they undoubtedly would had they been there. Joseph's portion *in Palestine* was not the "land" alluded to for another reason, it did not lie in the right place; for Jacob said it should be "unto the utmost [the outermost, the farthest, the extreme] bound of the everlasting hills" (Gen. 49: 26). To go from Goshen, in Egypt, where Jacob was when uttering this prophecy, to "the utmost bound of the everlasting hills," would bring us to the mountain ranges of America, to the land claimed for Joseph by the Book of Mormon. And that America is the special portion of Joseph may be gathered from the prophetic blessing put by Jacob upon the seed of Joseph, as follows:

"And he blessed Joseph, and said, God, before whom my fathers, Abraham and Isaac did walk, the God which fed me all my life long unto this day, the Angel which redeemed me from all evil, bless the lads; and let my name be named on them, and the name of my fathers Abraham and Isaac; and let them [Ephraim and Manasseh] grow into a multitude *in the midst of the earth*."

"The *midst of the earth*" geographically considered, measuring from where Jacob pronounced the blessing, would be *the land of America, precisely*. Nor is this all; Jacob predicts in verse 19, that Ephraim's "seed shall become a multitude of nations." In America we find "a multitude of nations"[*] of one common stock, whose traditions, religious rites and customs, language and language relics, clearly demonstrate their Israelitish origin; and we find them in the very place marked in prophecy, as the land of Joseph and his seed. Here is another strong proof of the truth of the Book of Mormon. Its claims in this respect are well sustained by the facts of both prophecy and history.

The Book of Mormon states that at the crucifixion of Christ the face of the land in Central America, and around it, was broken up

---

[*] The Book of Mormon states that Lehi was of Manasseh, and some argue thence that "the multitude of nations" found in America cannot be in any sense of Ephraim. We would remind such reasoners that the seed of Ishmael and his sons, and of Zoram, who accompanied Lehi, and the seed of those who accompanied Mulek, who finally became blended with the Nephites and Lamanites, may all have been of the lineage of Ephraim. This is neither impossible nor improbable. This, if true, would give large preponderance to Ephraim. Besides this Ephraim and Manasseh, together, were sometimes called Ephraim.—Hosea 5: 3, 13; 6: 4, 10; Isaiah 7: 8, etc., etc. And this is not strange when we remember that Jacob "set Ephraim before Manasseh."—Gen. 48: 20.

by earthquakes, and that many cities were sunk.—Book of Nephi 4 : 2–6. Evidences of such a catastrophe have been of late discovered. Baldwin, in "*Ancient America*," pages 274 and 275, says that James S. Wilson, Esq., in 1860, "discovered on the coast of Ecuador, ancient or fossil pottery vessels, images, and other manufactured articles, all finely wrought. Some of these articles were made of gold. The most remarkable fact connected with them is that they were taken from 'a stratum of ancient surface-earth' *which was covered with a marine deposit six feet thick.* * * * The ancient surface-earth or vegetable mould, with its pottery, gold-work, and other relics of civilized human life, was, therefore, *below the sea when that marine deposit was spread over it.* This land, after being occupied by men, had subsided and settled below the ocean, remained there long enough to accumulate the marine deposit, and again be elevated to its former position above the level of the sea." Of these discoveries, Sir Roderick Murchison, at a meeting of the Royal Geological Society, in 1862, says:

"The discoveries which Mr. Wilson has made of the existence of the works of man in a stratum of mould beneath the sea level, and covered by several feet of clay, the phenomenon being persistent for sixty miles, are of the highest interest to physical geographers and geologists. The facts seem to demonstrate that, *within the human period*, the lands of the west coast of Equatorial America were *depressed* and *submerged*, and that, after the accumulation of marine clays, above the terrestial relics the whole coast was elevated to its present position."

Now we submit, that, when these lands were "depressed and submerged" it was done, not gradually, but suddenly, as the presence of these valuable relics attests. Had they been depressed gradually, through a lapse of years, or months, or even weeks, these valuables would have been removed to places of safety. But the presence, under this marine deposit, of "fossil pottery, vessels, images," "all finely wrought" and "some of the articles made of gold," demonstrates that the catastrophe by which they were sunken and overwhelmed, was as sudden as that which buried Herculaneum and Pompeii.

The Book of Mormon, we see, tells us of the sudden depression and submergence of lands, towns, and cities, in these very regions, and travelers and antiquarians, after the coming forth of that book, and near 2000 years after the marvellous event occurred, find abundant evidence to confirm the statement. Hence, in this, we find another remarkable proof of the Book of Mormon.

The Book of Mormon states that there were horses on this continent more than 3,800 years ago.—Ether 4:3. Now it was commonly thought at the time when the Book of Mormon was first given to the world, that there were no horses in America till they were brought by the Spaniards in the sixteenth century. But recent discoveries of the fossil remains of the horse, in many places in America, go to confirm the statements of the Book of Mormon. Prof. Winchell, in his "*Sketches of Creation*," page 210, says:

"It is a curious fact that so many *generi*, now extinct from the Continent, but living in other quarters of the globe, were once abundant on the plains of North America. Various species of the *horse* have dwelt here for ages, and the question reasonably arises whether the wild horses of the Pampas may not have been indigenous. Here, too, the camel found a suitable home."

Recently discoveries have been made of the fossil remains of the horse and some of the other animals mentioned in the Book of Mormon. A correspondent of the Eugene City (Oregon) *Guard* gives the following account of a visit made June, 1877, by himself and another person to the so-called fossil beds of Lake county, that State:

* * * "We found fossil bones of the elephant, camel, horse, and elk, or reindeer, the horse being much more abundant than either of the others, but all being so clearly marked as to leave no doubt of their identity. There were other bones, apparently of large animals, but your correspondent was unable to name the animal they once belonged to. Among the fossils found, the smaller quadrupeds had a representation; bones answering to the fox and wolf were found; also others answering to the sheep or goat in size and appearance."

This affords good proof, from the fact that the book stated that which was contrary to the common belief, and subsequent discoveries confirm that *apparently* false statement.

The Book of Mormon predicts the rapid downfall of "the great and abominable church" after the coming forth of that book:

"And it came to pass that I beheld that the wrath of God was poured out upon the great and abominable church, insomuch that there were wars and rumors of wars among all the nations and kindreds of the earth, and as there began to be wars and rumors of wars among all the nations which belonged to the mother of abominations, the angel spake unto me, saying, Behold, the wrath of God is upon the mother of harlots; and behold, thou seest all these things; and when the day cometh that the wrath of God is poured out upon the mother of harlots, which is the great abominable church of all the earth, whose foundation is the devil, then, at that day, the work of the Father shall commence, in preparing the way for the fulfilling of his covenants, which he hath made to his people, who are of the house of Israel."—1 Nephi 3:51.

"And after our seed is scattered, the Lord God will proceed to do a marvelous work among the Gentiles, which shall be of great worth unto our seed; wherefore, it is likened unto their being nourished by the Gentiles, and being carried in their arms and upon their shoulders. And it shall also be of worth unto the Gentiles: and not only unto the Gentiles, but unto all the house of Israel, unto the making known of the covenants of the Father of heaven unto Abraham, saying, In thy seed shall all the kindreds of the earth be blessed. And I would, my brethren, that ye should know that all the kindreds of the earth cannot be blessed, unless he shall make bare his arm in the eyes of the nations. Wherefore, the Lord God will proceed to make bare his arm in the eyes of all the nations, in bringing about his covenants and his gospel, unto those who are of the house of Israel. Wherefore, he will bring them again out of captivity, and they shall be gathered together to the lands of their inheritance: and they shall be brought out of obscurity, and out of darkness: and they shall know that the Lord is their Savior and their Redeemer, the mighty one of Israel. And the blood of that great and abominable church, which is the whore of all the earth, shall turn upon their own heads; for they shall war among themselves, and the sword of their own hands shall fall upon their own heads, and they shall be drunken with their own blood. And every nation which shall war against thee, O house of Israel, shall be turned one against another, and they shall fall into the pit which they digged to ensnare the people of the Lord."— 1 Nephi 7:2.

That this is particularly true of the Papacy, one division of the great and abominable church, all may know who seek to inform themselves. The shock it received by the "Young Italy" party under Mazzini and others in 1831, and forward; the staggering blows it sustained in 1848-9, at the hands of the Provisional Government and the Roman National Assembly; the wounds it received in 1864 by means of the Pope's Ecyclical letter; and the rapid decline of that form of religion in all its former strong-holds since the king of Italy, in August, 1870, wrenched from the hand of the Pope the sceptre of civil power, has left that church broken, divided, and tottering to its final fall. And there is not, probably, one Catholic nation that has not been engaged in war since 1830. In these things the predictions of the book prove true.

The Book of Mormon predicts, 1 Nephi 7:2; 2 Nephi 5:5; 11:3; 12:13; Nephi 2:12; 10:1; Mormon 1:9; 2:6, etc., etc., that soon after the coming forth of that book the Lord will begin to prepare the way for the speedy restoration and gathering of Israel—including the Jews. The interest taken by England, France, and America in the civilization and enlightenment of the aborigines of America and of the adjacent islands, the restored state of the land of Judea, and the highly improved and favored condition of the Jews, go very far to confirm the truth of these remarkable predictions.

The Book of Mormon predicts that soon after its coming forth "the Lord God shall cause a *great division* among the people; and the wicked will he destroy; and he will spare his people, yea, even if it so be that he must destroy the wicked by fire."—2 Nephi 12: 14. And now we see *division* everywhere, in all departments of society, especially in matters of religion, politics, and civil government, and between labor and capital.

The Book of Mormon predicts with clearness the corrupt state of the world as it is to-day, and the means by which it is caused:

"And it shall come to pass, that those who have dwindled in unbelief, shall be smitten by the land of the Gentiles. And the Gentiles are lifted up in the pride of their eyes, and have stumbled, because of the greatness of their stumbling block, that they have built up many churches; nevertheless they put down the power and the miracles of God, and preach up unto themselves their own wisdom, and their own learning, that they may get gain, and grind upon the face of the poor; and there are many churches built up which cause envyings, and strifes, and malice; and there are also secret combinations, even as in times of old, according to the combinations of the devil, for he is the foundation of all these things; yea, the foundation of murder, and works of darkness; yea, and he leadeth them by the neck with a flaxen cord, until he bindeth them with his strong cords forever. For behold, my beloved brethren, I say unto you, that the Lord God worketh not in darkness. He doeth not any thing save it be for the benefit of the world; for he loveth the world, even that he layeth down his own life that he may draw all men unto him. Wherefore, he commandeth none that they shall not partake of his salvation. Behold, doth he cry unto any, saying, Depart from me? Behold, I say unto you, Nay; but he saith, Come unto me all ye ends of the earth, buy milk and honey, without money and without price. Behold, hath he commanded any that they should depart out of the synagogues, or out of the houses of worship? Behold, I say unto you, Nay. Hath he commanded any that they should not partake of his salvation? Behold, I say unto you, Nay; but he hath given it free for all men; and he hath commanded his people that they should persuade all men to repentance. Behold hath the Lord commanded any that they should not partake of his goodness? Behold I say unto you nay; but all men are privileged the one like unto the other, and none are forbidden. He commandeth that there shall be no priestcrafts; for, behold, priestcrafts are that men preach and set themselves up for a light unto the world, that they may get gain, and praise of the world; but they seek not the welfare of Zion. Behold, the Lord hath forbidden this thing; wherefore, the Lord God hath given a commandment, that all men should have charity, which charity is love. And except they should have charity, they were nothing: wherefore, if they should have charity, they would not suffer the laborer in Zion to perish. But the laborer in Zion, shall labor for Zion; for if they labor for money, they shall perish. And, again, the Lord God hath commanded that men should not murder; that they should not lie; that they should not steal; that they should not take the name of the Lord their God in vain; that they should not envy; that they should not have malice; that they should not contend one with another; that they should not commit whoredoms; and that they should do none of these things; for whoso doeth them shall perish; for none of these iniquities come of the Lord; for he doeth that which is good among the children of men; and he doeth nothing save it be plain unto the children of men; and he inviteth them all to come unto him, and partake of his goodness; and he denieth none that come unto him, black and white, bond and free, male and female; and he remembereth the heathen, and all are alike unto God, both Jew and Gentile. But behold, in the last days, or in the days of the Gentiles; yea, behold all the nations of the Gentiles, and also the Jews, both those who shall come upon this land, and those who shall be upon other lands; yea, even upon all the lands of the earth; behold they will be drunken with iniquity, and all manner of abominations; and when that day shall come, they shall be visited of the Lord of hosts, with thunder and with earthquake, and with a great noise, and with storm and with tempest, and with the flame of devouring fire; and all the nations that fight against Zion, and that distress her, shall be as a dream of a night vision; yea, it shall be unto them even as unto a hungry man, which dreameth, and behold he eateth, but he awaketh and his soul is empty; or like unto a thirsty man which dreameth, and behold he drinketh, but he awaketh, and behold he is faint, and his soul hateth appetite: yea, even so shall the multitude of all the nations be that fight against mount Zion: for behold, all ye that do iniquity, stay yourselves and wonder; for ye shall cry out, and cry; yea, ye shall be drunken, but not with wine; ye shall stagger, but not with strong drink; for behold, the Lord hath poured out upon you, the spirit of deep sleep. For behold, ye have closed your eyes, and ye have rejected the prophets, and your rulers, and the seers hath he covered because of your iniquity."—2 Nephi 11: 14, 15, 16.

"And now, behold, my brethren, I have spoken unto you according as the spirit hath constrained me; wherefore, I know that they must surely come to pass. And the things which shall be written out of the book shall be of great worth unto the children of men, and especially unto our seed, which is a remnant of the house of Israel. For it shall come to pass in that day, that the churches which are built up, and not unto the Lord, when the one shall say unto the other, Behold, I, I am the Lord's; and the other shall say, I, I am the Lord's. And thus shall every one say, that hath built up churches, and not unto the Lord; and they shall contend one with another; and their priests shall contend one with another; and they shall teach with their learning, and deny the Holy Ghost, which giveth utterance. And they deny the power of God, the Holy One of Israel; and they say unto the people, Hearken unto us, and hear ye our precept; for behold, there is no God to-day, for the Lord and Redeemer hath done his work, and he hath given his power unto men. Behold, hearken ye unto my precept: if they shall say there is a miracle wrought by the hand of the Lord, believe it not; for this day he is not a God of miracles; he hath done his work. Yea, and there shall be many which shall say, Eat, drink, and be merry, for to-morrow we die, and it shall be well with us. And there shall also be many which shall say, Eat, drink, and be merry; nevertheless, fear God, he will justify in committing a little sin: yea, lie a little, take the advantage of one because of his words, dig a pit for thy neighbor; there is no harm in this. And do all these things, for to-morrow we die; and if it so be that we are guilty, God will beat us with a few stripes, and at last we shall be saved in the kingdom of God. Yea, and there shall be many which shall teach after this manner, false, and vain, and foolish doctrines, and shall be puffed up in their hearts, and shall seek deep to hide their counsels from the Lord; and their works shall be in the dark; and the blood of the saints shall cry from the ground against them. Yea, they have all gone out of the way; they have become corrupted. Because of pride, and because of false teachers, and false doctrine, their churches have become corrupted; and their churches are lifted up; because of pride they are puffed up. They rob the poor, because of their fine sanctuaries; they rob the poor because of their fine clothing; and they persecute the meek, and the poor in heart; because in their pride, they are puffed up. They wear stiff necks and high heads; yea, and because of pride, and wickedness, and abominations, and whoredoms, they have all gone astray, save it be a few, who are the humble followers of Christ; nevertheless, they are led, that in many instances they do err, because they are taught by the precepts of men.

"O the wise, and the learned, and the rich, that are puffed up in the pride of their hearts, and all those who preach false doctrine, and all those who commit whoredoms, and pervert the right way of the Lord; wo, wo, wo be unto them, saith the Lord God Almighty, for they shall be thrust down to hell.

"Wo unto them that turn aside the just for a thing of nought, and revile against that which is good, and say that it is of no worth; for the day shall come that the Lord God will speedily visit the inhabitants of the earth; and in that day that they are fully ripe in iniquity, they shall perish. But behold, if the inhabitants of the earth shall repent of their wickedness and abominations, they shall not be destroyed, saith the Lord of hosts. But behold, that great and abominable church, the whore of all the earth, must tumble to the earth; and great must be the fall thereof: for the kingdom of the devil must shake, and they which belong to it must needs be stirred up unto repentance, or the devil will grasp them with his everlasting chains, and they be stirred up to anger and perish: for behold, at that day shall he rage in the hearts of the children of men, and stir them up to anger against that which is good; and others will he pacify, and lull them away into carnal security, that they will say, All is well in Zion; yea, Zion prospereth, all is well; and thus the devil cheateth their souls, and leadeth them away carefully down to hell. And behold, others he flattereth away, and telleth them there is no hell; and he saith unto them, I am no devil, for there is none: and thus he whispereth in their ears, until he grasps them with his awful chains, from whence there is no deliverance. Yea, they are grasped with death and hell; and death, and hell, and the devil, and all that have been seized therewith, must stand before the throne of God and be judged according to their works, from whence they must go into the place prepared for them, even a lake of fire and brimstone, which is endless torment. Therefore, wo be unto him that is at ease in Zion. Wo be unto him that crieth, All is well; yea, wo be unto him that hearkeneth unto the precepts of men, and denieth the power of God and the gift of the Holy Ghost. Yea, wo be unto him that saith, We have received, and we need no more. And in fine, wo unto all those who tremble, and are angry because of the truth of God. For behold, he that is built upon the rock, receiveth it with gladness: and he that is built upon a sandy foundation, trembleth, lest he shall fall.

"Wo be unto him that shall say, We have received the word of God, and we need no more of the word of God, for we have enough. For behold, thus saith the Lord God: I will give unto the children of men line upon line, precept upon precept, here a little and there a little: and blessed are those who hearken unto my precepts, and lend an ear unto my counsel, for they shall learn wisdom;

for unto him that receiveth, I will give more: and from them that shall say, We have enough, from them shall be taken away even that which they have. Cursed is he that putteth his trust in man, or maketh flesh his arm, or shall hearken unto the precepts of men, save their precepts shall be given by the power of the Holy Ghost.

"Wo be unto the Gentiles, saith the Lord God of hosts; for notwithstanding I shall lengthen out mine arm unto them from day to day, they will deny me; nevertheless, I will be merciful unto them, saith the Lord God, if they will repent and come unto me: for mine arm is lengthened out all the day long, saith the Lord God of hosts.

"But behold, there shall be many at that day, when I shall proceed to do a marvelous work among them, that I may remember my covenants which I have made unto the children of men, that I may set my hand again the second time to recover my people, which are of the house of Israel; and also, that I may remember the promises which I have made unto thee, Nephi, and also unto thy father, that I would remember your seed; and that the words of your seed should proceed forth out of my mouth unto your seed. And my words shall hiss forth unto the ends of the earth, for a standard unto my people, which are of the house of Israel. And because my words shall hiss forth, many of the Gentiles shall say, A bible, a bible, we have got a bible, and there cannot be any more bible. But thus saith the Lord God: O fools, they shall have a bible; and it shall proceed forth from the Jews, mine ancient covenant people. And what thank they the Jews for the bible which they receive from them? Yea, what do the Gentiles mean? Do they remember the travels, and the labors, and the pains of the Jews, and their diligence unto me, in bringing forth salvation unto the Gentiles?

"O ye Gentiles, have ye remembered the Jews, mine ancient covenant people? Nay; but ye have cursed them, and have hated them, and have not sought to recover them. But behold, I will return all these things upon your own heads; for I, the Lord, hath not forgotten my people. Thou fool, that shall say, A bible, we have got a bible, and we need no more bible. Have ye obtained a bible, save it were by the Jews? Know ye not that there are more nations than one? Know ye not that I, the Lord your God, have created all men, and that I remember those who are upon the isles of the sea; and that I rule in the heavens above, and in the earth beneath; and I bring forth my word unto the children of men, yea, even upon all the nations of the earth? Wherefore murmur ye, because that ye receive more of my word? Know ye not that the testimony of two nations is a witness unto you that I am God, that I remember one nation like unto another? Wherefore, I speak the same words unto one nation like unto another And when the two nations shall run together, the testimony of the two nations shall run together also. And I do this that I may prove unto many, that I am the same yesterday, to-day, and forever; and that I speak forth my words according to mine own pleasure. And because that I have spoken one word, ye need not suppose that I cannot speak another; for my work is not yet finished; neither shall it be, until the end of man; neither from that time henceforth and forever.

"Wherefore, because that ye have a bible, ye need not suppose that it contains all my words; neither need ye suppose that I have not caused more to be written: for I command all men, both in the east, and in the west, and in the north, and in the south, and in the islands of the sea, that they shall write the words which I speak unto them: for out of the books which shall be written, I will judge the world, every man according to their works, according to that which is written. For behold, I shall speak unto the Jews, and they shall write it: and I shall also speak unto the Nephites, and they shall write it; and I shall also speak unto the other tribes of the house of Israel, which I have led away, and they shall write it; and I shall also speak unto all nations of the earth, and they shall write it."—2 Nephi 12: 1–8.

"Hearken, O, ye Gentiles, and hear the words of Jesus Christ, the Son of the living God, which he hath commanded me that I should speak concerning you, for, behold he commandeth me that I should write, saying, Turn, all ye Gentiles, from your wicked ways, and repent of your evil doings, of your lyings and deceivings, and of your whoredoms, and of your secret abominations, and your idolatries, and of your murders, and of your priestcrafts, and your envyings, and your strifes, and from all your wickedness and abominations, and come unto me, and be baptized in my name, that ye may receive a remission of your sins, and be filled with the Holy Ghost, that ye may be numbered with my people, who are of the house of Israel."—Nephi 14: 1.

"And behold, their prayers were also in behalf of him that the Lord should suffer to bring these things forth. And no one need say, that they shall not come, for they surely shall, for the Lord hath spoken it; for out of the earth shall they come, by the hand of the Lord, and none can stay it; and it shall come in a day when it shall be said that miracles are done away; and it shall come even as if one should speak from the dead.

"And it shall come in a day when the blood of the saints shall cry unto the Lord, because of secret combinations and the works of darkness; yea, it shall come in a day when the power of God shall be denied, and churches become defiled, and shall be lifted up in the pride of their hearts; yea, even in a day when leaders of churches, and teachers, in the pride of their hearts, even to the envying of them who belong to their churches; yea, it shall come in a day when there shall be heard of fires, and tempests, and vapors of smoke in foreign lands; and there shall also be heard of wars and rumors of wars, and earthquakes in divers places; yea, it shall come in a day when there shall be great pollutions upon the face of the earth; there shall be murders and robbing, and lying, and deceivings, and whoredoms, and all manner of abominations, when there shall be many who will say, Do this, or do that, and it mattereth not, for the Lord will uphold such at the last day. But wo unto such, for they are in the gall of bitterness, and in the bonds of iniquity. Yea, it shall come in a day when there shall be churches built up that shall say, Come unto me, and for your money you shall be forgiven of your sins. O ye wicked, and perverse, and stiff-necked people, why have you built up churches unto yourselves to get gain? Why have ye transfigured the holy word of God, that ye might bring damnation upon your soul? Behold, look ye unto the revelations of God. For behold, the time cometh at that day when all these things must be fulfilled.

"Behold, the Lord hath shown unto me great and marvelous things concerning that which must shortly come at that day when these things shall come forth among you. Behold, I speak unto you as if you were present, and yet ye are not. But behold, Jesus Christ hath shown you unto me, and I know your doing; and I know that ye do walk in the pride of your hearts; and there are none, save a few only, who do not lift themselves up in the pride of their hearts, unto the wearing of very fine apparel, unto envying, and strifes, and malice, and persecutions, and all manner of iniquities; and your churches, yea, even every one, have become polluted because of the pride of your hearts. For behold, ye do love money, and your substances, and your fine apparel, and the adorning of your churches, more than ye love the poor and the needy, the sick and the afflicted. O ye pollutions, ye hypocrites, ye teachers, who sell yourselves for that which will canker, why have ye polluted the holy church of God? Why are ye ashamed to take upon you the name of Christ? Why do you not think that greater is the value of an endless happiness, than that misery which never dies, because of the praise of the world. Why do ye adorn yourselves with that which hath no life, and yet suffer the hungry, and the needy, and the naked, and the sick, and the afflicted to pass by you, and notice them not? Yea, why do ye build up your secret abominations to get gain, and cause that widows should mourn before the Lord, and also orphans to mourn before the Lord, and also the blood of their fathers and their husbands to cry unto the Lord from the ground, for vengeance upon your heads? Behold the sword of vengeance hangeth over you; and the time soon cometh that he avengeth the blood of the saints upon you, for he will not suffer their cries any longer."—Mormon 4: 2–4.

These predictions clearly portray (1) the condition of the world for the past fifty years, and (2) point clearly to the terrible apostasy in the church of the saints, and (3) to the important fact that said apostasy would be caused by the ministry, of whom it says, "O ye pollutions, ye hypocrites, ye teachers, who sell yourselves for that which will canker, why have you polluted the holy church of God." "Yea, why do ye build up your *secret abominations* to get gain, and cause that widows should mourn before the Lord, and also orphans to mourn before the Lord; and also the blood of their fathers and their husbands to cry unto the Lord from the ground for vengeance upon your heads. Behold, the sword of vengeance hangeth over you," &c. These prophecies are plain, and full; and they are having most precise and literal fulfillment. Surely, these prophecies were inspired of God, for no man, learned or unlearned, could have conjectured so many strange and unlikely events—events so contrary to what was fondly expected in the times at, and before the coming forth of the Book of Mormon. The moral doctrines of the book are fully equal to any ever given to man. No purer system can be conceived of. It embraces all the moral excellencies of the New Testament, whilst it is quite free from teachings of such questionable morality as are found in 1 Cor. 7 chapter; Rom. 7:17, 25; 3:7; 1 Cor. 6: 12, etc., etc., as found in the common version.

Its theology is strictly Biblical, and Christian; its religious rites and ceremonies are identical with those of the New Testament, as also its church polity and organization, though they are more clearly defined, and promulgated, and with greater emphasis.

Its style is plain, and ancient; its language is simple, comprehensive, and utterly free from cultured finish, scholarly taste, or learned structure and order.

That any one of judgment, on reading the book, could for one moment think that Rev. Mr. Spaulding, a man of poetic nature, romantic tastes, and high scholastic attainments, ever wrote the book, or even one page of it, is more than we can believe. Had he, or any man of finished education written the book, their scholarly attainments would have been manifest in the style, language, and arragement of the book.

Further; if Mr. Spaulding, a Congregational (or Presbyterian) minister wrote the book, he would have filled it with his doctrine instead of advocating in it such doctrines as are found in the book, many of which are in no sense Congregational, but rather un-Congregational. Every chapter, and every paragraph, in the book, utterly refutes the idea that a cultivated minister, Protestant or Catholic, ever wrote a page of the book. Such an idea is too palpably false to need a lengthy refutation. And as for the inexperienced and uneducated youth, Joseph Smith's writing or dictating the book, as is rather claimed by Mr. Sheldon, none but those possessed of prejudice and a partisan spirit, or those wanting fair common sense, could endorse such an idea. That Joseph Smith, without the inspiration of God, could write that book, abounding as it does in the most accurate items of history, declaring improbable historical facts, facts which have since been fully attested by the antiquarian and the geologist; disseminating a system of morals and religion that challenges the criticism, and that is worthy of the admiration of the race; and publishing a series of prophecies the most important and startling, many of which are being fulfilled under our own observation,—that he could do such a work, under such conditions, it would be for more difficult to believe, than to believe what he claims, viz., the guidance and inspiration of God.

Mr. S. avers that "the Book of Mormon makes the finder and translator of that book a Gentile." This is another of that large class of false assumptions we have had to deal with all the way through this work. That "the finder and translator" of the Book of Mormon was a citizen of a Gentile nation, and in that sense was a Gentile, we freely admit; but that he was of Gentile lineage, the thing claimed by Mr. S., we deny. Paul was a Roman citizen, Acts 22:27, and yet a Jew by lineage, v. 3. The "Parthians, and Medes, and Elamites," of Acts 2:9, were by lineage Jews, no doubt, and only *citizens* of those nations, v. 5. So Joseph Smith was a Gentile in his citizenship, though an Israelite by lineage, as is claimed by the Book of Mormon, 2 Nephi 2:2, 3.

Mr. S. says:

"It is insisted that the true church is a miracle-working church—and that such are the people called Mormons. Both the Josephites and the Brighamites use this argument to outsiders."

Whilst it is insisted by the "Josephites" that the church of Christ should enjoy miraculous powers and blessings, it is also true that the Utah Mormons, in Utah, are not only barren of these divine favors, but that they there in Utah teach that they are no longer needed, they having "the living oracles" to edify and perfect them. It is unquestionably true that ministers belonging to the Utah organization, who received their priesthood in a regular line from Joseph and Oliver, did, so long as they faithfully preached the gospel and ministered in righteousness, possess and enjoy the Spirit of God, and at times in great power, and very notably before the doctrines of polygamy, Adam-God, and corrupt tithing were thrust upon, and forced into, the church.

Mr. S., in order to throw discredit upon the claim of the Saints that the same kind of church organization is needed now in the perfect Church of Christ as was had in the times of the Apostles, says:

"In the true church order, God has set apostles, it is true, but simply as material for the foundation, and not as rafters to the building.

Very well, but is it not essential that the church should always have the same kind of a foundation? And when one part of the foundation of the church is removed by death or apostasy, is it not essential that the want created by such removal should be supplied? If not, why was Matthias, the thirteenth apostle in number, chosen to fill the place of Judas? and why were "the apostles, Barnabas and Paul," (Acts 14:14), chosen of the Holy Ghost, and ordained by the ministry? (Acts 13:1-4), and why did the church at Ephesus, ninety-six years after Christ, willingly consent to try them who said they were apostles? (Rev. 2:2). Paul, in speaking of the church, says Christ "gave some, apostles; and some, prophets; and some, evangelists; and some, pastors and teachers."—Eph. 4:11. Now there is just as much authority for discarding the evangelists, and pastors and teachers, as for discarding the others. Paul says the officers, *all of them*, were given for the "perfecting of the Saints, for the work of the ministry, for the edifying [building up] of the body of Christ."—Eph. 4:12. And he tells us how long the Lord intended them to continue in this church:—

"Till we all come in [into] the unity of the faith, and of the knowledge of the Son of God, unto a perfect man, unto the measure of the stature of the fullness of Christ."—Eph. 4:13.

And he tells us *why* these officers were given:—

"That we henceforth be no more children, tossed to and fro, and carried about by every wind of doctrine, by the sleight of men, and cunning craftiness, whereby they lie in wait to deceive."—Eph. 4:14.

No one questions but that evangelists, pastors, and teachers, should now be in the church, yet there is more reason for setting them aside as unnecessary, than for setting aside apostles and prophets, for the latter are the most important.

Again, Paul, after describing the gifts and administrations of "the one Spirit," proceeds to say to the Church:

"Now ye are the body of Christ, and members in particular. And God hath set some in the church, first apostles, secondarily prophets, thirdly teachers, after that miracles, then gifts of healings, helps, governments, diversities of tongues."—1 Cor. 12:27, 28.

Here the Church of Christ is compared to the body of man, united, compacted, and vitally connected together in all its parts. Of this another wisely remarks:

"If his illustrations be worth anything, then a church which has not for its members persons possessed of all these varied gifts, is no more a [perfect] Church of Christ than a body is a human body without its members. A Christian, living church must have members qualified and endowed from the Spirit, with all these gifts, or it is destitute of its members. They are no more living, real members than a wooden leg, or an artificial hand, or a glass eye is a member of the human body. A church must have its spiritual members, living and complete, or it is no body of Christ."

CHAPTER IX.

We now propose to consider the direct question, Was Joseph Smith a prophet of God?

And before we proceed with the main thread of our argument, and the chief lines of our proof, we pause to briefly notice what Mr. S. urges as a clear proof that, if Joseph was a prophet at all, then he was a false prophet. Mr. S. says:

> "If Joseph really introduced polygamy, it is another proof to Josephites that he is a false prophet."

Mr. S. should not stop here, but slash away at the prophetic and apostolic claims of others on similar grounds. He should tell us that, if Noah got intoxicated on wine, then he was a false prophet; and that if Abraham and Jacob practiced polygamy, then they were false prophets; and that if Moses killed an Egyptian and hid him in the sand, and if Aaron turned to idolatry while Moses was in the mount, then they were false prophets; and if Samuel hewed Agag, the prisoner, to pieces; and if David murdered Uriah and committed adultery with Bathshebah, and if Gideon went into polygamy and idolatry, then they were false prophets; and, finally, that if Peter cursed and swore, and denied Christ, and dissembled, then he was a false apostle, and was never an apostle of Christ. O consistency! thy name is not Sheldon!

In the first place, we know not whether Joseph the Seer did or did not practice and teach polygamy. If he did either, it was done very secretly, and it was done against the law and order of the Church, and against the teachings and protests of himself and Hyrum up to as late as the Spring of 1844.

Many good men of times gone by have gone into polygamy and kindred evils, and yet it did not prove that they were never the servants of God. Mr. S. tells us that "Mrs. Young, No. 19, mentions a plural marriage performed by Joseph himself." Mrs. Young is not a competent witness in this case, as she was not born until near the time of Joseph's death. All she could know of the case would be simply by rumor. And when one so incompetent makes charges of such a grave character their evidence should be treated as of no great or certain value. Besides this, "Mrs. Young, No. 19," has in other ways shown herself an utterly unsafe witness, when she publishes that Joseph claimed to be a new Messiah! And when she publishes that Joseph counselled a man at Nauvoo to go down the river to a Gentile saw mill and steal a lot of black walnut lumber for coffins! And that the man went and did as counselled, and rafted the lumber up the river to the city of the Saints! Mr. S., can't you see how easy this thing was done?—can't you see the man stealing that lumber, and making that raft, and floating it *up over the rapids*, against a current running from four to eight miles per hour, and no one to see or hear this lumber thief till he safely lands his booty in the city? Of course you can see it, for "No. 19" is just your kind of a witness; her testimony is of the same piece with that you are using to prove Joseph a false prophet and the Book of Mormon untrue; and of course you can see the "eternal fitness" of her testimony, and accept it for diamond truth! But you must pardon others if they don't see quite so easily as you do.

Joseph Smith; was he a prophet of God? Popular opinion answers no; and if we were to judge of the divinity of Jesus Christ, or any of the ancient prophets, by the same rule, it would give us the same result; for not one-fifth part of the human family now even profess to believe Christianity.

Popular opinion is not the rule of evidence by which to determine the truth or falsity of any fact or principle. The rankest errors in religion, in philosophy, and in science, have been highly popular in their time. *Known truth* is the touch-stone by which to try everything claiming to be true or divine.

All true principles harmonize. The truths of philosophy, of the sciences, of history, and of divine religion and revelation, do not, and cannot conflict. They will ever, when rightly understood, be found to perfectly agree.

We test the divinity of the mission of Moses and the prophets by comparing their teachings with known truths. The grandest principles connected with geology, astronomy, chemistry, and physiology, are outlined in their teachings. The facts of written history, and of universal tradition, and of history as lately discovered chiselled on the stony walls of ancient Egyptian and Assyrian cities, and their crumbling tombs and monuments are also found in their writings. All these are witnesses for Moses and the prophets. But the strongest external evidence that can be had,—evidence that should fully satisfy every one,—is the exact agreement between the predictions of these men, and the facts of subsequent history. They predict, with a "Thus saith the Lord," that certain events will transpire,—events which human sagacity could not foresee,—and history, the faithful chronicler of events as they occur, testifies that the events predicted *did* transpire.

True prophecy was always regarded by God's people as one of the crowning evidences of divinity; and it was so taught by Jesus and the prophets, as may be seen by Isaiah 41:21–23; Ezek. 33:33; John 13:19, etc.

We read that the early Christians vanquished their opponents successfully by showing the fulfillment of the predictions of Moses and the prophets, and especially of Jesus and the apostles.

We propose to discuss the prophetic character and mission of Joseph Smith, in the light of historical facts, mainly, if not entirely, as compared with his prophecies.

Joseph, when a boy aged seventeen years, began to know his marvelous and wonderful mission. This was as early as 1823. At that time, and from that time on, the chief part of Christendom was solacing itself with the thought that the world was rapidly improving in morals and religion. Many thought that the millennium would soon be ushered in through the joint efforts of the pulpit, the press, and missionary labors. And it was under the inspiration of this idea, no doubt, that the "World's Peace Congresses" were projected. In the midst of these things, and in opposition to these sentiments, Joseph pronounced the "Thus saith the Lord," and predicted the rise and rapid spread of social, political and spiritual corruption. He declared that iniquity would increase and abound, and that judgment would rapidly multiply among the wicked; that there would be great "divisions" among the people; that there would be great contentions, strifes and wars; that there would be unusual tempests, earthquakes, plagues, pestilences and famines; that there would be terribly destructive fires; that the sea would be greatly troubled; and that these things would continue to occur till the glorious appearing of the Lord Jesus, which, he said, was near at hand.

In short, he predicted the very opposite of what was taught by the worldly-wise and prudent, and what was fondly believed by the masses. In May, 1829, he predicted that the church he was about to found and organize, would become "a great and marvelous work among the children of men."—D. & C. 11:1. Such is its history already, though it has but fairly begun its work. In March of the same year he predicted the coming of the cholera "scourge;" and that it would continue its ravages among the nations, from time to time, till the earth became "empty."—D. & C. 4:3. The first case cholera in Western Europe occurred in 1831; in Great Britain in 1832; and in North America, in the summer of the same year; though it had existed in some parts of Asia for many years before this. The most eminent physicians pronounce it a "dreadful scourge," and state that its "essential character, and true origin are yet entirely unknown."

He predicted that "the weak and simple" would proclaim the fullness of the gospel "unto the ends of the world, and before kings and rulers."—D. & C. 1:4. And an unlettered and inexperienced ministry has been fulfilling this since 1830.

In 1831 he predicted that the time was near "when peace shall be taken from the earth, and the devil shall have power over his own dominion; and also the Lord shall have power over his Saints, and shall reign in their midst, and shall come down in judgment on Idumea, or the world."—D. & C. 1:6. Here is predicted the marked development of Satanic influence and working; its prevalence and power in contradistinction to the power of God. The last twenty-six years have witnessed the fulfillment of this prediction in a most wonderful degree, as the reader must be aware, at least so far as relates to the doings of those "spirit manifestations," so utterly opposed to Bible Christianity.

In March, 1831, he prophesied that soon there would

"Be heard of wars and rumors of wars, and the whole earth shall be in commotion, and men's hearts shall fail them, and they shall say that Christ delayeth his coming until the end of the earth. And the love of men shall wax cold, and iniquity shall abound; * * * and there shall be earthquakes, also, in divers places, and many desolations; yet men will harden their hearts against me, [Christ], and they will take up the sword one against another, and they will kill one another. * * * And it shall come to pass that he that feareth me, [Christ], shall be looking forth for the great day of the Lord to come, even for the signs of the coming of the Son of Man; and they shall see signs and wonders, for they shall be shown forth in the heavens above, and in the earth beneath; and they shall behold blood, and fire, and vapors of smoke; and before the day of the Lord shall come, the sun shall be darkened, and the moon be turned into blood, and stars fall from heaven; and the remnant [Jews] shall be gathered unto this place, [Jerusalem], and then they shall look for me, and behold I will come; and they shall see me in the clouds of heaven, clothed with power and great glory, with all the holy angels, and he that watches not for me shall be cut off."—D. & C. 45:4, 6.

Many of the items in the foregoing prophecies have been fulfilled, or are in process of fulfillment, while some remain to be fulfilled at no distant day. In December, 1832, he prophesied to the Elders as follows:

"And, after your testimony, cometh wrath and indignation upon the people; for after your testimony cometh the testimony of earthquakes, that shall cause groanings in the midst of her, and men shall fall upon the ground and shall not be able to stand. And also cometh the voice of thunderings, and the voice of lightnings, and the voice of tempests, and *the voice of the waves of the sea heaving themselves beyond their bounds.* And all things shall be in commotion; and surely men's hearts shall fail them; for fear shall come upon all people."—D. & C. 85:25.

Within the past twelve years "earthquakes" have been more frequent, wide-spread, and terrible; "thunderings" have been more common and frightful; "lightnings" have been more fearful, terrific, and disastrous; "tempests," tornadoes, cyclones, and whirlwinds, have been more prevalent and destructive than ever known before in the same length of time. These are facts beyond successful question.

In October, 1864, in India, the waves of the sea were driven by a *cyclone* inland, and many thousands of lives and many millions of property were destroyed. In November, 1876, in the same region, a *cyclone* drove the waters of the sea over one of the largest and most populous islands, destroying 257,000 human lives, with an immense amount of property. In 1867, at the Island of St. Thomas, the waves rose sixty or seventy feet higher than common, and "heaved themselves beyond their bounds," carrying upon their crests a United States war steamer, and leaving it high and dry on land. In 1868, I think in June, at the Sandwich Islands, the waves rose fifty to sixty feet higher than was their wont, and "heaved themselves beyond their bounds," washing away a number of the little coast towns, destroying life and property. In August of the same year occurred "the great tidal wave" which beat along the Pacific coast from the bay of San Francisco on the north, to near Cape Horn on the south. At the bay of Valparaiso, and other contiguous sea ports, the waves rose fifty to seventy feet higher than usual, tearing the shipping loose from its anchorage in many places, and

bearing the largest vessels in upon the dry land, destroying a great
many lives and millions of dollars worth of property. By what
means could Joseph predict these numerous and remarkable events
so clearly? Only by the Spirit that foresees and foreknows!—the
Spirit of the living God!

In the same prophecy he also tells us that "all things shall be in
commotion." How true we find this to-day! Every department of
society, political, social, commercial, scientific, and religious, is greatly agitated—is in great commotion. This is true of America, of
Europe, of Asia, of Africa,—of every place. The humblest peasant,
and the mightiest prince; the Pope with his triple crown, and the
cloistered monk; high church-men and low church-men; Pagan,
Parsee, Christian, and Jew,—all partake of this portentous spirit of
restlessness,—this ceaseless commotion. And the elements, too, are
unusually agitated, in all parts of the earth; and it is no wonder
that "men's hearts fail them," and that "fear" has come, and is coming, "upon all people."

On the 25th of December, 1832, Joseph Smith received a revelation foreshowing the desolating wars and fearful judgments of the
latter days. In this revelation is foretold the war of the late rebellion through which our nation passed from 1860 to 1866, which resulted in the death of 600,000 persons, and in crippling and disabling by disease 400,000 more. The revelation was first printed at
Liverpool, in England, in 1851, in a pamphlet entitled "The Pearl
of Great Price," though many of the Saints had known of it from
1832. Thousands of copies of this work are still in existence, in
the hands of the Saints and others. It was published in many languages, and in various other works, at different times *before* the rebellion took place, and among them the "True Latter Day Saints
Herald," "The Seer," and "The Compendium." It is also published in Beadle's work against the Mormons, issued in 1870. It reads
as follows:

"Verily, thus saith the Lord, concerning the wars that will shortly come to
pass, beginning at the rebellion of South Carolina, which will eventually terminate in the death and misery of many souls. The days will come that war
will be poured out upon all nations, beginning at that place; for behold the
Southern States shall be divided against the Northern States, and the Southern
States will call on other nations, even the nation of Great Britain, as it is called,
and they shall also call upon other nations, in order to defend themselves against
other nations: and thus shall war be poured out upon all nations. And it shall
come to pass, after many days, slaves shall rise up against their masters, who

shall be marshaled and disciplined for war, And it shall come to pass also, that the remnants who are left of the land shall marshal themselves, and shall become exceeding angry, and shall vex the Gentiles with a sore vexation; and thus, with the sword, and by bloodshed, the inhabitants of the earth shall mourn: and with famine, and plague, and earthquakes, and the thunder of heaven, and the fierce and vivid lightnings also, shall the inhabitants of the earth be made to feel the wrath and indignation and chastening hand of an Almighty God, until the consumption decreed hath made a full end of all nations, that the cry of the Saints, and the blood of the Saints, shall cease to come up into the ears of the Lord of Sabaoth, from the earth, to be avenged of their enemies. Wherefore, stand ye in holy places, and be not moved, until the day of the Lord come: for behold it cometh quickly, saith the Lord. Amen."

This is one of the most remarkables prophecies of this or any other age. It is lengthy, definite, precise, full of eminent points, without "ifs," or "buts," and was the very opposite of the popular ideas of the times in which it was given, and in which it was first published.

Some claim that it has been gotten up *since* the rebellion to suit the events transpiring during that time. They see that it contains a true and definite summary of the history made during that period, yet they dislike to believe that Joseph Smith uttered the prophecy. Such persons usually laud and glorify the prophets of the long-ago, but they will neither hear, investigate the claims of, nor respect modern prophets. They are of that class who revere the seers of the misty past who lived, and taught, and suffered two thousand or five thousand years before them,—but God, they conclude, will hold no direct communication with man in this age of the world, and a claim that he may, and does, should be scoffed at as an imposture.

As we have shown, there is an abundance of documentary evidence of the genuineness of the revelation; at least to show that it was in existence—in print—as early as 1851, nine years before the rebellion. Mr. Beadle, in his work against the Mormons, states that he copied it out of "The Seer," a work published by O. Pratt, in Washington, D. C., in 1853, seven years before the rebellion. And Mr. John Hyde, who wrote a work against the Mormons, entitled "Mormonism," which was issued by Fetridge & Co., of New York City, in 1857, cites on page 174, this same revelation, and he did it in order to prove that Joseph was a *false prophet.* He verily thought within himself, no doubt, that such a series of wars and calamities as Joseph Smith had predicted could never occur; and he probably felt fully justified in denouncing the prophecy as false. Nor was he alone in the thought that such things could never occur.

It was the universal sentiment with all people, except well-informed Latter Day Saints. They knew of the prophecy and confidently looked for its fulfillment.

Such an event as the rebellion of the Southern States was improbable—highly improbable at that time—as were many, if not all the other events predicted in the prophecy. The prophecy states what was very improbable, that "the Southern States shall be divided against the Northern States." And yet every Southern State *was* arrayed against the Northern States in the rebellion. The prophecy said the war would *begin* at the rebellion of South Carolina. South Carolina began the rebellion, December 20th, 1860; and on the 12th of the following March, war actually began by the Confederacy, her troops firing upon, and capturing Fort Sumpter.

The Southern States *did* "call on other nations,"—upon Great Britain and France, and this, too, in order to "defend themselves [diplomatically] against other nations;" for, by this time, they had assumed the *defensive*, as the revelation teaches they finally would do. They sought to be recognized by the nations as belligerents, and thus secure themselves against the influence and co-operation of other nations in favor of the Northern States; and further, to obtain material aid in order to defend themselves against the invading armies of the Northern States.

"And thus war shall be poured out upon all nations;" that is, *beginning* with our national rebellion, war would go forth, and finally occur among *all nations*. It is a prominent fact, that, since the beginning of the rebellion, war has been unusually prevalent, widespread, and sanguinary.

Taking advantage of our national troubles, Louis Napoleon, Emperor of France, and Francis Joseph, Emperor of Austria, sought, by a bloody war, to establish an empire in Mexico, and to place Maximillian upon its throne, but they failed in the attempt.

South America, Central America, France, Italy, Austria, Denmark, Spain, Cuba, Holland, Russia, Germany, Greece, Turkey, Egypt, Algeria, China, Japan, Corea, with many districts in Asia and Africa, have been visited with the war-fiend since the rebellion of South Carolina in 1860.

In these wars millions of lives have been lost and oceans of treasure expended; but the end is not yet. The spirit of war seems rife in every land and among all nations. Russia, the "Gog" of Ezekiel 38th chapter, is just now entering upon a war with Turkey, of huge dimensions, and one likely to embroil all Europe, and Asia, and northern Africa; and one that will materially change the boundaries of the nations, and go far to prepare the way for the restoration of Israel and Judah.

The war equipments of the nations, by land and sea, are far more extensive and highly perfected, than ever before known. For instance, the forces of Austria amount at present to 856,980 men. Russia has augmented her armies to 1,519,810 men. The aggregate military strength of Italy is 605,200. The German empire can summon to the field 1,261,160 men. The French army is 977,660 strong. The land-forces alone of Great Britain number 478,820 men; besides which her navy is the largest in the world. The Swedish army numbers about 274,510. The number of soldiers now at the disposal of all the European governments amount to between 6,000,000 and 7,000,000, an increase of over one-third in number since 1859. And still they are arming. The trust of nations to-day is mainly in their strength, their wealth, their wisdom, and their military prowess, rather than in truth and righteousness before God, and with man.

"After many days, slaves shall rise up against their masters, who shall be marshaled and disciplined for war." Not less than 200,000 of the blacks were enrolled in the armies of the North; and they were, as the prophecy indicates, "marshaled and disciplined," by white officers; and their arms were directed against their former masters.

These are facts so patent that comment is not needed.

And "the remnants who are left of the land, [the Indians], will marshal themselves, and shall become exceeding angry, and shall vex the Gentiles with a sore vexation." This is precisely what has been done. For the Indians *did* "marshal themselves" against the whites as early as August, 1862, and they have been waging war against them from time to time until the present. The massacre in Minnesota, which took place August, 1862, was a terribly cruel and heart-rending affair. 2,000 persons were barbarously slaughtered in a few hours. Nameless outrages were perpetrated; and the losses sustained, pecuniarily, by the government and by individuals, amounted to over $2,500,000:

"From the landing of the Pilgrim Fathers on the rock-bound coast of New England, in the winter of 1620, until their descendants had passed the center of the continent, and reached the lovely plains of Minnesota, no exhibition of

Indian character had so afflicted and appalled the soul of humanity, as the fearful and deliberate massacre perpetrated by them in August, 1862. * * The blow fell like a storm of thunderbolts from the clear, bright heavens. The storm of fierce, savage murder, in its most horrid and frightful forms, rolled on. Day passed and night came, until the sad catalogue reached the fearful number of *two thousand* human victims, from the gray-haired sire to the helpless infant of a day, who lay mangled and dead on the ensanguined field. * * In two days the whole work of murder was done, with here and there exceptional cases in different settlements. And, during these two days, a population of *thirty thousand*, scattered over some eight counties, on the western borders of the State, on foot, on horseback, with teams of oxen and horses, under the momentum of the panic thus created, were rushing wildly and frantically over the prairies to places of safety."—*Indian Massacres.*

The Indians "marshaled themselves," as foreshown in the prophecy,—no whites having a hand in that matter. The bad treatment which they had received from the whites—the Indian agents and traders in particular—had much to do in *causing* these outrages,—it made them "exceeding angry,"—yet, as we have said before, the whites had nothing to do in *marshaling* them, or directing them in their sanguinary work.

These Indian wars are *costly* as well as cruel; and hence, in more ways than one, are they "a sore vexation" to our tax-burdened nation. It has been reported that for every Indian captured and killed during some of the Indian wars since 1862, it has cost the whites the lives of nine white men, and $5,000,000 in money. This may be a slight exaggeration, yet it is probably not far from the truth. The enormous expense, with the loss of human life, and the various perplexities connected with these wars, and the whole Indian question, are sources of "sore vexation" to the whites, and from which there are no prospects of speedy and permanent relief.

As for the terrors of "famine and plague" predicted, they have been so widespread and destructive since 1860 that the bare mention of them ought to satisfy the reader of the truthfulness of this item of the prophecy. In India alone there has been numerous famines with terrible loss of life since 1860, prominent among them that which occurred in 1866, in which thousands perished of starvation weekly. The official report showed that there were a million of deaths in all. And famine is raging in India now.

In 1867 and 1868 there was a great lack of food supplies in the Southern States; and in England and France hundreds of thousands were in a state of semi-starvation. Germany and Eastern Prussia were in a similar condition, while in Russia both pestilence and famine raged terribly. In Finland, in Algeirs, in Tunis, and in other localities in Europe and Asia, it was no better. "Fully 100,000 Arabs have fallen victims within the last six months," wrote the Archbishop of Algiers. Persia has been nearly *annihilated* of late by famine and pestilence. Of the year 1871, the *Chicago Tribune*, November 15th, 1871, says:

"War, famine, pestilence, fire, wind and water, and ice, have been let loose and have done their worst, and with such appalling results, and with such remarkable phenomena accompanying them, that it is not to be wondered at, men have sometimes thought the end of the world had come."

Want of space forbids our itemizing at any length in regard to the calamities predicted; suffice it to say, that in nearly all parts of the world "famine and plague have sorely afflicted the sons of men, and sent many millions to an untimely grave."

The latter part of the prophecy states that the "chastening hand of an Almighty God," through the judgments mentioned in the prophecy, will be upon the nations until God "hath made a full end of all nations; that the *cry of the Saints, and of the* BLOOD *of the Saints*, shall cease to come up into the ears of the Lord of Sabaoth to be avenged of their enemies." "The cry of the Saints," and the "blood of the Saints" here mentioned, pointed to their coming persecutions, barbarously cruel, fiendish, and bloody, as they proved to be. The first very serious persecution of the Saints began at Independence, Missouri, July 20th, 1833. An armed mob was organized under the leadership of George Simpson, and was either countenanced or abetted by many ministers of religion and government officials.

The printing press of the Church was principally destroyed, including book-work, furniture, apparatus, and type, also the printing office, with the dwelling house of the editor. *The Evening and Morning Star*, and the *Upper Missouri Advertizer*, the one a monthly and the other a weekly paper, were forcibly stopped, and their further publication forbidden.

A number were whipped, tarred and feathered, among them Edward Partridge and —— Allen, late of Council Bluffs. Some received a pelting with rocks and a beating with guns and sticks Ten houses were partly demolished, and standing grain in some places destroyed; but, worst of all, one, a Bro. Barber, was killed, and some others seriously wounded.

The grounds upon which this persecution began, were, to use the language of those connected with it, as seen in the published proceedings, printed in *The Western Monitor*, August 2d, 1833, for the mobbers "to rid themselves of the sect of fanatics, called Mormons;" "this singular sect of pretended Christians;" "they now number 1200 souls in this [Jackson] county." "Elevated, as they mostly are, but little above the condition of our blacks, either in regard to property or education, they have become a subject of much anxiety on that part, serious and well grounded complaints having been already made of their corrupting influence on our slaves." "We are daily told, and not by the ignorant alone, but by all classes of them, that we (the Gentiles) of this county, are to be cut off, and our lands appropriated by them for inheritances. Whether this is to be accomplished by the hand of the destroying angel, the judgments of God, or the arm of power, they are not fully agreed among themselves." "They openly blaspheme the most high God, and cast contempt on his holy religion, by pretending to receive revelations direct from heaven; by pretending to speak unknown tongues by direct inspiration; and by divers pretences derogatory to God and religion, and to the utter subversion of human reason." "What would be the fate of our lives and property in the hands of jurors and witnesses, who do not blush to declare, and would not upon any occasion hesitate to swear, that they have wrought miracles, and have been the subjects of miraculous and supernatural cures, and have conversed with God and his angels, and possess and exercise the gifts of divination, and of unknown tongues, and fired with the prospect of obtaining inheritances without money and without price—may be better imagined than described." "One of the means resorted to by them in order to drive us to emigrate, is an indirect invitation to the free brethren of color in Illinois, to come up like the rest, to the land of Zion. True, they said this was not intended to invite, but to prevent their emigration; but this weak attempt to quiet our apprehension, is but a poor compliment to our understandings."

Here, dear reader, are the main charges upon which over 1200 souls were, with violence, sorely persecuted and driven out of Jackson county, Missouri, the persecutors themselves being the witnesses.

From July 20th, when the violent persecutions began, till November of the same year, the Saints had but little rest from their enemies, though they sought patiently for that protection which was assured by the laws of Missouri, and of our nation, but they sought in vain.

While the Saints were fleeing from their merciless persecutors into Clay and adjoining counties, the Lord displayed his glory in the heavens, to the comfort and delight of his smitten and afflicted people. The heavens, on the night of the 12th of November, were made grandly beautiful by the "falling stars,"—a sign to the Saints that the coming of Christ is near:

"In Zion [Missouri] all heaven seemed enwrapped in splendid fire-works, as if every star in the broad expanse had been suddenly hurled from its course, and sent lawless through the wilds of ether. * * * Beautiful and terrific as was the scenery, which might be compared to the falling figs, or fruit, when the tree is shaken by a mighty wind, yet it will not fully compare with the time when the sun shall become black like sackcloth of hair, the moon like blood, and the stars fall to the earth."—*Joseph Smith.*

Most of those driven from Jackson county went to Clay county, where they were received with some degree of kindness. The Saints continued to gather into Missouri, chiefly into Clay, Ray, Davies, and Caldwell counties, until 1837, when persecution again stretched forth her merciless and bloody hand against them, and they were mobbed, robbed, and finally, in the late fall of 1838, driven out of the State into Illinois, under the exterminating orders of Gov. Lilburn W. Boggs. The Church in Missouri numbered at this time 12,000 or more. In this persecution, well nigh every barbarity was practiced that brutal lust or fiendish cruelty could suggest. Property was stolen and burned; persons beaten and maimed; others wounded nigh unto death, and many killed. An infirm old revolutionary soldier, when pleading for mercy, and telling of his services as a soldier in procuring our dearly-bought liberties, was hacked to death with a corn cutter; a little innocent lad, who, when hunted like a beast, had taken refuge in a blacksmith shop at Haun's Mills, was shot to death through the head, in cool blood; women were ravished, and an amount of exposure and suffering forced upon many that resulted in death, or in permanently impairing their health and usefulness.

Surely "the *cry* of the Saints, and of the *blood* of the Saints," did now, from seven months to five years after the prophecy was uttered, ascend up into the ears of the Lord of Sabaoth.

Professor Turner, sometime of Illinois College, an open and bitter opponent of the Church of the Latter Day Saints, in writing of the conduct of Missouri towards the Mormons, says:

"Who began the quarrel? Was it the Mormons? Is it not notorious, on the contrary, that they were hunted like wild beasts, from county to county, before they made any desperate resistance? Did they ever, as a body, refuse obedience to the laws, when called upon to do so, until driven to desparation by repeated threats and assaults from the mob? Did the State ever make one decent effort to defend them as fellow citizens in their rights, or to redress their wrongs? Let the conduct of its govenors, attorneys, and the fate of their final petitions answer. Have any who plundered and openly massacred the Mormons ever been brought to the punishment due to their crimes? Let the boasting murderers of begging and helpless infancy answer. Has the state ever remunerated, even those known to be innocent, for the loss of either their property or their arms? Did either the pulpit or the press throughout the State raise a note of remonstrance or alarm? Let the clergymen who abetted, and the editors who encouraged the mob answer."

Thus speaks one of our bitterest, yet comparatively honorable opponents.

Nor did persecution stop even here. Its fires were again kindled in Illinois, in Hancock county and vicinity in 1844 to 1846, resulting in terrible suffering and great loss of life.

The persecutions of 1838, in Missouri, were clearly set forth in a prophecy given through Joseph Smith, at Kirtland, Ohio, July 23d, 1837, one year and more before the persecution occurred. See Doctrine and Covenants 105:9. It reads:

"Verily, verily, I say unto you, darkness covereth the earth, and gross darkness the minds of the people, and all flesh has become corrupt before my face. Behold, vengeance cometh speedily upon the inhabitants of the earth—a day of wrath, a day of burning, a day of desolation, of weeping, of mourning, of lamentation—and as a whirlwind it shall come upon all the face of the earth, saith the Lord. And upon my house [the church] shall it begin, and from my house shall it go forth, saith the Lord."

The "wrath," the "burning," the "desolation," the "weeping," the "mourning," and the "lamentation" here predicted, which are to go forth among all nations, *did* come upon the Church suddenly, "as a whirlwind," with all its fearful and terrible destructiveness. No one, unless inspired of God, could have foretold, with such precision and clearness, the bitter persecutions suffered by the Saints in Missouri.

The persecutions and the scattering of the Saints from Nauvoo, were foretold by Joseph. His death, likewise, he himself foretold. On parting with his wife, at Nauvoo, when he went to Carthage jail, under promise of protection from Governor Thomas Ford, he told her he would never see his family again,—that his work was done, —that he was going to rest,—that the Church would be broken up and scattered, and instructed her to remain with the family at Nauvoo, or take them to Kirtland, Ohio. More than once, just prior to his death, he predicted that if Brigham Young should get the lead of the Church he would lead it to hell.

It would be the height of folly to say that these prophecies of Joseph, so numerous, so definite, and so unlikely to be fulfilled, were mere conjectures or guesses, like many made by human wisdom alone. That military genius, Napoleon, tried his skill in making predictions. He said, "In fifty years all Europe will be either Cossack or Republican." More than the "fifty years" have passed away, and the prediction is found false.

Vettius Vallens, a wise man of Rome, and a Pagan oracle, predicted that, "If it be true as historians say, that Romulus saw twelve vultures at the founding of Rome, that signifies that it should exist for twelve centuries." But, Rome, under its eight different forms of government, has existed for more than twenty-six centuries.

Shameful failure is the fate of *human predictions*, however wise their authors.

Joseph was assassinated in Carthage jail, Hancock county, Illinois, June 27th, 1844, at the age of thirty-eight years and six months, after a most eventful life, seventeen years of which were marked with great activities, great perplexities and numerous persecutions. Those who knew him best loved him most. He was misunderstood and misapprehended by the masses; blindly opposed by the pulpit and the press, in many instances; maligned and slandered by his enemies, and his sentiments perverted, misconstrued and misstated by those who should have been his truest friends.

His work was great in the foundations which he laid, rather than in the immediate results which he wrought out. The great truths of God, and the exalted principles of life and salvation given to the race through him, will live, and be earnestly cherished by the faithful and true, when the hoary errors, and the gilded and flimsy theories of uninspired men, will be remembered only with sorrow, and mentioned only with pity and contempt.

Joseph uttered many predictions concerning the spiritual manifestations with which the world is now being deluged and deceived. This he did long before Spiritualism was introduced. In May, 1831, while he was young in years, and limited in worldly wisdom, the Lord said through him to the Elders of the Church:

"Behold, verily I say unto you, that there are many spirits which are false spirits, which have gone forth in the earth, deceiving the world; and also Satan hath sought to deceive you, that he might everthrow you."—D. & C. 50:1.

In June, 1831, the following was revealed to the Elders through him:

"And again I will give you a pattern in all things, that ye may not be deceived; for Satan is abroad in the land, and he goeth forth deceiving the nations; wherefore he that prayeth, whose spirit is contrite, the same is acccepted of me, if he obey mine ordinances. He that speaketh, whose spirit is contrite, whose language is meek, and edifieth, the same is of God, if he obey mine ordinances. And again, he that trembleth under my power shall be made strong, and shall bring forth fruits of praise, and wisdom, according to [*i. e.*, in harmony with] the revelations and truths I have given you. And again, he that is overcome and bringeth not forth fruits, even according to this pattern, is not of me; wherefore by this pattern ye shall know the spirits in all cases under the whole heavens. And the days have come, according to men's faith it shall be done unto them."—D. & C. 52:4, 5.

A short time before this revelation was given a number of persons in the Church at Kirtland had been deceived and strangely handled by false spirits. Some were so far possessed by them as to lose all control of either mind or body. The physical manifestations were startling and peculiar; while those of a mental or spiritual character were such as to bewilder and mislead the unwary and unskillful. Joseph and Hyrum readily detected the arch enemy and proclaimed against him. Of this Joseph wrote in his Church History:

"On the 6th of June, the Elders from the various parts of the country where they were laboring came in, and the Conference, before appointed, convened in Kirtland, and the Lord displayed his power in a manner that could not be mistaken. The *man of sin* was revealed, and the authority of the Melchisedec priesthood was manifested, and conferred for the first time upon several of the Elders. It was clearly evident that the Lord gave us power in proportion to the work to be done, and strength according to the race set before us, and grace and help as our needs required."—*Times and Seasons*, vol. 5, page 416.

The origin, character, operations, and final state of these spirits, had been revealed to Joseph before this. In September, 1830, the Lord said of them:

"Behold, the devil was before Adam, for he rebelled against me, saying, Give me thine honor, which is my power; and also a third part of the hosts of heaven turned he away from me because of their agency; and they were thrust down, and thus became the devil and his angels; and behold, there is a place prepared for them from the beginning, which place is hell; and it must needs be that the devil should tempt the children of men, or they could not be agents unto themselves, for if they never should have bitter, they could not know the sweet."—D. & C. 28:10.

Of spirit manifestations Joseph wrote in A. D. 1839:

"We are to try the spirits and prove them, for it is often the case that men

make a mistake in regard to these things. God has so ordained that when he has communicated no vision is to be taken but what you see by the seeing of the eye, or what you hear by the hearing of the ear. When you see a vision, pray for the interpretation; if you get not this, shut it up; there must be certainty in this matter. An open vision will manifest that which is more important. Lying spirits are going forth in the earth. There will be great manifestations of spirits, both false and true. Being born again, comes by the Spirit of God through ordinances. An angel of God never has wings. Some will say that they have seen a spirit; that he offered them his hand, but they did not touch it. This is a lie. First, it is contrary to the plan of God; a spirit cannot come but in glory; [as Moses and Elias, Matt.]; an angel has flesh and bones; we see not their glory. The devil may appear as an angel of light. Ask God to reveal it; if it be of the devil he will flee from you; if of God, he will manifest himself, or make it manifest. We may come to Jesus and ask him; he will know all about it; if he comes to a little child he will adapt himself to the language and capacity of a little child. Every spirit, or vision, or singing, is not of God. The devil is an orator; he is powerful; he took our Savior on to a pinacle of the temple, and kept him in the wilderness for forty days. The gift of discerning of spirits will be given to the Presiding Elder. Pray for him that he may have this gift. Speak not in the gift of tongues without understanding it, or without interpretation. The devil can speak in tongues; the adversary will come with his work; he can tempt all classes; can speak in English or Dutch. Let no one speak in tongues unless he interpret, except by the consent of the one who is placed to preside; then he may discern or interpret, or another may."
—*Millennial Star* 17: 312.

By the foregoing we see that Joseph was thoroughly informed in regard to spirit manifestations; and that he foreknew, clearly, the going forth of lying spirits in the earth, and that there would "be great manifestations of spirit, both false and true."

Nothing short of the Spirit of God, by revelation and prophecy, could impart such facts and information, and so plainly make known the future. Bancroft

Having examined a few of the many fulfilled prophecies of Joseph Smith, we will add as further evidence of his prophetic character, that he organized the Church of Christ after the Apostolic pattern, given in 1 Corinthians 12:28, Ephesians 4:11; and restored the primitive doctrines and ordinances, as taught and practiced by the first Christian ministry, in all their divine power and simplicity, (Heb. 6:1–3; Acts 2:38; 8:18; 9:12; 19:6; 13:3; 1 Timothy 4:14; John 13:4, 5; 1 Cor. 11:23–31; James 5:14, 15; Mark 10:13–16). He also revived and renewed the same general promises (John 7:16, 17; Mark 16:15–18; Acts 2:38, 39; John 14: 26; 15:26; 16:7, 13; 1 Cor. 12 ch.; 1 John 2:27; 3:24; Luke 20:35, 36; John 5:28, 29; 1 Cor. 15:22, 23, 41–44; Phil. 3:20,

21; John 17:20-24; Rev. 20:4, 5, 6, 12, 13; 2 Pet. 3:13, 14; Matt. 5:5; Rev. 5:10). This he claimed to do in fulfillment of Rev. 14:6, 7; Mal. 4:5, 6; Isaiah 11:11, 12; 18:3; Luke 14:16-24; Matt. 20:6.

He brought forth by inspiration of God the record of Joseph, in fulfillment of Ezekiel 37:16, 17, 18, 19,—the "sealed book" of Isaiah 29:11, 12, 18,—the "truth" of God, hidden in the earth, predicted by David, Ps. 85:11, as we have demonstrated in the former pages of this work.

His was the usual fate of God's prophets—hated, persecuted, and destroyed by his enemies (Matt. 23:34; Acts 7:52); yet tenderly and passionately beloved by all those who knew him and who believed him to be a servant of God. When the murky clouds of prejudice, and the blinding mists of falsehood and superstition shall have passed away, the character and work of Joseph Smith will appear in honor, and millions will revere him as a martyr.

Joseph Smith, in his religious effort did not introduce "another gospel," nor "preach another Christ;" but he simply preached "him of whom Moses in the law and the prophets did write, Jesus of Nazareth;" and, under God, he restored the very gospel taught by the Saints of the first century after Christ, in fulfillment of Rev. 14:6, 7. He organized the church after the primitive pattern, and set in order the ordinances, rites, and ceremonies, as they were in the apostolic age. He proclaimed the same gifts of the Holy Ghost as were promised by Joel, 2:28, 29; by the Lord Jesus, Mark 16:17, 18; John 14:26; 15:26; 16:7, 8, 9, 10, 11; by Peter, Acts 2:38, 39, and Paul, 1 Cor. 12:1-31; 14:1-40, etc. He prophesied of men within and without the Church; of events that pertained to the Church in blessing and in cursing; of events to transpire in our own nation and among the nations of the earth—of wars, famines, pestilences, plagues, earthquakes, tempests, destructions and desolations; of the waves of the sea heaving themselves beyond their bounds; of the rapid increase of pride, of spiritual iniquity, and of all kinds of crime and wrong doing. He prophesied of "great changes in the times and in the seasons;" and of the great incoming of satanic power, and the rapid spread and general prevalence of demon-spirit power among the nations. He prophecied of the "temptations and great tribulation" and apostasy of the Twelve; and of B. Young, that "if he got the lead of the Church he would lead it to hell." He prophecied of the rebellion of the Southern States; of their calling on other nations for aid in defense; of the slaves being "marshaled and disciplined for war;" and of the Indians becoming exceeding angry, of their marshaling themselves and vexing the Gentiles with a sore vexation; and of the wars terminating "in the death and misery of many souls." He also prophesied of his own death, of the manner of it, and about the time it would occur, with many other things we have not time nor space to mention.

He translated, between September 22, 1827, and July, 1829, a period of nearly two years, the Book of Mormon, which abounds in historical statements relative to the two great and enlightened nations which once possessed North, and South, and Central America, and which speaks of their civilization and industries, and of the locality of the great centers of their skilled and cultivated populations; and these things, highly improbable when the young seer gave the Book of Mormon to the world, are now, for the last fifty years, being confirmed by scientific travelers, explorers, and antiquarians.

This same book abounds with prophecies touching Jew and Gentile, churches and nations, priests and people;—of Roman Catholic, Protestant, and Latter Day Saints—of their corruptions, their evils and their fate. It speaks of the rapid and favorable changes that would take place in the physical condition of the land of Judea soon after the coming forth of the Book of Mormon—that the land which was given by the oath of God to Abraham and to his seed forever, should be turned into "a fruitful field." It speaks of the rapid downfall of "the mother of harlots" soon after the coming forth of "the book," an event which has been transpiring since 1848, and in a striking manner since August 18th, 1870. It speaks also of the work of the Lord beginning at that time for the restoration of the literal seed of Israel to their own lands of promise, and of the favor and honor which the seed of Israel should receive at the hands of the Gentiles. It speaks of the fact that the ancient civilizations of America were built up by two separate and distinct peoples, one succeeding the other in dominion—a matter largely agitated by antiquarians and travelers of late, and now generally admitted—nations differing widely in their language and their architecture. It tells of the marvelous wealth of the land in gold and silver and all manner of mineral products, a matter of which little comparatively was known till long since the coming forth of the book. Its moral teachings and influence are unsurpassed in purity, while its doctrines, plainly expressed, and embraced in simple forms of speech, are the doctrines of the Holy Scriptures.

Besides translating the Book of Mormon, Mr. Smith revised, corrected, and translated the Old and New Testaments—or portions of them—restoring much that had been lost from the text, and removing from the text many things of a hurtful tendency which had been added by uninspired men. In this translation, in the first eleven chapters, is furnished the easy answer to the question now agitating the enlightened world, as to why, among all the leading ancient nations, among them the ancient Mexicans and Peruvians, and many of the Pagan nations of to-day, we find nearly all the leading religious ideas of the Old and New Testaments, though in a mutilated and corrupted form. It informs us that the creation, the fall of man, the scheme of redemption in all its details, the punishment of the wicked, the rewards of the righteous, and the glory of the redeemed, were all revealed and taught to man from Adam down to Noah, and from Noah to his posterity, thus reaching down to the tower of Babel and the confusion of languages. We can readily see, on reflection, how natural, how easy and certain it was that these wonderful and important ideas should flow out with all the streams of immigration from the Tower, to all parts of the world, and be perpetuated under variously corrupted forms as they have existed in the past, and as they exist to-day. And with this view of the matter, as furnished us by the Inspired Translation, (as also by the Book of Mormon and the revelations of Joseph), we can see why it is that Jesus Christ our Lord was, and is, and is to be, "the Desire of all nations" (Hag. 2:7). Every movement of the wheels of time— every important change among the nations or among religionists, every discovery in the heavens above or in the earth beneath, every hidden thing uncovered and every secret thing revealed, the revelations and miracle-wonders of "the spirits of devils," the revelations and testimony of God's Spirit to man, all bear witness, directly or remotely, to the important and cheering fact that God has spoken from the heavens in these latter days, and caused his "truth to spring out of the earth;" and that he called and inspired the youth,

Joseph Smith, as his prophet, seer, revelator, and translator, whom he honored in the founding and building up of his church and kingdom, preparatory to the glorious appearing of our Lord Jesus Christ, and the ushering in of the age of millennial glory. And to these facts tens of thousands of honest, rejoicing hearts can bear truthful testimony. Joseph Smith was a prophet of God, and every effort to disprove that fact only makes it the more apparent that he was.

INDEX.

Adam—Michael, an Angel 88
American Antiquities........................... 143, 153, 158
Apocrypha 83
Apostasy of Latter Day Saints....................... 171, 173
Baptism................... 47, 48, 50, 51, 80, 81, 133, 144
    "   For the Dead 145
    "   Object of..51, 81
    "   Of Ancient Date............................... 48
    "   Mode of....................................... 50
Bible and Book of Mormon Compared...................36, 128
Bible Defects in History 7, 27, 33, 86, 135
    "   Miracles *vs.* Those Now 141
    "   More Truth Than it Alone......................... 54
Book of Lehi... 77
Book of Mormon, Coming forth of 148, 150
    "   "   Historical Errors Possible................. 6
    "   "   Morals and Theology.....................171
    "   "   Not Found by a Gentile 173
    "   "   Prophecies of.......................165, 166
Christ's Appearing Before His Birth and After His Resurrection 18
    "   Birth, Place of 12
    "   "   Time of.................................8, 134

INDEX.

Christ's Crucifixion, Time of	7
" Genealogy	46
" Second Coming	17
Christian Doctrine Among the Heathen	49
" Name of	22
Christians Not All Priests	57
Church Organization	173, 191
Cities Sunk at Time of Crucifixion	163
Confusion of Languages	130
Consciousness after Death	106
Covenant Breaking	87
Criticism on Mormonism Invited	5
Destruction of Jaredites and Lamanites	129, 142
Doctrine of Christ	191
Egyptian Art in Peru and Mexico	159
" Reformed	138
Elias—Gabriel	98
Endless Punishment	146
Errors in Book of Mormon History Possible	6
" in Bible	7, 27, 33, 86, 135
Feet Washing	87
Finder of Book of Mormon not a Gentile	173
Fossil Remains	164
Generation, What Constitutes	74
Grammar, Joseph's	38
Inspiration, Degrees of	40
Inspired Translation	35, 41, 78, 84, 128, 134
Interpreters	30, 32, 34, 84, 94, 141, 142
Jaredites, Destruction of	129, 142
" Longevity of	127
Jaredite Kings	127
John the Baptist Resurrected	63
" Evangelist to Tarry	88
Joseph's Land	162
Joseph and Oliver's Ordination	52, 64
Joseph as a Translator	6, 94
Joseph's Ministry and Writings	191, 195

INDEX.

Joseph's Prophecies Fulfilled:	Brighamite Apostasy	192
"	"	"	Famines	.................184, 185
"	"	"	His Own Death	193
"	"	"	Persecution of Saints	185–188
"	"	"	Pestilences and Scourges	..177, 178
"	"	"	Slaves Marshaled for War	183
"	"	"	Spiritualism	189–191
"	"	"	Wars, Foreign	182
"	"	"	" Indian	............183, 184
"	"	"	War, Not Peace	177
"	"	"	War of Rebellion	.........180, 181
"	"	"	Waves of the Sea	179

Laban Killed 131
Lamanites, Destruction of 129, 142
Land of Joseph..162
Longevity, Jaredite.......................................127
     "   Nephite..144
"Mormon," Word 82
Mulek, Son of Zedekiah 138
Nephi, a King 124
     "   Builds a Temple 124
Nephites, Destruction of 129, 142
     "   Longevity 144
     "   Numbers of 125, 126
     "   Perpetuated 132
New Jerusalem... 74
Oliver to Translate.......................................137
Ordination, Joseph and Oliver 52, 64
Organization of the Church........................173, 191,
Papacy, Fall of, Foretold 165
People of Zarahemla 24
Plagiarism, Charge of, Refuted.........................20, 96
Plates of Book of Mormon.....23, 26, 28, 66, 71, 99, 137, 142, 152
Polygamy Not Joseph's Doctrine 175
Pre-existence 41
Priesthood, Aaronic........................16, 52, 53, 59, 63
     "   Melchisedek....................13, 55, 59, 61, 136

INDEX.

Printing House	82
Prophecies of Book of Mormon	165, 166
" " Joseph	177–193
"Relics"	1531–55
Reformed Egyptian	138
Second Coming of Christ	17
"Seventy Weeks" of Daniel	9
Soul of Man	41, 93, 106
Spiritual Creation	41
" Gifts	192
Stone,—Hiram Page	135
Testimony of Cowdery, Whitmer, and Harris	70, 99, 135, 137
Three and Eight Witnesses	99
Three Glories	90, 147
" Nephites	23
Tithes	15
Translator, Joseph as a	6, 94
" Responsible Only for the Faithfulness of his Work	6
Truth, All, Harmonious	176
Urim and Thummim	94
Witnesses, Three and Eight	99
Zarahemlaites	25
Zion not Removed	132

Printed at Herald Office, Plano, Kendall County, Illinois.

www.ingramcontent.com/pod-product-compliance
Lightning Source LLC
Chambersburg PA
CBHW020925230426
43666CB00008B/1570